City Peregrines

City Peregrines

A Ten-year Saga of New York City Falcons

Saul Frank

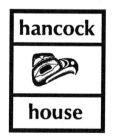

hancock

house

ISBN 0-88839-330-X
Copyright © 1994 Saul Frank

Cataloging in Publication Data
Frank, Saul.
City Peregrine

ISBN 0-88839-330-X

1. Peregrine falcon—New York (N.Y.)   I. Title.
QL696.F34F73 1994   598.9'18   C93-091836-3

Edited: Herb Bryce
Production: Herb Bryce & Lorna Lake

Published simultaneously in Canada and the United States by

HANCOCK HOUSE PUBLISHERS LTD.
19313 Zero Avenue, Surrey, B.C. V4P 1M7
(604) 538-1114   Fax (604) 538-2262

HANCOCK HOUSE PUBLISHERS
1431 Harrison Avenue, Box 959, Blaine, WA 98231-0959
(206) 354-6953   Fax (604) 538-2262

Contents

Foreword 6

Preface 8

Acknowledgments 13

Introduction 15

1 Beginnings 24

2 Transition 35

3 In Full Swing 42

4 Bridge Rescues 47

5 Bridge Disasters 55

6 Expansion 63

7 Hands On 102

8 Riverside Church 124

9 The Queenies 147

10 Migrations and Movements 158

11 Trouble 164

12 Roundup 181

13 Oops! 191

14 Limited Success 197

15 Bikes and Films 207

16 Training and Instincts 217

17 Marine Parkway 226

18 A Record Season 238

19 Queen's Reign Ends 251

20 Most Productive Season 259

21 Our First Decade 285

Epilogue 288

Appendix 291

Glossary 309

Foreword

The peregrine falcon ranges naturally over more of the land surface of planet earth than any other species of bird. Its migratory peregrinations carry it from eyries on cliffs in "Greenland's icy mountains" to winter quarters in Brazil. Its spectacular dives in pursuit of prey have made it the preeminent favorite of both falconers and bird watchers.

In the New York metropolitan area, the peregrine had nested since time immemorial on cliff ledges along the Hudson River Palisades, despite attrition in modern times by egg collectors, falconers, and irresponsible gunners who shot every bird of prey that came within range. These perils the Hudson River peregrines survived. In the winter, some even moved across the river to Manhattan, where, from lofty perches on skyscrapers, they had their pick of the city's teeming pigeons. Once or twice only, did a pair attempt to nest on a high window ledge of a skyscraper.

Then, in the late 1940s, began a mysterious decline, not only in the falcons but also in bald eagles and ospreys. Rachel Carson's *Silent Spring* rang the alarm bell: it was the insecticide DDT and other chemicals that were wreaking havoc with the peregrines. Even when exposed to only low doses, the birds laid thin-shelled eggs that were crushed by the incubating bird. By the late 1960s, the peregrine falcon was gone as a nesting bird in the eastern United States. Finally, laws were passed curtailing the use of the worst chemicals—which were threats to humankind as well as to bird and beast. But when, if ever, would the peregrine return?

To give them a hand up, The Peregrine Fund, Inc. was established at Cornell University and began to raise falcons in captivity. This was easier said than done, but under the skilled leadership of Professor Tom Cade, it was accomplished.

Within a few years, some dozens of young birds were being reared and set free by a process falconers, whose skills were indispensable, called "hacking." In the east, especially, great horned owls proved to be a surprisingly potent enemy of the inexperienced young falcons. It proved more successful to release them from isolated towers or build-

6

ings, rather than from owl-infested cliffs. But these young peregrines, most familiar with man-made structures, began to nest on buildings and bridge girders. To this day, none of the introduced, laboratory-reared or wild peregrines have returned to their traditional eyries on the Palisades of the Hudson, although they do now nest in other eastern cliffs. Meanwhile, the numbers of metropolitan eyries has increased to nine, which, in 1993, produced thirty-four young, as set forth in Saul Frank's vivid account. He has become the enthusiastic chronicler of these city peregrines, at times pedaling on his bicycle from eyrie to eyrie, at risk to his own life and limb. Minutes later may find him on the terrifying catwalks of the huge Throgs Neck Bridge, binoculars in hand and camera at the ready. He can distinguish the individuals of each pair at a glance or follow the first hazardous flights of the nestlings as they try to avoid crashing into glass-walled skyscrapers or falling into the East River or New York Bay.

Saul Frank's enthusiasm and dedication make *City Peregrines* exciting reading. But the book will be of value to the professional biologist as well as to the layman. It tells of a successful effort to reintroduce a threatened species, a species that is becoming adapted to one of the most man-modified urbanized habitats in the world!

Are other similar triumphs possible?

DEAN AMADON
CURATOR OF BIRDS EMERITUS
AMERICAN MUSEUM OF NATURAL HISTORY

Preface

Admired down through the centuries by falconers and naturalists alike for its spectacular aerobatics in pursuit of flying prey, the peregrine falcon has become one of the most evocative symbols of endangered wildlife in the closing decades of the twentieth century. Catholic in habits, worldwide in occurrence, the peregrine has proved to be resilient and adaptable in the aftermath of the grave threat to its existence posed by the excessive use of pesticides from the late 1940s to the 1970s. The story of its catastrophic decline to endangered status, both in Europe and North America owing to the effects of residual DDT and dieldrin in its food supply, is too familiar to require repeating here. Suffice it to say that by the late 1960s not a single pair of peregrines could be found breeding anywhere in North America east of the Great Plains and south of the boreal forest, a region where a stable population of more than 400 pairs had nested annually until the end of World War II. Similar reductions in the number of falcons occurred in many other parts of North America and in Europe, and for a time conservationists feared that the species would disappear completely from most of its range in the temperate regions of the northern hemisphere.

Today, thanks to the restrictions placed on the use of DDT and dieldrin in the early 1970s and to a successful captive-breeding and releasing program, about 175 pairs have become reestablished at eyries in eastern North America. The species has also increased in number in most other regions where it had declined, and in some areas it is now more abundant than before the widespread use of pesticides. No longer endangered in the biological sense, the peregrine's recovery on two continents is an outstanding example of what can be done to save a species when men and women of goodwill and determination work together for constructive change.

Many of these reestablished peregrines have taken up habitation in cities, nesting on man-made structures such as buildings and bridges and leading lives like those which Saul Frank describes in such interesting detail in *City Peregrines,* his chronicle of how the peregrine falcon colonized New York City and became a celebrity among the skyscrapers. Over the whole of Canada and the United States there are now, in 1993, more than seventy pairs of peregrines residing in at least fifty cities and towns, from Baltimore, New York, and Boston on the east coast, north to Winnipeg, Saskatoon, and Edmonton in Canada, west to San Francisco and Los Angeles, and south to San Diego and Atlanta. Once considered to be mere oddities or the unnatural outcome of elaborate stunts to educate the public about an endangered species, urban-dwelling peregrines have quite clearly established a commanding presence in the land and have become a significant element in the overall recovery of the species.

Soon after The Peregrine Fund began releasing the young falcons being bred at Cornell University in 1975, biologists became interested in the possibility of establishing some of the peregrines in cities because of frequent problems encountered with natural predators of young falcons at the cliff-side eyries where the falcons had nested in former times. In the years since the disappearance of peregrines, raccoons, foxes, and especially, great horned owls had become numerous around these cliffs. Many of the young falcons were being killed before they could become strong, independent fliers. It seemed likely that metropolitan environments would be free of these predators, and the young falcons might have a better chance of surviving. Moreover, cities abound in pigeons, generally considered to be the peregrine's favorite food, while starlings and other suitable prey are also abundant. In addition, tall buildings are similar to cliffs and provide the falcons with high hunting perches and nesting sites.

All that is needed to convert a skyscraper into a suitable falcon eyrie is to provide a tray on a window ledge with sand and gravel to give the falcons the necessary substrate in which to make their nest scrape and lay their eggs. The effectiveness of this simple trick had already been demonstrated in the case of the famous peregrines that resided in Montreal on the Sun Life Assurance building, where the same female nested continually from 1940 to 1952 and reared twenty-two young. Peregrines were also known to have nested on the St. Regis Hotel in Manhattan and on the old City Hall tower of Philadelphia in the 1940s, and for centuries in Europe falcons have used various man-made structures as eyries, old castles, cathedrals, and towers. In fact, as long as they are not unduly persecuted, peregrines have demonstrated their ability to live in close proximity to human beings in many parts of the world.

Encouraged by these bits of historical information about urban falcons, The Peregrine Fund began releasing falcons in several eastern cities in the late 1970s. In 1980 we released peregrines in Manhattan on top of the old Metropolitan Life building on West 57th Street, and the following year, we also released them on the Consolidated Edison Building in lower Manhattan not far from the World Trade Center.

I remember an early planning meeting with Mayor Ed Koch and other city officials. The Mayor was concerned that introduced peregrines might become "another problem like starlings." When we told him that we would be extremely lucky to get two or three pairs established in the city, he relaxed and made a public announcement that "these falcons are better than pigeons." Later, his enthusiasm for the bird bubbled over to such an extent that he declared June 30, 1981 "Peregrine Falcon Day," and he persuaded a reluctant Interior Secretary, James Watt, to participate with him in a public ceremony at City Hall Park to herald the peregrine's return to the city. It probably was as close to an endorsement of the endangered species program as Jim Watt ever came.

We had no idea then how successful these captive-reared and released peregrines would be in entering the cities and that by the 1990s there could be as many as ten pairs in the greater New York metropolitan area. Although they are not as numerous as starlings, the peregrines have certainly adapted to urban life to a far greater degree than anyone could have predicted. No city has more peregrines than New York, and the municipal Department of Environmental Protection even has its own falcon expert, Chris Nadareski, to look after them.

As far as we know, none of the peregrines originally set free in New York City has become a member of a nesting pair there. Falcons released in other places have found the city attractive; but there is poetic justice in the fact that a pair of peregrines now nests on the renamed MetLife Building (the old Pan Am Building), a fitting recognition for the company that helped so much to get peregrines started in the city.

Wherever peregrines have settled in cities they have invariably attracted a small coterie of special people who become enthusiastic and devoted falcon watchers. The romance with city falcons started in Baltimore in 1977 when Scarlett, the first of our released peregrines to take up residence in a city, adopted the United States Fidelity and Guaranty Insurance Company's home office building as her eyrie, and John Barber became the company's guardian of the falcons. From there it spread to Los Angeles and the Union Bank building, where the CEO, John Harrigan, had a video monitor installed in his office so he could keep regular watch on the activities at the eyrie. In New York City, Dr. John Aronian attends to the welfare of the falcons that nest on the New York Hospital, Cornell Medical College, overlooking the East River. One of the luckiest and most avid of these observers is Saul Frank, who now shares his experiences in *City Peregrines*.

In 1983, Saul and his wife, Dolores, first heard on the radio that a pair of peregrines was nesting on the Throgs Neck Bridge, practically in their backyard. Saul soon discovered that from the terrace of his apartment in Beechhurst he could look over to the Throgs Neck and watch all the comings and goings of the peregrines at their eyrie. Later, one of the fledged young used the top of his apartment building as a perch. He became hooked on watching the falcons, and since 1983 he has logged more than 2,500 hours of observations. He has seen details in the lives of peregrines seldom or never reported before. He tells us that peregrines can make it in the big city just as easily as they can survive on the wildest reaches of some Arctic river, truly cosmopolitan birds.

Soon after the first peregrines released in New York flew from their hack box on the top of the Metropolitan Life building on West 57th Street, the company arranged for a cocktail party on the roof of the nearby Barbizon Plaza Hotel for guests to view the falcons; birds that I had seen hatch from our incubators at Cornell University. Watching the young peregrines flying at dusk around Barbizon Plaza, essaying to attack their first pigeons and sportively hawking monarch butterflies out of the air and then dropping them, street lights just starting to flicker below, I was struck with the feeling of how different their city world among the tops of the skyscrapers is from the world we human pedestrians experience at street level or in the confines of our offices and apartments. Theirs is a cleaner, quieter world up there— almost pristine, almost wild. One can sense it best, perhaps, atop the World Trade Center, around which falcons often soar these days.

It is a world in which breathtaking aerial pursuits and escapes, and a thousand natural dramas take place daily against a backdrop of steel spires, glass, and sheer granite walls, unseen by all but a few singular people who have learned to look skyward to find "that cloud-biting anchor shape, that crossbow flinging through the air." Saul Frank is one of those people.

TOM J. CADE
THE PEREGRINE FUND, INC.

Acknowledgments

First and foremost I thank my wife Dolores for initiating our decade-long peregrine odyssey and supporting my writing of *City Peregrines* in far too many ways to catalog here.

Dr. Tom Cade first urged me to write the New York City peregrine story. His confidence in the project and my efforts has helped me work through the difficult times.

Ted LeViness has generously shared with me his prodigious knowledge of raptors, and recounted his ten years of peregrine observations. Together, we have invested many hundreds of hours at hawk watches in addition to our legion observation sessions at peregrine nesting sites.

Bill Van Meter ably critiqued in detail an early draft of a portion of *City Peregrines* and has consistently provided morale boosting comments.

Drs. Anne A. Paolucci and Lynn Quitman Troyka read some of my earliest material and provided valuable advice.

Stephen Settanni reviewed the entire manuscript in detail and provided corrections and suggestions regarding grammar, clarity, and presentation. His unflagging vigor in trying to develop a reader-friendly document required hundreds of hours of dedicated effort. Any improvement in my writing technique is the result of Stephen's tenacity.

Dr. Dean Amadon reviewed several chapters of the manuscript and provided corrections and suggestions which were very helpful. His knowledge of the historical facets of peregrine nesting and its relation to current patterns was a most valuable resource for me.

David Hancock embraced my peregrine treatise immediately with a confidence born of knowledge and a sharing attitude. His suggestions regarding the inclusion of raptor topics and tales and the deletion of repetitive material yielded a more interesting work.

Dave Gardner has selflessly pursued the New York City peregrines with his camera and provided many superb photos. His observations at the Throgs Neck Bridge site have been a valuable source of information.

Barbara Loucks of the New York State Department of Environmental Conservation's Endangered Species Unit (DEC) provided personal service contracts for me for four nesting seasons, 1989-1992 inclusive, recognizing the value of my monitoring efforts and enabling me to become a more productive volunteer in the peregrine program. Many peregrine watchers reported their observations, which helped to safeguard the peregrines and assisted me greatly in documenting their behavior. The following observers are listed in alphabetical order. I apologize to those individuals whose names have been omitted. Persons mentioned in the text are not listed here.

Georges Buon, Murray Brettschneider, Peter Capitelli, Mike Colapietro, Scotty Jenkins, Steven Kazianis, Bob Kurtz, Elliott Kutner, Manny Levine, Harold Lustbader, Mary Normandia, Larry Plotnick, Robert Ruckh, George Siatos, Vivienne Sokol, Joe & Virginia Sbano, Len Schrier, Enzo Volpe, and Bob Williams.

Introduction

Friends introduced my wife Dolores and me to bird watching in the late 1970s. It was from a marsh located within walking distance from their home that we first enjoyed observing and identifying birds. Dolores and I birded infrequently during the ensuing years. How could we possibly have realized that those early faltering steps were on a pathway that would lead us to a whole new world of beauty and growth?

The year 1983 presaged no change in our inconsequential birding endeavors. However, in the spring, there appeared on the scene a pair of peregrine falcons which had other plans in mind, both for themselves and for us. A two-year-old wild-raised female peregrine from New Hampshire and her one-year-old mate set up nesting quarters on the Throgs Neck Bridge. We learned of this event when Dolores heard a brief announcement of it on a May 5 radio newscast. Luckily, we live on the ninth floor of a twenty-story building, just a long stone's throw from the Throgs. Amazingly, from our apartment, we were able to see directly into the eyrie.

We were galvanized. Leaping into action, we scanned the Throgs for the peregrines, and Dolores began a detailed log the moment we made our first sighting. She recorded not only our personal observations but also any and all other information that we received. During our first peregrine watching season, Dolores contacted the DEC and The Peregrine Fund to obtain information regarding our peregrine neighbors and, in turn, we related our observations. These two organizations were collaborating in the monitoring and managing of known peregrine nesting sites and potential new locations in New York State. Later, we became acquainted with other peregrine watchers and incorporated their observations into our log in our efforts to create as complete a record as possible. Dolores made all the entries, single-handedly, for the first two years. In 1985, I took over the delightful chore of recording the peregrine observations and have continued to do so to the date of this writing.

The reasons for our embracing our peregrine neighbors right from the beginning and, as we learned to know them better, for our ever-deeper relationship with them is still not absolutely clear to us. We had never seen any peregrines nor had we known anything about peregrines until that momentous day in May. Even after we had observed the peregrines for several months during that first season, we could not differentiate among the adult male, female, or fledgling. Yet we were strongly motivated to observe and to learn what we could about them.

During that very first year, a monitoring role developed, allowing us to render assistance to the peregrine program. We became the eyes of DEC at the Throgs, especially during the part of the year other than the breeding season. For the breeding season, DEC hired a monitor to observe the Throgs Neck and Verrazano-Narrows nesting sites and to follow up on any peregrine sighting reports concerning other locations in the New York City metropolitan region. Starting with the 1986 breeding season, the hired monitor service was discontinued, giving rise to the opportunity for Dolores and me and a few other devoted peregrine watchers to become an informal volunteer monitoring group. A DEC employee directed the entire New York State peregrine program. In later years, in addition to observing the nesting sites, I performed "hands on" work, usually in conjunction with a DEC staffer. This work consisted of inspections of bridge- and building-based nesting sites, nest-box-installation, chick banding, relocation of chicks at bridge-nesting sites, and placing nestlings that had prematurely fallen from their nests in safer locations.

I was given personal service contracts by DEC to provide monitoring and hands-on services for the 1989 through 1992 breeding seasons. It was immensely gratifying to have progressed from merely watching peregrines in unknowing awe to holding chicks in my hands in an attempt to save their lives.

In the decade ending in 1992, I have invested 2,000 hours observing at the Throgs Neck Bridge site and 350 hours at others. I have been fortunate to have witnessed more than 180 successful prey captures and many more times that number of hunts. "City peregrines" have prospered in urban environments, thereby providing outstanding observational opportunities for raptorphiles. In many cities, the home or workplace now also becomes a window to the wild world of peregrines.

Peregrines have captured the interest and hearts of humans throughout recorded history. Their haughty beauty, eye-dazzling

16

speed, consummate flying ability, and skill in capturing prey are some of the most outstanding characteristics that have combined to make them the most desired raptor for use in the ancient and modern sport of falconry. Their rarefied lifestyle of usually dining only on birds which they have caught alive requires them to be in top flying condition at all times. Peregrines are reputed to be the fastest creatures on earth. In a stoop attack, they approach speeds of 200 miles per hour. Peregrines live on all the continents except Antarctica. Humans have always found a special attraction in those qualities which represent the ultimate limits of achievement and peregrines possess some of those essences.

The modern love affair with the peregrine, however, has new origins and a new class of devotees. By 1968, there were no known peregrine nesting pairs east of the Mississippi River, a region that had previously supported more than 400 peregrine pairs. Pesticides, such as DDT and related chemicals, that had been used to safeguard food crops from devastation by insects, produced concentrated residues which worked their way through the peregrines' food chain. In the peregrine, and other raptors such as the bald eagle and osprey, the ingestion of pesticide residues caused the formation of thin-shelled eggs, which resulted in reproductive failure.

The dramatic turnaround in the fortunes of these pesticide-impacted raptors developed because two beneficial events occurred. In 1972, the United States, among other nations, banned the use of DDT-based pesticides, some of which were known to cause eggshell thinning. In addition, reintroduction programs were created to hasten the reestablishment of viable breeding populations. The success in increasing nesting populations in some raptor species designated as endangered has intrigued growing numbers of environmentally interested citizens. The concept that wildlife that has become endangered, especially through human intervention, can and should be restored to an independent, viable status is a positive force in today's society. The great interest in peregrines now derives from factors that did not exist prior to their decline. The poisoning of wild creatures and their recovery has seized the imagination of many. It provides another beacon of hope for a renaissance in the restoration of respect for the world of nature.

The majority of people who are involved in watching, monitoring, or studying peregrines do so from a distance and are not remotely interested in possessing or intimately getting involved with a peregrine on a one-to-one basis or in "getting their hands on" one. They do not have the space, the time, the resources, or the inclination required for the onerous responsibility involved in providing for the well-being of a raptor. They want to relate to peregrines in a nonintrusive way. As a significant number of current peregrine nests, in the United States, are located on bridges or buildings in or close to large cities, millions of city dwellers now are able to observe one of the most stupendous, wild creatures known to man. The marvelous element of this phenomenon is that the peregrines are, for the most part, not disturbed by their human watchers and, in many cases, are saved by them from potentially life-threatening situations.

Peregrines had been residents of New York City for at least fifty years and probably much longer. Renowned naturalist Roger Tory Peterson recalled a weekend in the early 1940s when he visited fourteen peregrine eyries within a hundred miles of New York City. He specifically mentioned winter "command posts," such as the Riverside Church, New York Hospital, and the Lincoln Building. Adult peregrines that nested on the Palisades cliffs overlooking the New Jersey shore of the Hudson River overwintered on New York City skyscrapers. They used these buildings for shelter and dined on the plethora of pigeons that lived there year-round. One extraordinarily interesting item concerning this historical perspective is that, starting in the late 1980s, peregrines have successfully nested on New York Hospital and the Riverside Church and have used the Lincoln Building in association with their successful nesting at the adjacent Pan Am/MetLife Building. So, after a hiatus of about thirty years, peregrines are again using buildings that their species had previously used. There is no genetic memory operative here because the present-day eastern peregrines do not derive from the same stock as did those in earlier periods. Certain structures, of the thousands of buildings from which to choose in New York City, doubtlessly possess special characteristics that are universally attractive to peregrines—for it seems to be more than a coincidence that sites that were used decades earlier are again hosting peregrines.

The noted ornithologists R. A. Herbert and K. G. S. Herbert made thousands of visits to peregrine nesting sites during the thirty-year period ending 1959, with 1,200 carried out during the last decade. Their study included eight eyries on the western shore of the Hudson River over a distance of fifty-five miles in New Jersey and New York, one eyrie in New York City, and several New York City wintering sites. Six of the eight Hudson eyries were situated on the sheer rock cliffs of the Hudson Palisades, which tower to a height of 400 feet over the Hudson River. The southernmost site was in New Jersey, across from New York City. Two eyries were located in abandoned rock quarries.

Height or a dominating vantage point relative to the surrounding landscape seemed to have been the most important factor in nest-site selection. However, other site conditions appeared to have been more important factors with regard to nesting success. These, as the Herberts stated, included: "(1) suitable ledges for nesting, feeding and perching; (2) absence of large trees that would impede visibility and flight; (3) length of cliff, a long cliff with several ledges being preferable to a narrow one; and (4) inaccessibility to disturbance from above." When these advantageous conditions were present at an eyrie, the resident peregrines became strongly attached to the site. Even the availability of a superior territory would not lure resident peregrines from their traditional eyrie. First-class sites were utilized year after year because of their universally recognizable advantages.

New York City had one pair of year-round peregrines from 1943 to 1953. They roosted regularly on the Grand Central Building during the winter and possibly nested on several different skyscrapers in midtown Manhattan. The city hosted as many as sixteen wintering peregrines in 1946. However, their number dropped to seven by 1952. Most were females and were believed to have originated from New England and other northeastern regions rather than from the Hudson eyries. The Herberts also reported that peregrines had roosted on the Riverside Church. It is gratifying to observe peregrines again nesting in territories within New York City that had been deserted for thirty years.

The story of the reintroduction of the peregrine in the eastern United States is itself an interesting one. The plight of the peregrine and its near extirpation in the United States was discussed at the 1965 International Peregrine Conference organized by the late J.J. Hickey at the University of Wisconsin. Hickey was dean of peregrine research and had studied the falcons in and around New York City in the 1930s and 1940s. The information presented led to the conclusion that if peregrines were to reestablish their nesting territories, to any meaningful extent in the near future, they would not be able to do so without human intervention. Breeding peregrines in captivity and releasing them, a process called hacking, at some of their historical eyries and at other protected, favorable nesting locations seemed to be the only solution for regions where the falcons had completely disappeared.

In 1970, Dr. Tom J. Cade of the Laboratory of Ornithology at Cornell University established a peregrine captive-breeding program known as The Peregrine Fund. Dr. Heinz Meng of the State University of New York at New Paltz had already successfully bred peregrines in captivity. He provided a pair of breeding peregrines and their progeny to the breeding program. Twenty peregrines were bred in captivity in 1973 and two were released in 1974, during the initial experimental phase of the program, in cooperation with Dr. Meng. In 1975, the U.S. Fish and Wildlife Service instituted an Eastern Peregrine Falcon Recovery Team which developed a recovery plan that set a goal of establishing a self-maintaining population at a level of 50 percent of the number of breeding pairs estimated to have occurred in the 1940s or to a level that the environment will support.

The first releases, carried out in 1974, were done both at historical cliff sites and at man-made towers erected at coastal marshes. It was an attempt to balance the goal of reintroducing the peregrine to their known historical nesting locations while meeting the peregrines' primal nesting needs and, of course, achieving as high a dispersal rate as possible. Peregrines hacked at cliff sites suffered substantial losses due to great horned owl predation. Therefore, the early and continued higher success rate at coastal towers led to an increase in their use. During the four-year period from 1975-1978, a total of 152 peregrines were hacked in the eastern United States. From this group, 108 dispersed satisfactorily.

The first reintroduced peregrine known to have attained maturity and to nest did so in 1979 on a tower in New Jersey. Although that first nesting attempt failed, an ever-increasing number of birds did succeed at nesting on towers, and, later, on bridges and buildings. Urban buildings were used as hack sites starting in 1979 and generated the highest success rate of all. During the 1975 to 1981 period, a total of 353 peregrines had been hacked in eighty-one releases at thirty-six locations in eleven eastern states and the District of Columbia. The successful overall dispersal rate was 74 percent. Then 1983 became known as the "year of the bridges" because the initial bridge nestings in the east took place at three locations. One was in Maryland and the other two were on New York City's Throgs Neck and Verrazano-Narrows bridges. Although the Maryland nest failed, five young were produced at the New York City bridges. This was a harbinger of the urban peregrine nesting explosion that was about to occur throughout the United States. On a personal level, it was 1983 that marked the entry of peregrines into the lives of Dolores and myself and in the lives of many of our newfound friends and associates.

By the conclusion of the 1985 breeding season, more than 750 peregrines had been released in the eastern United States. This decade of tremendous effort yielded very gratifying results. There had been sixty-three documented nesting attempts of which 75 percent had been successful, producing 128 young. In 1985 alone, forty pairs were observed and at least twenty-five pairs made nesting attempts. Of these twenty-five pairs, nine pairs failed and the remaining sixteen successful pairs produced forty-seven young. However, this did not meet the standard set by the Eastern Peregrine Recovery Plan, which called for approximately 175 nesting pairs to indicate a recovered peregrine population. While only one-seventh of the goal amount had been reached, the increasing number of active nests and the advent of bridge sites were very encouraging signs that the goal would eventually be achieved.

In 1991, a milestone was reached in the eastern peregrine reintroduction program. The Peregrine Fund decided to stop releasing captive-produced falcons at the end of the 1991 season. A total of 1,207 had been released in the east of the more than 4,000 released throughout the entire United States by The Peregrine Fund and two cooperators. More than 630 young had been produced by the reestablished nesters whose numbers had grown to ninety-one known territorial pairs.

Despite the slowing of the growth rate for the reestablished population during the 1989-1991 period, the expectation was for a continued increase in nesting pairs with a doubling of that population in one or two more decades. The current peregrines had shown a marked tendency to use many nesting sites other than cliffs: buildings, bridges, and towers. About half the pairs were nesting on these types of man-made structures and the region contained an abundant supply.

The New York City metropolitan region was a barometer of the urban expansion of peregrine nesting. Only two bridges had working nests for the five years ending in 1987. Then, in 1988, the Tappan Zee Bridge came on stream, as did the New York Hospital/Cornell Medical Center Building. These new sites produced a total of four chicks that developed to independence; a wonderful achievement for initial nesting sites.

The upward trend continued in 1989 with three additional nesting locations. Two were on buildings and one was on a bridge. The Riverside Church produced two young that year. Eggs were laid at 40 Wall Street in a failed nesting attempt, and finally there was a failed nesting at the Hell Gate Bridge.

In 1990, the Pan American Building in midtown Manhattan became the seventh known egg-producing site. Fifteen chicks were produced at five sites in New York City during 1991. The first season Marine Parkway Bridge contributed two fledglings to this total, somewhat mitigating the failures experienced at established sites.

The 1992 breeding season produced decade-record-high numbers in all categories: seven productive sites, twenty-six eggs, twenty-one chicks, nineteen fledglings, and thirteen young dispersed satisfactorily. The Pan American Building site produced one chick in its initial successful breeding season.

Then 1993 was a banner year with twenty-six chicks hatched at the seven established sites and four at each of the two first-time producing sites, 48 Wall Street and the Goethal's Bridge for a total of thirty-four young. The New York Hospital site produced five young, a rare event in the wild.

This book was written in the hope of sharing with the reader the experiences that we so fortunately were able to enjoy over a ten-year period. We observed the entire life cycle of the peregrines: bonding, nest-site selection, courtship, copulation, egg incubation, chick development, fledging, and the "training" of the fledglings. Of course, there was always the lengthy "quiet" period that began during each summer after the fledglings of the season had dispersed and the following February when the breeding cycle had begun anew. If this work were to add to our understanding of this majestic raptor, at any level, I would treasure that contribution.

Is it any wonder that Dolores and I, and hundreds of devout peregrine watchers, have developed a serious case of "Peregrine Passion"?

A glossary is appended to assist those readers who are not conversant with terms used in the text. Some explanations are very detailed in order to enhance the reader's understanding of the story without the necessity of consulting other materials.

1

Beginnings

(1983)

In the fall of 1971, my wife Dolores and I moved into a twenty-story apartment building in Queens County, New York City. Situated on a six-acre site 200 yards west of the Throgs Neck Bridge, our new home, called Cryder House, is only several yards from the high-water mark of the East River. Our ninth-floor apartment offers us a magnificent panorama, facing east with oversized windows measuring more than five feet in height and ten feet in width. Water surrounds us and gives us a feeling of serenity, and of unity with the spirit of the wildlife that flourishes in the area. We have a terrace that enables us to enter the outside environment and yet enjoy the comforts of home.

The Throgs Neck Bridge, a beautiful suspension bridge, dominates our view. We see the sun rise beyond the bridge structure. Sunsets bathe it in a golden hue. It appears graceful, though its movements are not visible to the naked eye. (Suspension bridge roadways hang by their cables and are in a constant motion due to winds and traffic.)

The bridge is located at the junction of the East River and Long Island Sound. Little Bay forms the southern perimeter. Two daily tides, averaging nine feet, produce dramatic surface effects on the water. These three bodies of water, with varying depths, force the tremendous tidal volumes of water to move alternately into the narrow East River and the broader Long Island Sound. Winds frequently create whitecaps in one area and only ripples nearby.

Dolores and I were amazed by the diversity of avian and water-based wildlife around the Throgs. The expected contingent of herring,

ring-billed, and great black-backed gulls, rock and mourning doves, is joined by many species of water birds. Great and snowy egrets, great blue and black-crowned night herons, double-crested cormorants and mute swans. Winter visitors include greater and lesser scaup, ruddy and bufflehead ducks. Local fisherman regularly pull lobster, bluefish, striped bass, and flounder from the waters. Menhaden are present seasonally in prodigious numbers, at times in the millions.

In the spring of 1983, our newest wildlife neighbors, a pair of peregrine falcons, nested on the Throgs. This circumstance was important because it was one of a series of significant events indicating that the peregrine falcon reintroduction program was making progress. By the 1960s there were no known nesting peregrine falcons east of the Mississippi River because of pesticide contamination. In 1979, released peregrines nested in New Jersey and continued there and in several other locations in the east. However, the adult female on the Throgs Neck Bridge in 1983 was the farthest documented dispersed wild-raised progeny of a pair of released peregrines to nest successfully in the eastern United States.

The Throgs peregrines produced three eggs. Two chicks hatched and one fledged after it had developed satisfactorily. This fledgling honed its flight skills, learned to capture prey, and apparently dispersed to independence. The other chick did not fledge, possibly due to interference by vandals.

But let's start at the beginning, when we first became involved with peregrine falcons. On May 9, 1983, a radio newscast reported a pair of peregrine falcons nesting on the Throgs Neck Bridge. The exact location of the nest was not indicated. Dolores and I hoped it would be on the Queens side of the bridge, rather than on the Bronx side, for our viewing benefit. Scanning the Throgs repeatedly produced no sightings. Our task was difficult because we didn't know what a peregrine looked like and we were using a very old, weak binocular.

We persisted in our search and began asking ourselves, "If I were a bird of prey, what spot might I choose for a nest?" One location seemed ideal to us. The bridge's weight-bearing cables tie into a massive concrete anchorage in the water. On its south side, over a hundred feet above the water, there is an opening that is nine feet wide and five feet deep. This cavity provides protection from bad weather, is difficult to approach, and is over water. We hoped that this very suitable

25

spot would be the nest because we could see directly into it from our apartment.

The next day, a neighbor excitedly told us that she had met some New York State Department of Environmental Conservation (DEC) staff in the parking lot of the old Hammerstein Estate across the street. The mansion is dilapidated but in its heyday it housed the renowned Oscar Hammerstein and attracted many famous personages. Our neighbor had observed the nest through the DEC spotting telescope. Wonder of wonders, the nest was in the exact spot we had thought of as the ideal location a day earlier. We felt as if we were in tune with the peregrines, even though we had not yet seen them.

The DEC staff made their observations from the Hammerstein Estate parking lot because it was the closest land area to the nest affording a view directly up into the nest. The disadvantage of viewing from that spot is that, at ground level, it is considerably below the nest ledge. Our apartment, however, is at the same height as the nest ledge, and from our vantage point, although the sightline is at an angle, we are nevertheless able to see into most of the eyrie. The DEC observers had spotted two adult peregrines at the nest cavity but the most dramatic news of all was that there were three eggs.

On our second day of watching, we observed a peregrine sitting atop the Queens tower of the bridge. Dolores and I felt as though we had made a discovery, although we realized that the event was special only to us. We couldn't conceive at that time how much impact these new neighbors would have on us. We were able to identify the peregrine only because it was so radically different from any other creature we had ever observed. Rarely had we seen a bird atop the Throgs tower and then only briefly. As this bird sat surveying its domain, we, as neophytes, were awed by its majestic mien. That special feeling that we experienced has proven to be an almost universal one.

Dolores started a diary to record our peregrine observations that very first day, and we still don't understand what motivated her to start it. She kept it going for two years, entirely on her own initiative. Then I took it over and have faithfully continued it to the day of this writing. The log expanded to include information and personal observations on the growing number of other peregrine nesting sites and potential sites in the New York City metropolitan area. Sighting reports and information received from others are also recorded.

One day we met three birders at the Hammerstein parking lot. We looked through their spotting scope into the nest and actually saw an adult peregrine sitting on eggs. The floor of the nest area was covered with debris, and grass had sprouted in some spots. The birds had chosen an environment much like a natural cliff ledge except for the safety chains across the front end of the cavity.

We borrowed a spotting telescope with a fifteen-to-sixty-variable-power magnification zoom lens. Mounted on a tripod, this instrument brought a new dimension to our observations. The sheer pleasure we derived from being able to see the minute details on these gorgeous birds is an experience not adequately describable in words. The black coloring around the eyes, on the head, and down the cheeks now was ours to study. These features are variously referred to in the vernacular as the helmet or moustaches but such descriptions just don't do justice to the magnificent beauty which they add to these creatures. Their bearing was regal as they sat upright, serenely, for what seemed very prolonged periods of time. We soon learned that peregrine time cannot be equated with human time. Hours go by without their displaying any appreciable movement.

Our improved optical equipment gave us superb coverage of the front of the nest and most of the adjacent perching spots. We did all our watching from our terrace, which was fortunate because the nest was the focal point of their activities. The chains at the front end provided convenient perches, and the birds sat there peering outward, usually appearing alert but frequently seeming to be alert yet relaxed at the same time.

Almost directly above the nest, there's a favorite roosting place for pigeons, which we watched fly in and out regularly with no evident fear of the peregrines, which regularly dine on their brethren. Although the distance between them is but yards, the peregrines normally showed only limited interest in the pigeons, merely glancing at them as they flew by.

For the next few days, we saw the peregrines soaring frequently above the Throgs. We learned to identify them from among the numerous gulls, pigeons, and doves that stream through the area. Slowly we developed the ability to discern various nuances in peregrine flight patterns as opposed to those of the other birds. As our observational skills improved, our appreciation of the wondrous flying machine we

27

were watching soared. The peregrine's ease in performing aerial maneuvers was such that sometimes their acrobatics went by too fast for the eye to decipher. We always enjoyed the action even when we could not see it in its entirety.

Exactly three weeks after we started our peregrine watching, we noted a significant behavioral change. The peregrines began to sit for long periods on the chains, looking into the nest. Up to that time, they were seen looking outward. We were sure that they must be looking at something interesting. We surmised that the chicks must have hatched.

The following morning, the peregrines were seen either perched at the nest or hunting for prolonged periods. That same afternoon, May 31, 1983, we were exhilarated to see two white, downy chicks huddled together. They were about ten days old and we saw them very clearly from our apartment terrace. Our many hours of watching, worrying, and recording our observations had finally been rewarded with an opportunity to study and enjoy wild, young peregrines.

Several days later, a group of birders came for a visit and the peregrines cooperated by actively soaring and hunting. The birders were thrilled at witnessing these spectacular sights. Their visit pointed up our good fortune in being able to observe nesting peregrines on a daily basis from our own home.

We savored being able to observe the chicks' development. The now two-week-old chicks usually huddled very close together, touching. After three days of observing the chicks, we saw that they had grown larger but were still pure white. On the fourth day, they seemed to be using their stubby wings for balance. By the ninth day of our observations, they had grown significantly larger and showed some darker feathers on their wings. The chicks remained at the outer edge of the nest cavity for longer periods by the tenth day, and they also ate there. More darker feathers grew in and preening sessions were more frequent.

Then one day the adults excitedly flew and wheeled about just outside their nest. Their tight turns and erratic flying was very uncharacteristic behavior. The cause of their disturbance became clear when we observed three men in the eyrie. We were horrified. Who were these interlopers? Were they vandals or thieves? But we drew some comfort when we observed that they were very deliberate in their actions and were measuring the nest area.

After the men left, the chicks appeared normal. However, the adults did not reenter the nest area for at least thirty minutes after the visitors had left. We learned later that these men were DEC and Peregrine Fund personnel who banded, photographed, and measured the chicks.

The chicks grew progressively darker and exercised more frequently. The adults increasingly sat on nearby piers where they could monitor the chicks without being directly with them. The feeding sessions were oftener and lengthier. Hunting forays were more frequent to provide the ever larger quantity of food needed for the growing chicks. One day we saw a peregrine, in flight, catch a pigeon. It was a spectacular sight to see the peregrine dive down at its prey at great speed. The pigeon was missed completely but as the peregrine zoomed past it, and rose upward again on the speed it had built up, it turned so quickly and skillfully that it was now pursuing its prey from the rear. Though the quarry was flying very fast, the peregrine overtook it and grasped it in its talons. We learned later that many devoted peregrine watchers had never, or rarely, had the good fortune of witnessing a kill. We were indeed lucky to have chosen this area as our home. It was doubly good luck that the peregrines also chose to live here.

More and more the chicks sat at the edge of the nest. They were much darker. Exuberant from observing these activities for three weeks, we telephoned DEC and were advised that the chicks at the Throgs were females. At the Verrazano-Narrows Bridge, linking Brooklyn and Staten Island, another peregrine pair had produced two males and a female chick. These two nestings were extraordinarily important. They were the very first successes in the New York City metropolitan area since the peregrine falcon had been eliminated as a nesting species east of the Mississippi River in the 1960s.

The chicks were at the front of the eyrie more often as they developed, which was wonderful for our viewing. Their wings had now become very dark and their chests buffy. They looked more and more like adult peregrines as each day passed. They started to show interest in the pigeons that flew by. Each day brought more darkening of their

29

wings and backs. Wing stretching, hopping around the eyrie, and food intake were their main activities.

On the twenty-sixth observation day, we saw the chicks running around in the eyrie. We described their gait as light-footed. They ran from the rear to the front of the eyrie, stopped at the edge, spread their wings, and ran to the rear. They sat at the front edge and bobbed their heads. In the twenty-six days we had observed them, they had progressed from almost helpless chicks to fairly well coordinated youngsters.

At this stage, the adults started to bring in whole birds and encouraged the chicks to feed themselves. Prior to this, the adults had stripped the meat from carcasses and fed the chicks. Four weeks had passed since we first had seen the young and the drama of their development heightened. A chick sat on the extreme edge of the eyrie. Occasionally she would drop one leg over the side or spread one wing out of the eyrie. It was nerve-racking to watch these antics. Would she fall out and down over a hundred feet to the forbidding water below? If she were to fall, would she fly? I was almost sure she could. The chicks now were as large as their parents and their wingspans were more than a yard.

The next day brought change: only one chick was seen at a time. Were we seeing two different chicks, one at a time, or the same one each time? We had strong feelings that one young falcon had fledged. An adult flew in and out of the eyrie. The young falcon's behavior was very much like the adults' but it did not fly out. It appeared agitated as it flapped and stretched its wings very close to the edge. It seemed to need encouragement to leave the only space it had ever known. It definitely looked sufficiently developed and ready to fledge.

The following morning we could find no adults or young. In the afternoon, two peregrines soared and then flew over and under the Throgs. The eyrie was deserted; surely both the young had fledged. It was truly wonderful to have seen them through to this stage but our worry quotient was sky high because of the many dangers at this site. The water was an ever-present snare. The roadway could bring an even quicker death. Nonhuman predators were not a problem but vandals could be a danger.

The first six days of observations in July produced varied results. Sometimes we saw one or two peregrines at a time. Often we couldn't

30

find a peregrine for an entire day. We were so concerned about this turn of events that we again called DEC. They advised us that one fledgling was missing but they had no additional information. The eyrie had been inspected but nothing had been found. DEC said that the missing chick may have fledged early, which could explain why we weren't seeing it. This possibility made us feel somewhat better because the chick might be alive.

We were out of town for the next six days but when we returned on July 13, happily, we saw a peregrine aloft. The following day, while sitting at the Cryder House pool, a little west of the Cryder House building, we saw a peregrine perched on the west roof parapet and then on temporary scaffolding beams. Then it soared directly over the pool area. The pigeons that normally frequented the west side of Cryder House were absent that day.

The next day we thoroughly enjoyed an aerial show at poolside. A peregrine was perched on the scaffolding, vocalizing loudly. Having had the foresight to bring our binoculars to the pool with us, we watched it circle the area and perform several lazy turns. It turned its head to stare down at the people assembled at the pool. On one go around, the peregrine made a very low pass at a pigeon and flew just over the trees adjacent to the pool.

When the wind picked up, the peregrine demonstrated its special flying skills. It fanned out its wings and tail against the prevailing flow of air and effortlessly gained altitude. Every so often it flapped its wings once or twice. Strangely, when it did beat its wings, the appearance was that of a bird having some difficulty in flying. This seemed so contrary to its great ability to move against a strong wind and the tremendous speed it attains when traveling with a wind. After it gained several hundred feet in altitude, it turned and suddenly streaked back toward Cryder House. Carried by the wind, it folded in its wings to streamline itself. We sensed that it couldn't possibly flap its wings fast enough to move at that speed. It had to use the wind's power and its own projectile shape to attain high speed. The bird zoomed toward its perch. Then, at the last second, it gracefully veered off and slowed so abruptly that it appeared to stop dead in midair. Everyone at the pool was awed at the magnificent flying show. Our "oohing and aahing" could be heard along with applauding. We wondered if the peregrine knew it had an audience.

We had been very worried, because we had seen only one peregrine during the past two weeks. Later that same afternoon, however,
we saw two peregrines circling the Throgs and were elated to see both
alive and well. The next day a peregrine perched on a Cryder House
twelfth-floor terrace railing for thirty minutes. It was undoubtedly one
of the young because the adults rarely perched in such exposed positions.

On July 19, 1983, a *New York Times* release stated that Dr. Tom
Cade, director of The Peregrine Fund, Inc. at Cornell University,
reported that one nestling at the Throgs had been lost, perhaps to
vandals, and that the peregrines were no longer at the bridge. How
could this be true, since we, contrary to this report, were observing
them regularly? He must have received some erroneous information.
Dolores immediately dispatched a letter to Dr. Cade to advise him that
we were observing two peregrines regularly.

One evening a week later, Dr. Cade called in response to Dolores'
letter. He thanked us for notifying him of our observations and for our
continuing interest. He was elated to learn of our detailed log. He
explained that DEC had employed a paid observer for the entire
breeding season to monitor the known peregrine nesting sites in the
New York City metropolitan area and to follow up on reports of other
peregrine sightings. Most of the monitoring was done at the Throgs
Neck and Verrazano-Narrows bridges and all observations were
logged.

Dr. Cade asked us to meet with the DEC observer to clear up her
mistaken report that the peregrines had left the Throgs. The next day
we received a letter from the reintroduction coordinator for The
Peregrine Fund, Jack Barclay. He provided us with more information
about the peregrines at the Throgs. The adult female's band number
identified her as being two years old and having been raised in the
wilds of New Hampshire. Her parents had both been released under
the auspices of The Peregrine Fund. This spelled a resounding success
for The Peregrine Fund's reintroduction program. They had released
peregrine chicks in New Hampshire, which had matured, mated, and
produced their own young. The young of the released birds then
moved down the Atlantic seaboard and established their own successful nesting territories. The accomplishment of the female at the
Throgs was a special breakthrough. It marked the longest distance

known, about 300 miles, that a wild-raised fledgling of two released parents had traveled to establish a successful breeding site of its own east of the Mississippi River.

The reading of the numbered band on our female was itself an accomplishment. Jack Barclay had lain prone on the eyrie floor, which was covered with wet, filthy debris, mostly pigeon droppings. He was hidden from the female's view but she knew he was there. Her instinct to flee to safety conflicted with that of remaining to protect her chicks. Her ambivalence was displayed in her nervousness. Fortunately, she opted to stay with her chicks, affording Barclay the chance of getting close enough to read her band numbers. Only a few numbers were visible because the rest were on the other side of the circular band. Amazingly, using a piece of wire, Jack was able to turn the band on her leg and to read the other numbers. The band had been placed upside down. This fortunate error would help in identifying her at a later time when we were not able to read all the numbers.

On August 3, Pamela Manice, the DEC observer, visited us to compare her observation log entries with ours. She had been watching the peregrines from the beach adjacent to the Hammerstein Mansion from the start of the 1983 breeding season. It's a shame we hadn't met her early in the breeding season. It would have been much more fun and far more fruitful. We compared the two logs and immediately found the answer to the apparent discrepancy in our observations. Since Pamela had not seen any peregrines on four successive mornings, she had assumed that they had left. We, however, had seen the birds at times when she was not at her site, frequently in the afternoons.

Our experience indicated that before chicks fledge, the adults usually hunt early each morning. To observers like us, eager to see peregrines in action, especially in that most thrilling activity, hunting, this propensity for early-morning hunting was a great boon. On many mornings, we had seen several kills in just a few hours of observing. However, once the chicks fledged, the hunting and feeding pattern changed dramatically, especially as to location. The fledglings did not use the nest itself nor did they return to it except by chance. Feeding took place wherever the fledglings perched and the feeding sessions were no longer concentrated in the early mornings or evenings.

Pamela provided additional facts and concepts for our heightened curiosities. She stated that the two peregrines we were seeing at the end of the breeding season were the adult female and a female fledgling. The female's mate, the one we had seen earlier, appeared to have been a one-year-old. A one-year-old male breeder is considered unusual but not entirely rare. Obviously, he was sexually competent; but he was not sufficiently mature to perform his other spousal duties properly, namely rearing the chicks. He showed his extreme youth by begging food from the female. Pamela thought that the female eventually forced him from the area. This theorizing was extremely interesting to us. Unfortunately, we were unaware of many pertinent facts during our first season of observation. Our optical equipment had been inadequate and we did not identify the sex or age of the peregrines we observed. If we had, we would have been able to interpret our observations more effectively. As it was, many behavioral nuances were lost to us.

However, our enjoyment of the peregrines was not greatly reduced by these missing components. I guess "ignorance was bliss" while watching the adults perform their wonderful aerial displays. Seeing the chicks' development and fledging was more than enough for novice observers. The more we learned, the more we were fascinated by our peregrines as we looked ahead to future seasons.

As noted, 1983 also marked the first nesting on the Verrazano-Narrows Bridge connecting Brooklyn and Staten Island. Three eggs were laid and three young developed and fledged. Both the adults had been hacked out; the female at a tower in southern New Jersey in 1980 and the male from a cliff in New York's Shawangunk Mountains in 1979. Interestingly, this was the first evidence of contact between coastal-zone peregrines and those released at inland locations.

2

Transition

(1984)

The 1984 breeding season opened for us in the depth of winter, on February 20. Jack Barclay, The Peregrine Fund's reintroduction coordinator, telephoned to inquire about our peregrine observations and advised us that The Peregrine Fund had placed a nesting box in the 1983 eyrie and another one on the Bronx anchorage. The boxes were partially covered and had gravel bases to provide protection from water. If the peregrines were to use a box for their second breeding season, we hoped it would be the one on the Queens side because our observations would have been significantly reduced if they nested on the Bronx end. Somehow we felt the peregrines wouldn't use either of the boxes, that they would pick another location on the bridge.

We had been observing the peregrines at the Throgs throughout the winter. Our most recent sighting had been just two days prior to Jack's call when we had observed a pigeon kill.

For use that second season, and for the many more we anticipated, we bought a spotting telescope identical to the borrowed one we had been using and new, improved binoculars.

In later years, our study of peregrine falcons and other raptors taught us that nesting failures far outnumber successes. One successful breeding season bodes well, but does not assure that the next one will be satisfactory. In addition to the physiological requirements the peregrine must bring to the breeding process, there are many external environmental factors which are crucial for success. Any single problem condition can ruin the nesting attempt, such as ongoing bridge maintenance, which can be disruptive if it occurs too close to the nest.

In early July, we observed one peregrine at a time at the Throgs and several hunting forays; but we could not discern a pattern which would lead us to a possible nest site. They definitely weren't using last year's eyrie.

Toward the middle of July, we observed two peregrines sitting close together on the Bronx tower. The larger one had a band on its right leg and looked like the female of the previous season. The smaller male was darker. We called Jack Barclay to inform him of our observations and to obtain additional information. He advised us that there were three chicks in a beam cavity beneath the roadway of the bridge near the Queens tower. They were expected to fledge in ten to fourteen days. The eyrie was not observable from our vantage point, or from any of the land-based points, but we were able to observe the adults flying in this area.

Our anticipation was buoyed by the fact that our prediction that the nest boxes would not be used had been proven correct. We felt as if we knew our neighbors and were in tune with them. The following day, we met Lorinda Lombardi, the DEC observer for the 1984 season. We were already becoming known as avid and meticulous observers, especially, of course, of the Throgs Neck peregrines. Lorinda confirmed the exact location of the eyrie. We shared the information we had and offered to collaborate for the remainder of the season. The prospect which now presented itself, of receiving first-hand information directly and regularly from an official observer, came as welcome news.

I went to the beach area adjacent to the Hammerstein Mansion on July 21 to observe the nest area from a different perspective and, also, to see who else might be observing. I met Ted LeViness, who had been observing very regularly from the start of the 1983 breeding season. He has an encyclopedic knowledge of raptors, gained from over forty years of assiduous study and personal observations. The event that kindled his lifelong pursuit of raptors occurred when he was only eight years old. Arriving early one morning at a baseball field, he was treated to a red-tailed hawk's attack on a rabbit. This stirring event motivated him to begin reading about raptors and he has continued studying them with undiminished vigor. He had invested many more hours watching the peregrines at the Throgs than anyone else, including Dolores and myself. We spoke for half an hour.

I was gratified to meet someone so knowledgeable and so devoted to the peregrines. He introduced me to the concept that the world of raptors could be as deep and as wide as one wants to embrace. There was a body of knowledge to study and a growing number of people engaged in studying and enjoying raptors. I knew then that he would be a valuable resource in our study of raptors and that he would provide observation coverage during times when we would not be available. In addition, there would be the shared pleasures in observing these gorgeous creatures. It was a turning point in my life as it relates to raptors. My serious studies can be marked from that point. We exchanged telephone numbers and I left saying I expected that we would be lifelong friends. That was my feeling based on the pleasure of this first intense discussion. Ted must have thought that I was a strange one to say something like that, but my feeling was right and we are close friends, and doubtless always will be.

My expectations regarding Ted's importance were proven correct the very next morning. He was the only person on watch at the Throgs at 6:00 A.M. to observe two chicks fledge. One attempted to alight on the anchorage ledge, which is several yards above the water. It missed, ending up in the water. While thoughts of various rescue methods streamed through Ted's brain, including his swimming out to rescue the youngster, the fledgling became a reluctant swimmer. Using his wings as oars, he propelled himself about seventy-five yards to a partially submerged barge and gained sanctuary there.

The tired, bedraggled youngster was very vulnerable to any predatory bird that might chance upon him, sitting in the open on the barge. There were many great black-backed and herring gulls in the area which were capable of dispatching a young, inexperienced peregrine. The adult female was very nervous in light of this situation. She uncharacteristically attacked avian species that she usually ignored. Black-crowned night herons and great egrets regularly hunt on and around the barge without interference from the peregrines. But now with the fledgling on the barge, the area was declared off limits. A great egret was unmercifully attacked with repeated diving passes until, finally, the female struck it forcefully enough to cause it to plummet into the water. Wading birds are not equipped for deep water and the egret quickly flew off, with the female continuing to dive at it. As the egret distanced itself from the barge, the peregrine's attacks subsided. When the female returned to the barge to check on her youngster, she found a black-crowned night heron there. She immediately dove at this new threat. The heron instantly took flight, thereby suffering no consequences except for the loss of its fishing post. The female monitored the barge area for several hours, continuing to attack potential predators, until the fledgling returned to the Throgs.

Dolores and I arrived while the fledgling was still drying out on the barge. He preened relaxedly as though his morning brush with a watery death had never happened. When he had every feather in proper condition, he flew to the main pier of the Bronx tower and joined his sibling. The adults then hunted successfully and fed the young.

One evening, three and half days after the chicks had fledged, we were treated to a beautiful sight. Looking eastward, with the sun setting behind us, we saw four peregrines flying in formation. There were two sets of two. Each set had one adult and one young. The small space between the birds in each set looked identical while there was a larger space between the two sets. They were all highlighted by the sun as they floated upward and toward us on a light northwest breeze. They held their relative positions like a precision fighter squadron. The late afternoon sun gave them a golden cast. We heard appreciative sighs and comments from our neighbors on adjacent terraces. Even onlookers, who were not devotees, were smitten with such natural beauty.

The next evening provided a different kind of show. The adults had hunted unsuccessfully. In one instance, they collaborated in attacking a pigeon. One made a pass at the intended victim and the other followed quickly with another dive at it. The pigeon employed some fantastic flying tactics of its own to avoid the peregrines' slashing talons. It executed a variety of dives and combined them with abrupt changes in direction. The moves seemed random so that no pattern could be discerned and therefore the peregrines would have to outfly their victim if they were to catch it. The pigeon escaped by flying through some trees at the edge of the Cryder House lawn and gained cover under some plantings. The peregrines broke off the chase at the perimeter trees, obviously unwilling to fly through them as the pigeon had.

The following days were filled with hunting forays, the peregrines' most dramatic flying activity. We also were extremely enthused in observing other types of interactions. One morning, both fledglings were in the 1983 eyrie. The adult female alighted with prey as they faced her expecting a meal. Instead, she deliberately pushed the carcass backward. It went overboard and plummeted toward the water below. One fledgling immediately understood what action was necessary. It rushed past its mother and flew down so quickly and adroitly that it was able to snare the carcass before it could reach the water. The second fledgling took the cue and followed close behind the first.

Breathlessly we witnessed two in-flight prey transfers. The adult flew down, took the prey from the first fledgling, and passed it off to the grasping talons of the second youngster. This was apparently a training exercise for the young. We had never seen a prey item treated this way. It surely accomplished its goal of motivating the fledglings to lightning quick action and skillful flying to get a meal. We were awed by their flying ability only one week after fledging.

That same afternoon, a fledgling alighted on a Cryder House terrace railing just three floors above ours and, later, landed on the roofs of Cryder House and adjacent buildings. When a fledgling perched on the roof of the closest building, we were able to read the oversized number (87) on its left leg band.

August yielded the usual activities of four healthy peregrines. We gloried in observing their inspiring hunting attacks. These included stoops, at tremendous speeds, which regularly exceeded 100 miles an hour, dives at prey from varied positions, tail chases combined with acceleration spurts, simple interceptions of the prey with no apparent course change by either antagonist, and captures from behind. We witnessed numerous feedings and watched the young share meals. One morning, a fledgling was enjoying breakfast on the Queens tower pier. Only several feet away, four pigeons were unconcernedly preening. As the second fledgling alighted on the pier, the pigeons flew off with great alarm. This phenomenon seemed very consistent. Pigeons do not recognize sitting peregrines as their mortal enemy. However, when a peregrine is in flight, pigeons aloft take evasive action even if the peregrine is not interested in them. Peregrines almost always attack by flying at a bird that is also in the air.

The relationship between predators and their prey has been widely studied. For example, lions on the African plains can evoke tremendous fear in their prey species when they're in the hunting mode. The same predator, when not hunting, is all but ignored by the prey species because its body language signals that this is a safe time. The predator exhibits specific approach patterns and body positions when hunting. Birds are not credited with the brain power of mammals but they show tendencies to recognize predators in the hunting mode. No doubt this survival response derives from instinctual mechanisms rather than decision making. Those creatures that can identify and evade danger more competently will be the ones to survive and pro-create. They will produce young who will be endowed with those survival skills. During that August, the young regaled us with their unbridled enthusiasm in pursuing their most outstanding natural gift, flying. On one occasion, we saw a youngster take off from the beach area in Queens and head toward the Bronx. Before disappearing over the Bronx, we saw it attack three birds. Whether these were serious attempts to capture prey or just exuberant displays of its natural incli-nation to pursue flying objects is an open question. A herring gull sitting in the water became the recipient of a long, graceful swooping dive executed by one of the young. Large gulls are not prey under the best of circumstances and certainly are not of any interest in the water. But to a young peregrine, every object in its territory is subject to its interest and pursuit.

The young often followed their parents on hunting expeditions. Usually they brought up the rear and did not affect the outcome. On one memorable evening, all four peregrines were aloft in the face of storm winds. It was wonderful to see them using the power of the wind to sculpt their flight trajectories as an artist utilizes his medium to express himself, and at the same time provide pleasure to others. We saw cooperative hunts, too, most often against pigeons. To the unini-tiated, it would seem nearly impossible for a pigeon to escape from several healthy peregrines intent on making it their next meal. But, after we had witnessed many hunts, it became very evident to us that pigeons are speedy and accomplished fliers. In most cases, they are not easily caught. Yet there are instances when the capture appears rou-tine. Part of the thrill in watching a real wildlife drama is that the outcome cannot be predicted.

One morning, before leaving for work, I observed the two fledg-lings on the Queens tower. It was a nice pick-me-up to start the day.

Later as I walked to my car, something caused me to look up at the roof of an adjacent building. I saw a youngster sitting on the parapet railing. It was as if it was beckoning to me to keep my interest on high. I was aware that I read too much into these chance events but it was fun and good for the soul.

That particular morning, I gave an important presentation at a business meeting at the World Trade Center. The meeting room was on the fifty-sixth floor of a 102-story tower. I sat facing a wall with many high, narrow windows, which gave me a segmented view to the south. Unreasonable as it seemed, I clearly saw two peregrines cavorting in the spaces between the tall buildings. Yes, even at work peregrines sought me out. I didn't for a minute think these were my peregrine friends from the Throgs, but they were beautiful nonetheless. The meeting adjourned shortly after my presentation ended. I immediately rushed to the window to improve my angle of observation, whereupon a colleague offered, "Don't jump, you did real good." It seemed funny at the time.

Toward the end of September and into October, we saw only one young peregrine at a time. It was banded on the right leg. We surmised that the other fledgling had dispersed. On October 29, we saw three peregrines hunting and then the fledgling eating a fresh kill. This is the last date of the year that we definitely observed a fledgling.

We expected the adults to overwinter at the Throgs as they had the previous year because the winter weather is not severe in New York City and there is a limitless supply of prey birds, even in the dead of winter. We learned later, however, that it is not so simple. Most peregrines migrate during the fall, following their breeding season after their young have dispersed, because their prey base increasingly becomes unavailable. We asked ourselves, "What does a peregrine do that nests in a climate that provides prey throughout the entire year?" We knew that migration is thought to be genetically determined, so that if a peregrine is of migrating stock, it will migrate regardless of weather conditions or prey base availability. We weren't sure why our peregrines overwintered in 1983-84 but we anticipated that they would do so again for the 1984-85 winter. They did.

3

In Full Swing

(1985)

On January 2, 1985, Dolores and I observed the adult female peregrine capture a bird at the Throgs. We had been seeing both adults regularly through the fall and winter until January 12 when we went on vacation. When we returned on January 29, we again immediately found them.

Early March was cold. The peregrines kept warm with courtship behavior. The male performed intricate flying maneuvers to demonstrate his prowess to his mate. He dove down at tremendous speed toward the water. An inexperienced onlooker would surely have feared that the peregrine would not have been able to pull up in time to avoid hitting the water. But he always did and did so with a spectacular maneuverability that took our breath away. He hovered motionless near or above his intended mate as she expectantly sat on the tower top. Sometimes he lowered his legs as he hovered. He captured prey, brought his catch to the female, and shared it with her. Courtship is designed to prepare the female for the breeding cycle. Five days later, Ted LeViness observed them copulate.

On May 4, Dolores and I met Eileen Jones, the DEC observer for the current 1985 breeding season, and discussed our experiences of the two prior seasons. It seemed we were becoming established as reliable observers, worthy of being consulted, and we looked forward to our third breeding season and to collaborating with Eileen.

We saw the adults, on June 1, flying around the eyrie in an extremely agitated manner. They repeatedly made tight, circular approaches at the nest box area, interspersed with larger loops outward.

This behavior signified an intrusion into the nest area. They were obviously exasperated with their inability to fend off the interlopers. Finally, whatever it was that had been disturbing them left the site and they resumed their normal activities. They hunted successfully, making two kills. We called DEC to report the disturbance we had witnessed. They informed us that The Peregrine Fund and DEC staff had been compelled to relocate four chicks because, on a previous visit to the eyrie, they had found that the eggs had been laid in a narrow box beam under the bridge roadway. The eggs would have been safe in that spot and any chicks that would have hatched would also have been safe. However, the cavity was unsuitable because chicks need a space wide enough to engage in wingflapping, a vital exercise that develops their flight muscles. Since their wingspreads would grow to more than a yard, the inadequate nest space would eventually cause them to move out of it prematurely and almost certainly to their death in the water below.

To remedy this, the chicks had been relocated into a nest box which had been installed close to the original cavity. During this intervention, the adult male did his best to defend his progeny. He flew at the transgressors repeatedly, trying to discourage them and force them away from his young. He flew within inches of them, but to no avail. Frustrated, he became discouraged and left while the female remained close by vocalizing forcefully.

During the next week, hunting was the major activity. One day the adults perched close to one another atop the Throgs tower and sat there for a full hour while a driving rain beat down on them. Usually, they took to cover when it rained. There was one particular area that they had used so often during times when it had rained or snowed that Dolores and I had dubbed it the "rain spot." Luckily, for us, it was located directly across from our apartment on the lower edge of the large steel beams that support the bridge roadway just south of the Queens anchorage. This area is sheltered from the inclement weather by a protective overhang which deflects the icy northwest and northeast winds. The peregrines, however, seemed impervious to the rigors of winter's cold, biting winds, heavy rain, the fumes and noise created by the bridge traffic, and the interventions of humans.

We first observed the fledglings on June 15, two females and a male, on the Queens pier. This location was a perfect area for them.

It provided a long, unobstructed runway on which they could clamber about and fly over without being directly over the surrounding water. Within a week, the fledglings were flying well and trying to emulate their parents. They began to join their parents on hunts. On the morning of June 26, Ted LeViness observed six kills. There are many peregrine watchers who have never had the good fortune of having seen even one kill. For example, the devoted individuals who monitor peregrine hack sites for many weeks rarely see their charges make a kill. The observation stations at hack sites are positioned to provide a favorable view of the hack-box without disturbing the birds. However, the fledglings usually capture their prey out of the observer's sight range. Watchers at other sites, such as buildings, although they are very close to the nest itself, may have narrow vistas.

In the morning of the last day of June in 1985, we were treated to an uncommon hunting session. While observing the peregrines from the beach in Queens, a mourning dove appeared over the water west of the Bronx tower. All five peregrines took off after the seemingly doomed bird. Each alternately made a pass at the quarry. The chase covered a distance of several thousand yards. The lucky dove escaped unscathed into Queens, leading us to believe that this was not a serious hunt but rather a training exercise for the young.

Several days later, we again saw all five peregrines hunting as a group. This time it was a pigeon that was the ill-fated recipient of their attention. After several unsuccessful passes by various members of the hunting party, the adult female rocketed in from the rear and applied the characteristic slash and grab for the capture. It was as if she were saying to the youngsters, "This is how it's done." Peregrines try to slash their victims with a rear talon to disable them. Prior to visual evidence of this technique provided by slow-motion photography, it was widely believed that peregrines hit their prey with a closed foot.

On another July morning, one of the youngsters had a bird securely in its talons. It started feeding while the prey was still very much alive. The victim's squirming was disconcerting to the peregrine as well as to the human onlookers. Because the pigeon continued to struggle in the youngster's talons, the peregrine realized that it would be better to dine on an inert object and dispatched it with one lethal neck bite. The importance of this observation lies in the fact that the pigeon was alive in the fledgling's talons, denoting that the youngster almost assuredly caught the bird itself.

I observed an astounding hunting session by the adult male one morning. He snared ten small birds in very rapid fashion. He cached his kills, then he carried each little victim, in turn, up into the Throgs and, almost immediately, he came out ready to hunt again. His speed, maneuverability, and tenacity were electrifying to watch. I had never seen such a determined, sustained display of a peregrine in the hunting mode as I had witnessed that morning. Cornelius Ward, an avid peregrine watcher, was the only other person with me to witness this natural wonder. We agreed that the rest of the world had missed a special event.

Dolores and I continued to observe all five peregrines until July 19. The last date any of the young were reported seen was August 18, but the adults were on territory to the close of 1985. We missed the youngsters after they dispersed but we rejoiced in the knowledge that they had developed to independence satisfactorily. The fledglings had been observed for more than a month after they fledged and at least one was seen, on the wing, for more than two months. Prior to our last sightings of them, they appeared to be hunting for themselves, the main prerequisite for fledglings to survive independently.

The first of two noteworthy events, during the last months of the year, occurred on November 23. Dolores and I stepped out of our car in the Cryder House parking lot and heard loud, insistent peregrine alarm vocalizations. We were ecstatic to discover three peregrines aloft. We rushed to our apartment and brought our binoculars and scope into action. The visitor was a second-year female with a red-taped left leg band and a black band on her right leg. She was perched on a bridge cable, a resident peregrine on each side of her. All three sat calmly. We could only imagine that the residents were explaining to the interloper that she could visit but she could not stay. She didn't.

The other event was an international conference on birds of prey held by the Raptor Research Foundation (RRF) in Sacramento, California, from November 1 to 11. The RRF is dedicated to the study and preservation of raptors. None of my raptorphile friends were able to attend this conference so I alone attended. The conference theme was the management of birds of prey and was of special interest to me because it was also the twentieth anniversary of the first major conference on peregrines ever held. The 1965 Madison conference had established the plight of the peregrine falcon populations as being in a steep decline. Three full days of the 1985 conference were convened as an International Peregrine Conference—Twenty Year Anniversary Meeting. Dr. Tom Cade, founder and director of The Peregrine Fund, spoke at the conference and acted as session chairman for the section on Status of Peregrine Populations Since 1965—North America.

I attended four days of the conference. There were more than 800 attendees from many different nations. The atmosphere was electric. The presentations, films, slides, and informal talk were chock full of new insights and information for me. I found them interesting and enjoyable and, like a sponge, I absorbed as much as possible. Dr. Cade and I discussed my observations. It was very gratifying to me to have my three seasons of peregrine watching considered as important. Undoubtedly, this accepting attitude motivated me to continue my monitoring efforts. The international flavor of The Peregrine Conference was evidenced by presenters from Europe (France, Great Britain, West Germany, Sweden, Italy, Switzerland, Spain), Ecuador, Arabia, South Africa, Australia, and Greenland. Peregrine Fund contributors included Barclay, Burnham, Gilroy, Heinrich, and Walton. A partial list of other well-known raptor experts who spoke includes Bird, Enderson, Fyfe, Hickey, Nelson, Newton, Ratcliffe, Redig, and Tordoff.

Some of the major topics covered were peregrine breeding, pesticide contamination, population dynamics, management strategies, and historical perspectives. There was no overwhelming statement of success but there were reports of many geographic areas where the population was increasing. The continued release of captive-bred falcons was a factor which did not allow for an accurate prognostication of whether the peregrine population was self-sustaining in many regions. The tenor was upbeat because of the accomplishments to date.

We looked forward to the next breeding season with great anticipation. Dolores and I had had three enjoyable and enlightening seasons with our peregrine neighbors. Our enthusiasm remained at a high pitch. We never tired of watching them and we enjoyed learning all that we could about them.

4

Bridge Rescues

(1986)

Dolores and I observed both adult peregrines at the Throgs
throughout the 1985-86 winter. The first notable event of 1986
took place on March 17. Despite all the sizable spaces within the
Throgs structure and the vast open expanse around it, an adult male
peregrine had somehow managed to entangle its wing on a rope hanging from the bridge. Picture this forlorn creature hanging by a wing,
from that massive structure, 150 feet above the water. I had not
actually seen this event personally but I have recreated it from talking
to DEC personnel and studying newspaper accounts.

An observant barge captain chugging along below the Throgs
discovered the peregrine's predicament. He radioed several official
agencies and DEC responded quickly. The Coast Guard positioned a
vessel beneath the trapped bird and a DEC conservation officer went
up on the Throgs. Unable to retrieve the peregrine, he cut the rope
that held the bird. The peregrine ingloriously fluttered down into an
impromptu safety net, a blanket. The fall did not add any injury to the
insult and he appeared healthy. As a precautionary measure, he was
taken to a raptor rehabilitator in Brooklyn for further examination.
His injuries were slight, but he was transferred to a rehabilitator in
Albany because there wasn't sufficient space in which to house him for
a convalescent period. This peregrine had a band on each leg. Records
identified him as "Rio" (Rio de Janeiro); he had been released at a
building hack site in Boston in July, 1984. Peregrine chicks were given
names of world famous cities at that particular release site.

Rio's right leg band was removed by the rehabilitator to help future observers differentiate him from the resident female who had a right leg band. Was he the resident male at the Throgs or had he just been passing through when he became trapped?

Meanwhile, Rio was healthy and merely needed exercise to regain his normal flying condition after the bridge incident. During that rehabilitation period, we met Kathy O'Brien of DEC's Endangered Species Unit who had the responsibility of handling the New York City metropolitan region peregrine activities. DEC had not hired a locally based observer for the 1986 breeding season, but we had the opportunity of reviewing the events of the past breeding seasons with her and together we assessed the prospects. Everyone hoped that the peregrines would not encounter too much trouble during the season but our experience indicated that there would be problems that humans could solve.

When Rio was ready for release at the end of March, Kathy called to confer with me regarding the selection of a suitable release site, because of my familiarity with the area. I was most flattered to be considered a sort of "local expert," and happily cooperated. A likely site was Little Bay Park in Queens, a large open area, within sight of the Throgs and about half a mile away from it. But a release within close sight range of the Throgs was possibly dangerous because if Rio were not the resident male, he might be seen and harassed by the resident adults. Kathy selected Ferry Point Park in the Bronx for Rio's release because, although it is within sight range of the Throgs, it is almost two miles distant. A portion of Ferry Point Park is situated directly beneath the Bronx-Whitestone Bridge. Rio was released with appropriate fanfare on April 1, 1986. He flew up high and alighted on the Bronx-Whitestone Bridge.

Several days later, while in conference with Kathy, she said something about Rio's release and this triggered my memory: I had observed two adults at the Throgs prior to Rio's release. Checking my log, I found that, indeed, I had recorded two adults on the wing, on March 30, 1986. This meant that during Rio's two-week convalescent period, another male had replaced him, if he were the resident male. Parenthetically, let me state that the recording of observations is extremely important and provides valuable information when monitoring nesting situations or other activities. Observations that seem routine at the moment of occurrence may at a future time prove to

48

have discovery value, as it had in the case at hand. Rio was again captured at the Throgs during the 1988 breeding season, leading to the inevitable conclusion that he had been the resident male, was replaced during his absence, and regained his position immediately upon his return.

On the morning of April 5, at the Throgs, Ted LeViness observed the Throgs peregrines copulate and Kathy saw them copulate four times during April 9. They were "doing their thing" and conditions seemed promising for the upcoming breeding season. On May 30, Jack Barclay, The Peregrine Fund's reintroduction coordinator, inspected the nest area, under the roadway at the Queens tower, and observed two chicks in the nest box which had been placed there the preceding year. They appeared to be about four days old. This was wonderful news; we had young for the fourth consecutive breeding season. He planned to return in several weeks to band the chicks. Jack also reported that there was a pair of peregrines at the Verrazano-Narrows Bridge incubating eggs.

Kathy and Jack returned to the Throgs eyrie on June 17 and were pleasantly surprised to find not two but three chicks. One chick must have been hidden from Jack's view during his May 30 visit. This undercount was understandable since his inspection had been conducted from a distance. They double-banded the chicks, two males and a female. One band was the universal Federal Fish and Wildlife type. The other had larger numerals and letters to allow for easier reading in the field.

The latest information regarding the Verrazano-Narrows was that one chick had hatched and that there were still two unhatched eggs. Subsequently, the one chick was banded and the two unhatched eggs were removed for laboratory analysis.

Early on the morning of July 8, 1986, Ted was observing at the Throgs and spotted a fledgling perched on the roof of the Hammerstein Mansion. The first fledgling of the season. He alerted me and I rushed down to join him. We worked our way to within twenty-five yards of the bird while the adult female nervously watched us from vantage points on the Throgs. Oddly, there was a group of small birds also perched on the roof of the mansion, only several yards from the fledgling, and they actually moved closer to the peregrine to inspect this unknown creature. The fledgling took little notice of his potential future meals. Ted cranked up the power on his variable-power zoom binoculars and was able to read the large figures "A22A" on the fledgling's left leg band. It identified him as one of the two male chicks from the Throgs. According to our observations, he had fledged that morning or the day before.

That evening, I was riveted to my scope by some very interesting behavior. The adult female and A22A were sitting in the "rain spot" several yards south of the anchorage. She flew off and returned shortly with a prey item. She started to feed on it only a few feet away from A22A, who immediately assumed the begging posture: bending forward and vocalizing plaintively. He called so loudly that we clearly heard him at our apartment. The adult female continued to feed, ignoring him completely. Slowly, he moved closer and closer, continuing to beg. She kept on eating for several minutes and then she abruptly flew off, leaving the carcass. A22A footed it anxiously and commenced feeding with a hungry quickness.

Half an hour later, the female arrived with another kill and left immediately. A22A certainly did not go to bed hungry that evening. At 8:00 P.M., I went out and left the scope positioned on A22A. I thought that it was likely that he would remain in that spot all night. At 6:30 A.M. the next day, I rushed to the scope, and did indeed find that A22A was still there. Had he remained in the same spot for over ten hours or had he moved and then returned to it? Regardless, it was a testament to the tenacity of the wild young predator.

Drama and peregrine fledglings are like a pair of wings: they go together. The following afternoon, A22A pursued a dove and they both ended up in the water. A22A was able to "swim" to the beach and haul out. He then scampered across the sandy beach, climbed up a low retaining wall, and perched on it. Though tired and bedraggled, he was unhurt. However, to some well-intentioned neighbors, he appeared possibly injured or in need of assistance. They knew of the peregrine monitoring program because we had educated them regarding the endangered species designation. One worried neighbor threw a jacket over the fledgling and took him up to his eighth-floor apartment. He put A22A in a plastic milk box provisioned with water and strips of raw meat and placed it on his terrace, facing the Throgs.

The good Samaritan then called the American Society for the Prevention of Cruelty to Animals and other agencies to obtain help but no one wanted any part of a wild peregrine. Dolores and I were notified by another neighbor of the fledgling's predicament. We rushed to the apartment where A22A was being held and when we approached to within two feet of his makeshift cage, A22A yelled loudly, reared back, and presented his talons. Talons are indisputably the most formidable weapons that a peregrine possesses and thrusting all eight of them in an opponent's face will frequently be a sufficient defense. He also made himself look as large and ferocious as possible by spreading his wings and fluffing out his feathers. This was the appropriate attitude a healthy peregrine should display under those conditions. He looked healthy and unhurt but we couldn't be certain without an examination. We could see the adult female on the Throgs, at that very moment, scanning the area in search of her wayward youngster. She would have been able to see him if the terrace had the usual see-through aluminum type of railings. Unfortunately, this terrace was hip high and had solid block construction walls, obstructing all view.

We notified DEC of the incident and also called Eileen Jones (the 1985 season observer) and asked for their assistance in returning the fledgling to the Throgs. Eileen arrived equipped with thick gloves and a large airline-type animal transport cage. She examined A22A and found him to be sound. We decided to try to place the youngster on the pier directly beneath the nest, which would enable the adults to reunite with their offspring. With A22A in the cage, we drove to Triborough Bridge and Tunnel Authority's (TBTA) administrative offices at the Throgs. It was wonderful to see the fledgling up close and interact with that truly wild creature. While in the car, we could readily detect the odor of his body. Even at this tender age, he had a distinct presence. I took the liberty of running my fingertips lightly over a few of his feathers that were accessible through the cage's air slits. Dolores and I were elated to have been able to help our peregrine neighbor.

TBTA personnel took us to the Queens tower and we gingerly climbed into an elevator. This was no ordinary elevator and we stood in it, shoulder to shoulder, with some trepidation. Dimly lit, our conveyor noisily descended and lurched to a stop. When the door opened, we were confronted with an exterior platform which was still twenty-five feet above our destination, the main pier. It was now almost dark and we still needed to negotiate twenty ladder rungs down to the pier.

We concluded that it would be impossible to get down the ladder safely while holding a wild peregrine. It would be wiser to effect the release during daylight. A release at nightfall increases the chances of a mishap when dealing with such an inexperienced youngster. Eileen took our ungrateful prisoner to her Brooklyn apartment for the night where she provided him with food and water. He was a quiet guest. The following afternoon, Eileen retraced our journey and released A22A. He flew immediately and was joined by his mother.

At that point, we had become very concerned because we hadn't seen Rio, the resident male, since July 3, almost a week earlier. Also, A22A had been on the wing for at least three days and, contrary to our expectations, no other chick had been observed. What had become of them? We notified DEC of our observations and concerns.

The following morning, I saw the female flying over the anchorage in an extremely agitated manner; she kept this up for three hours. I could neither see nor determine the cause and called TBTA. They advised me that a dog had wandered onto the roadway from Queens. The peregrines obviously considered the dog as a predator and therefore a danger to their young. In a more natural setting, such as a cliff ledge, any four-legged mammal usually would be a predator.

Later that day we saw A22A sitting on a cable. The female landed on the cable close to him and presented him with a carcass. The aplomb shown by this recently fledged creature in sitting on a perfectly round cable was very reassuring. But he wasn't able to manage the prey at the same time and it fell from the cable. The female dove down and snatched the falling meal before it had dropped twenty yards; and there, this lesson ended.

On July 15, Kathy inspected the Throgs in response to our report that we hadn't seen Rio or the awaited fledglings. She found absolutely nothing. No Rio, no other fledglings, no remains. There was not a clue as to what had transpired. We could only speculate that Rio and the other fledglings disappeared during the July Fourth period when there were special celebrations creating much noise and increased waterway traffic about the Throgs. Since noise, activity, fumes, and other human pollution had never bothered them before, unless it had occurred very close to their nesting site, we considered the possibility that the peregrines might have been abducted or otherwise harmed.

Whatever the truth of the matter might be, there was a somber sense of loss.

Nine days later, we saw the female aloft, accompanied by what appeared to be an adult male. He wore a dark band on each leg. He was definitely not Rio, which substantiated our determination that Rio was no longer at the Throgs. Several days later, Ted observed an adult male, in full view of the female, repeatedly diving at A22A. Although the adult was highly aggressive, no contact was made. Ted opined that it would have been uncharacteristic for the natural sire to act so hostile toward his own progeny, which seemed to corroborate our premise that Rio had been replaced when he disappeared around July 4.

A22A was last seen at the Throgs on August 19. The adults were observed regularly and strong winds, especially those from the northwest, frequently brought them out directly in front of our terrace. These winds hit the west face of the anchorage, creating a strong uplift upon which the peregrines loved to ride. We dubbed this technique "riding the elevator." They would ride the elevator as high as possible and there seek additional uplifting air currents. Sometimes they were able to start a hunting foray from this position, a process called "waiting on" by falconers. Waiting on describes a raptor's holding position above a hunting area. When the aerial hunter locates prey, it dives down to make the kill.

These same northwest winds spill over the top of Cryder House and create a sustained torrent of air, upon which the peregrines love to rise. They approach Cryder House from the east and enter this invisible wind stream with their wings set so that there is tremendous lift applied to their undersides. Effortlessly, they rise slowly and pass over the top of the building. It reminds us of sailors beating into the wind and slowly going against the natural force opposing them. The peregrines would often return with the wind behind them, at a high rate of speed, again with wings set. Both against and with the wind they travel, effortlessly. It tantalizes our minds to see their mastery of the skies.

On November 2, 1986, the Cape May Bird Observatory Hawk Watch enumerators tallied 140 peregrines and 800 ospreys migrating past their station. Both totals were daily records for the species at Cape May. The importance of observing and recording migratory raptors was demonstrated during their drastic decline in the 1960s due to pesticide poisoning. Declining hawk-watch counts were one of the first indicators of reduced populations. The steadily increasing migration numbers in recent years and the development of urban peregrine nesting centers is evidence of the resurgent nesting success of these raptors.

We observed two adult peregrines at the Throgs regularly through to the end of the year. We saw them hunt together, share meals, and transfer prey in midair, among other activities. Their fidelity to each other and to the site was a joy they shared with us. They became members of our family. Or we of theirs!

5

Bridge Disasters

(1987)

As Dolores and I were driving across the Bronx-Whitestone Bridge on January 5, 1987, we observed a peregrine atop the Bronx tower. The next day, we again saw a peregrine on the Whitestone Bridge. The New York City Rare Bird Alert reported that four peregrines had been sighted in the vicinity of the Whitestone Bridge during the Christmas bird count, conducted on January 3 and 4. The Throgs peregrines had been seen at the Whitestone and no doubt traveling peregrines are unable to resist the temptation to inspect these attractive structures.

In the period spanning January through March, Dolores and I regularly observed Rio and his mate at the Throgs. Sometime during the period after Rio had disappeared from the Throgs around July 4, 1986, he had returned and regained his position as resident male. The male that had replaced him was no longer at the Throgs.

On March 7, Ted LeViness, conducting a lone vigil at the Throgs, observed the peregrines mating on the Bronx tower. The breeding season was off to a promising start. On April 5, Kathy O'Brien (DEC) and William Sugg of The Peregrine Fund conducted an inspection of the Throgs. They found the female sitting in a cavity, formed by the junction of several steel beams, below the roadway close to the Bronx tower. She hunkered down and sat tight while the observers were near the nest. Usually such behavior signifies that the bird is on eggs. Because she did not move throughout their visit, they were unable to positively determine whether or not she had eggs. The nervous adult male remained nearby during their inspection. The nest cavity faced west and it was difficult to see into it, even from on the bridge, and impossible from any location off the bridge. Clearly, it was going to be much more difficult to conduct our observations this season.

Kathy and William had also made an inspection of the Verrazano-Narrows Bridge that day and had observed a similar set of conditions near that bridge's Brooklyn tower. The female had maintained her brooding posture and the male had hovered nearby.

April 12 provided an amusing story. William Sugg had spent most of the day observing the Throgs site but could not find a single peregrine. After having been "shut out" all day, he came to confer with us about the nesting peregrines. As William stood with Dolores and me on our indoor-outdoor carpeted terrace, a pigeon alighted a mere five feet from us. I flushed it off the terrace but it immediately returned to the exact spot. I again chased the pigeon off and again it determinedly returned to its spot. After our futile attempts were rebuffed twice more, I jokingly remarked, "That bird seems to have chosen that particular spot and I wouldn't be surprised if she were to lay an egg." She then turned her back to us, squatted down, and squeezed out an egg. She had selected that particular spot and even three humans standing so close could not deter her.

The first day of May was noteworthy because we had a visitor at the Throgs. An immature peregrine flew the length of the Throgs, progressing very slowly as if it were "checking out" the Throgs. Shortly thereafter, I saw our resident female perched on the Bronx tower. I was sure that she had not seen the young visitor because she would undoubtedly have challenged it.

The State University of New York Maritime College at Fort Schuyler occupies the land directly adjacent to the Bronx tower of the Throgs. To facilitate monitoring of the nest, DEC had obtained permission for observers to gain admittance to Fort Schuyler. Starting on May 3, Ted and I regularly traveled across the Throgs to Fort Schuyler to make our observations. That very morning, we saw two peregrines on the Throgs. That evening, William Sugg advised me that he had inspected the Throgs during the afternoon and that he had observed the female sitting on three eggs. We were ecstatic; we had eggs for the fifth consecutive breeding season.

On the Saturday morning of the next week, before 7:00 A.M., Ted and I were at Fort Schuyler to conduct our usual vigil. We were suddenly jolted by the sight of a crew of riggers clambering about all around the nest cavity. They were installing lines, ladders, and other equipment in preparation for a major painting project. What atrocious bad luck it was that they should start at that particular area. A disturbance of this magnitude so close to the nest site could ruin the season's nesting attempt or, even worse, force the peregrines off the Throgs entirely.

We could see the female peregrine defending her nest area very vigorously. Of course, riggers are also "tough birds" and they were not going to succumb to the protestations of a two-pound creature, regardless of its ferocity. I called Dolores, who was at home, to relate the impending disaster. To notify DEC immediately, Dolores called Kathy at her home. Kathy said she would do what she could but we knew it was difficult because she was 150 miles away in the Albany area. Dejectedly, we waited and hoped for the best.

We tried to enjoy the remainder of the day's observations despite the fearful condition we surveyed each time our binoculars were trained on the nest area. A peregrine visitor appeared at the Bronx tower and was immediately pursued by the resident female. The interloper wisely offered no resistance and flew away over Long Island Sound. Nesting peregrines will not abide another raptor anywhere near their eyrie, especially during the breeding season; and that includes their own kind.

The subject of unwanted visitors in the vicinity of a peregrine's eyrie brings to mind their particular dislike for crows. Many crows frequent the land areas adjacent to both ends of the Throgs. In fact, crows have nested for several consecutive years directly across from my terrace. On one occasion, a crow was feeding its nestlings when the screaming female peregrine zoomed down to harass it. The crow cowered in its nest and cawed in response. The peregrine dove by the crow tirelessly for half an hour. There was no doubt that the crow would have suffered injury or death had it left the security of its tree. The crow was in its own nest and far away from the peregrine's nest at the Bronx tower. We thought that the peregrine had an abundance of nerve to harass the crow since it obviously did not have any relevance to the peregrine's nest.

At Fort Schuyler, Ted and I observed the female peregrine chase a crow, which was hundreds of yards inland over the Bronx and well away from her eyrie. We had never seen a crow near any of the peregrine eyries. Whether crows are too smart to imperil themselves by flying into open areas without cover or the vigilant peregrines keep them at a distance is unclear. It is probably a combination of both factors.

As we watched from our vantage point at Fort Schuyler, an interesting drama was next on our bill of fare. The adult male caught a blue jay over the open water west of the Throgs. The peregrine flew toward the Throgs with his prize but obviously had not yet killed it because we could easily hear its strident calling. The jay was being held firmly, upside down, facing his captor. Plucky to the very end, it was reaching up and trying to hit the peregrine with his bill. Finally, the peregrine bent toward his victim and delivered the fatal, spine-severing neck bite.

Jim Weaver of The Peregrine Fund inspected both the Throgs Neck and Verrazano-Narrows bridges on May 18 and found three unhatched eggs at each eyrie. We still hoped for a successful breeding season at the Throgs but the odds were stacked against it because of the ongoing work there. Subsequently, we learned that the bridge workers were frequently directly at the nest cavity, causing the incubating female to react violently and periodically abandon her eggs.

We did not flag in our observations and were rewarded with views of the peregrines hunting, capturing prey, and chasing crows. Several times we saw the female fly to the Whitestone Bridge and alight on it, prompting many discussions as to whether a second pair of peregrines could nest there successfully. True, the resident adults at the Throgs would have direct visual contact with any peregrines on the other bridge, but since there is so much prey available at both sites, there would be no need for either pair to hunt near the other's domain. The critical question was the territorial needs of the Throgs resident pair. Would they accept another pair at a distance of less than two miles? It would be wonderful to have a second pair of peregrines close by but it seemed too much to expect. Peregrines like to have their airspace free of other raptors and the distance seemed inadequate in peregrine terms.

We witnessed and enjoyed a courtship flying session. The male performed spectacular aerial maneuvers, diving down at great speed and pulling up abruptly into a graceful glide to display his flying prowess. He hovered above and near his mate as she perched on the top of the Throgs tower. He captured a bird and presented it to her as evidence of his ability to be a good provider. Peregrines are known to perform these rituals even though they have already mated and produced eggs for the season. Mock copulation, the mounting of the female without insemination taking place, is another behavior in which mated pairs engage, despite their having a successful clutch of eggs, as a reaffirmation of their fidelity.

The end of June brought changes in the activity patterns of the adults that corroborated our worst fears. The female was seen away from the eyrie much more frequently and increasingly returned to the Queens tower after her hunting forays. If she had young, she should have been seen almost exclusively at the Bronx tower where the nest was located. This change in behavior accelerated in the ensuing weeks so that the Queens tower became the pair's main focal point, as it always had been in previous years. The nesting season was most certainly beyond remedy at this point. In fact, the nest area had been completely draped with tarpaulins for several days, seemingly bringing down the final curtain on our saga of human interference. Unfortunately, I did not have official status and could not intervene to prevent the disturbances at the eyrie.

The nest was inspected and two of its three eggs were recovered and transported to the DEC laboratory for analysis. We despaired that the breeding season had been a failure after the four successful ones that we had enjoyed.

The adults appeared to be in excellent condition at the conclusion of their Bronx ordeal. The only degradation that we observed was the usual one: their plumage was not as clean as it would normally be. Sitting on eggs is a dirty job because the nest cavity is filthy. The tremendous torrent of traffic constantly flowing across the bridge produces a downpouring of dust, automotive exhaust emissions, and other materials, which cover all of the bridge's surfaces. The female's breast feathers were especially soiled because she had spent many more hours on the eggs than the male. However, we saw the gradual brightening in her plumage and this served as a beacon to light our way forward, away from our sadness of the lost breeding season.

We continued observing the peregrines and felt privileged to witness their intimate interactions; these were daily routines for the

59

peregrines, of course, but thrilling for us. Our pleasure was heightened because we did not intrude into their lives, which provided continual, anecdotal events. One afternoon as I observed the female feeding, for example, she suddenly jumped off the carcass and dove down toward a pigeon that was flying low over the water. I had never seen an attack initiated directly from a feeding position. I thought that there must have been something particularly appetizing about this pigeon, but the peregrine failed to capture her intended quarry. On another day, I saw the adults alight close to one another. The female started feeding on a cached pigeon. After she had eaten very determinedly for fifteen minutes, the male moved closer and pulled the remains to himself. She did not protest and flew away. The male fed for half an hour.

Kathy O'Brien called on August 10 to exchange information and divulged the fact that at the Verrazano, the adult female had been found dead. The body had decomposed but a leg band was recovered. The band number enabled DEC to ascertain that she was the 1984 offspring of the famous female "Scarlett," who reigned at a Baltimore, Maryland, skyscraper from 1977 to 1984.

Throughout the autumn period until December 17 when we went to Florida for a vacation, we continued to observe the adult peregrines at the Throgs. One September evening, we saw a peregrine visitor at the Throgs just after we had seen both resident adults. The visitor left the area without being challenged by the resident peregrines, who were not in view. Whenever we see a visiting peregrine at the Throgs, we wonder how many there are out there just waiting to move into an established nesting territory. It is very important to have a reservoir of unattached adult peregrines in the New York City metropolitan region because it enables a surviving adult to quickly replace its missing mate. It is especially vital that the replacement be made immediately if the loss occurs during the breeding season because that season's breeding opportunity would otherwise be lost. There is ample evidence to support the conclusion that such a reservoir does indeed exist in our area. In each instance where a resident adult at a nesting site has died or disappeared, it has been replaced in a timely manner. For example, on two occasions when Rio was absent from the Throgs, he was quickly replaced. Several adult females and at least one male have been lost at the Verrazano-Narrows Bridge. In each case, they were replaced in time for the next breeding cycle.

In October, the Raptor Research Foundation's 1987 annual meeting was convened in Boise, Idaho. Ted and I attended the meeting and enjoyed it immensely. A field trip to The Peregrine Fund's World Center for Birds of Prey and the Snake River Canyon was very rewarding. Golden eagles were observed several times at great distances but we viewed three prairie falcons at close range as they flew wonderfully acrobatic routines above the picturesque canyon.

Oliphant (Department of Veterinary Anatomy, University of Saskatchewan), in a paper on Peregrine Falcon Breeding Strategies, suggested that migratory female peregrines, which had engaged in active courtship behavior, including prey transfers, copulation, etc., and then disappeared, might be ". . . tundra peregrines using territorial *anatum* males to supply food prior to finishing their migration to move to northerly breeding grounds." Sands, in a paper on nesting peregrines in southwestern Oregon, remarked that, at one eyrie, the female took migrating gulls as they passed within a mile or two of the eyrie.

One evening at an informal presentation session, Friedrich (Fritz) Reilmann, a German ornithologist, held the audience spellbound with his description and slide presentation of a peregrine nest in a Bremerhaven Harbor lighthouse. He had been working on a cormorant nesting platform project when he discovered that peregrines were nesting in the abandoned living room while thirty-five pairs of cormorants were nesting above on the roof and balcony. He installed a blind in the eyrie chamber itself and spent an entire weekend photographing the peregrine family at a distance of several yards. His fantastic slides depicted slices of the life of a pair of wild peregrines. Although the blind intruded into their home, they nevertheless continued to minister to their young. So powerful is their procreative drive that they will suffer extremely distressing molestations rather than abandon their young.

One series of slides showed the female flying in toward the eyrie. Mr. Reilmann stood in her flight path and she demonstrated her great displeasure by adroitly snaring the cloth hat from his head and delivering a blood-letting scratch to his forehead. She presented the hat to her chicks, footing it repeatedly. Other remarkable slides showed the female actually picking at an eggshell that was also being laboriously worked on from within by her soon-to-hatch chick. There was no question that she was assisting in the hatching process. To our knowledge, this was an important behavioral discovery because the literature in the field contains no observations of this phenomenon.

I invited Mr. Reilmann to visit Dolores and me in New York City prior to his return to Germany so that I could show him peregrines in an urban setting. He accepted my offer and spent the better part of the last week in November with us. He greatly enjoyed his observations of the Throgs adults and of New York City in general. The three of us visited Heinz Meng at his home in New Paltz, New York. Heinz Meng was one of the first Americans to successfully breed peregrines in captivity and provided expertise and some of the peregrine stock that helped initiate The Peregrine Fund's reintroduction program.

As we drove along the Hudson River Palisades on the trip to New Paltz, Fritz enthusiastically viewed the former prime peregrine habitat. He positively glowed at the sight of the beautiful cliffs, the wide expanse of the Hudson River, and the floral environment. He effusively concluded that if the peregrines were not using this wonderful terrain, efforts should be made to reestablish them in the area. I advised him that the building of the Palisades Interstate Parkway above the cliffs and the tremendously increased human activity pattern seemed to have precluded peregrines from ever returning to this historical nesting location. He was not quite convinced by my arguments but the absence of peregrines on the cliffs spoke more eloquently than my words.

When we arrived at Heinz Meng's home, he graciously moved all his raptors from their commodious cages and placed them in a yard outside where we could leisurely view and photograph them. We ogled several peregrines, a peregrine x gyrfalcon hybrid, and a Harris' hawk. The next treat was a falconry session at a remote location that gave the peregrines freedom to fly unhindered over the countryside. Heinz released live quail and we watched as the peregrines dove down on their doomed quarry. The peregrines flew with great zeal. The quail were snared very quickly and consumed right there in the field. I had one of the peregrines feed as it sat on my gloved hand. We left New Paltz with many new images imprinted in our minds.

6

Expansion

(1988)

Dolores and I were out of town for most of January, 1988. Upon our return, I observed Rio as he was eating, on the ledge above the 1983 eyrie. The upper "bib" area of his chest was very white and he sported a bracelet on his left leg. Seeing Rio in prime condition in the middle of the winter gave us reason to hope that he and his mate would produce viable eggs and have a successful nesting season after the 1987 debacle.

On March 5, Ted LeViness observed the adults hunting collaboratively; they captured a pigeon. They alighted on the Throgs with their prize and shared the meal. Several days later, I saw an immature peregrine fly along the entire length of the Throgs, obviously attracted to its height, pigeons, and water view.

Then two new peregrine nesting sites in the New York City region were in the offing. In the case of the first, Dr. John Aronian, a surgeon at the New York Hospital/Cornell Medical Center whose office is on the twenty-fourth floor, had observed three peregrines using the building as their headquarters since November of 1987. This twenty-seven-story structure is adjacent to the East River at 69th Street in Manhattan. Marty Gilroy, reintroduction coordinator for The Peregrine Fund, inspected the site in March and was able to read one of the adult female's bands which identified her as having been hacked at Acadia National Park, Maine, in 1986. More and more peregrines released through the reintroduction program were reaching maturity and establishing nesting territories of their own. When the breeding season arrived, the immature male of the three that were seen regularly left the territory. Marty installed a nest box on an east-facing twenty-fourth-floor ledge which was the focal point of the peregrines' activities.

The second new potential peregrine nesting location was the Tappan Zee Bridge. Peregrines had been observed copulating on the Tappan Zee in mid-March. This bridge has two identical tower super-structures that rise eighty feet above the vehicular roadway. Several years earlier, a nest box had been installed on each of the towers in an attempt to attract peregrines. Our hopes for an increase in nesting sites in the region were apparently coming to pass. We looked forward to being able to visit several peregrine nesting sites within a half-hour's drive.

At the Verrazano-Narrows Bridge, meantime, Marty had observed two adult peregrines frequenting its Brooklyn tower. The New York City area seemed to be off to an encouraging start in 1988 with three pairs of adult peregrines at bridges and one at the New York Hospital. We recalled only too vividly the 1987 breeding season in which none of the eggs had hatched young at the two bridge sites.

Toward the end of March, at the Throgs, we noted that the pere-grines had been using the area below the roadway adjacent to the Queens tower with increasing frequency. It was the same area in which the peregrines had successfully raised six youngsters in the three breeding seasons 1984-1986. This was an indication that the birds were about to select a cavity for their forthcoming eggs.

At the end of March, we saw only Rio. This indicated to us that his mate was very probably on eggs. Peregrine mates share incubation duties but not equitably. Females usually take the entire night shift and most of each day. The male's contribution to the nesting attempt, prior to the hatching of the chicks, is threefold: he sits on the eggs whenever his mate needs relief to take care of personal needs such as exercise or preening; he supplies the female with her sustenance during the approximate six-week period starting with the first egg being laid to the last chick being hatched; and he defends the eyrie area and the larger territory that they have established.

I called Dr. Aronian, at the New York Hospital, to talk with him about the conditions at that site and to exchange notes on other experiences. He was exuberant about having the good fortune of observing the pair of peregrines regularly at very close range. More

View of the author's apartment from Throgs eyrie.   *Photo: Author*
Inset: Queen on the hunt at Throgs.   *Photo: Dave Gardner*

Rio and Queen, male and female peregrine falcons at Throgs, 1990.   *Photo: Dave Gardner*

Queen defending eyrie at Throgs site, 1991.

Photos: Dave Gardner

Inset: Rio defending eyrie.

Queen cacking at departing banders, 1991.

Rio on eggs at Throgs, 1990.
Photo: Dave Gardner

Female fledgling at Throgs, 1993.
Photo: Dave Gardner

Three chicks relocated to nest box at Throgs, 1989.
Photo: Author

Author assisting in banding chicks at Throgs, 1991. *Photo: Dave Gardner*

Red-Red disturbed while feeding at New York Hospital, 1989. *Photo: Author*

Enlargement of Red-Red feeding.

Queen soaring at Throgs.

Photos: Dave Gardner

Red-Red on nest box perch pole at New York Hospital.

Three chicks in original nest box at Hospital site, 1989.

Chick on nest ledge at New York Hospital, 1989.

Photos: Dave Gardner

Warning sign at New York Hospital.

NESTING FALCONS
DO NOT DISTURB

PLEASE BE AWARE THAT THERE ARE FALCONS

OUT HERE, NESTING.

THEY LIKE THEIR PRIVACY AND CAN BECOME

AGGRESSIVE.

SO PROCEED AT YOUR OWN RISK !

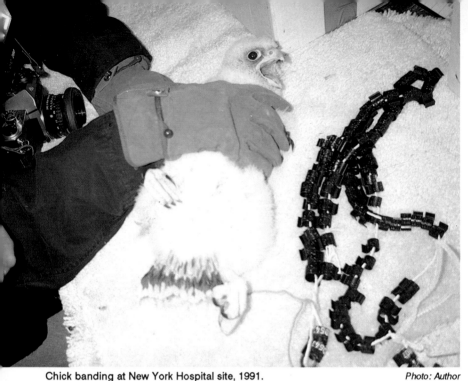

Chick banding at New York Hospital site, 1991.

Photo: Author

Inset: Six-week-old female fledgling at Throgs, 1991.

Photo: Dave Gardner

Female fledgling being released at the New York Hospital site by Dr. John Aronian after visiting the hospital, 1989.

Photo: Author

Hell Gate Bridge, 1990. Arrow shows position of birds. *Photo: Author*

Dr. John Aronian, Dr. Tom Cade, author, and Ted LeViness observing Hell Gate site, 1989.
Photo: Robert DeCandido Jr.

Pan American/MetLife building site.

Inset: Adult on perch pole at Riverside Church nest ledge.

Opposite: Palisades cliffs, New Jersey; historical peregrine nesting site.

Red-tailed hawk nesting site at building in New York City.

48 Wall Street site.

Photo: Author

Red-tailed hawk nest on building.

Photo: Dave Gardner

Holyoke, Massachusetts Hawk Watch site.

Photos: Dave Gardner

Inset: Chelsea retrieving starling at Throgs, 1992.

Tappan Zee Bridge site.

Marilyn England releasing migrating immature peregrine after banding at the Fire Island Hawk Watch.   *Photo: Author*

Adults and fledglings soaring at Cryder House.   *Photo: Dave Gardner*

Red-Red, resident adult female at New York Hospital site.   *Photo: Dave Gardner*

importantly, he reported, they had been observed copulating many times. During a site visit on which I was accompanied by Ted LeViness, we observed both adults aloft and the nest box. It was an open box with a bed of sand, for drainage, as eggshells are permeable and will spoil if they are in water. The female had not yet laid any eggs.

Kathy O'Brien called me during the first week of April and informed me that Marty had inspected the Throgs and had found four eggs in a steel beam cavity beneath the roadway at the Queens tower. That was the good news. The bad news was that the cavity, while safe for the eggs, would not provide nearly enough space for any hatchlings. Furthermore, if a chick were to take one step beyond the edge of the cavity, it would also be one long, deadly step directly down to the water more than a hundred feet below. It was Marty's considered opinion that something would have to be done or the nesting attempt would be doomed to failure. This news was disheartening after our hopes had risen, buoyed by the activity pattern at the Queens tower where the birds had been so successful.

Kathy related other very optimistic news. The Verrazano-Narrows adults were apparently in the nesting mode. Both double-banded birds were in excellent physical condition. Dolores, Ted, and I felt very fortunate to be involved in such a growing situation. We looked forward, with great anticipation, to the future with our increasing number of peregrine neighbors.

The Throgs

But then a series of observations that we made in April distressed us. One day when the outside temperature was 36 degrees Fahrenheit, we observed both adults away from the eyrie at the same time, for extended periods. At temperature levels approaching the freezing point, eggs require almost continual application of external warmth to retain their viability. This is provided by the adults who place their brood patches (two featherless areas on their chest) against the eggs. The tissue beneath the skin, in the brood patch area, becomes heavily vascularized in order to provide increased surface heat. Also, we observed prenuptial behavior: the peregrines perched very close to one another and flew in tandem. If they had eggs, they would not be engaged in this type of display behavior. We could only surmise that there must be a problem with the eggs. Despair was setting in—and it was so early in the season.

Kathy enlightened us: the four Throgs eggs had been removed and transported to The Peregrine Fund laboratory in Boise, Idaho. There, the eggs were to be incubated and the expected chicks nurtured until they were ready for release.

The eggs had been taken pursuant to an agreement between The Peregrine Fund and DEC. Their statistical analyses had revealed that the success rate for the fledging and dispersal of chicks reared at bridge sites was significantly lower when compared to natural locations in the wild and other urban settings such as buildings. Bridge nesters fared even worse in comparison to release locations. A plan had therefore been developed to take eggs from several bridge sites where the conditions appeared to be unfavorable.

The eggs were taken early in the breeding-season cycle and it was expected that the peregrines would lay a second clutch. Peregrines will usually attempt to renest if it is early enough in the breeding season to enable the full breeding cycle to be completed in a timely fashion and the nesting conditions at the site have remained satisfactory. Both requirements were present at the Throgs and there was an excellent chance that the peregrines would double clutch. The peregrines' biological drives were still in gear.

While the cadre of devoted peregrine watchers at the Throgs suffered through this period of exasperation, the big picture was not quite as bleak as it appeared on the surface. If a second clutch of eggs were laid, it would serve to double the productivity of this pair. The Peregrine Fund had had great success in increasing the productivity of the breeding birds via their laboratory by removing first and second clutches of eggs. If this plan worked at the Throgs, two sets of chicks might well develop to the point of dispersal from our one peregrine pair. In the event that a second clutch was not forthcoming, a good case could still conceivably be made that the intervention was a success. The dispersal success rate for chicks released at fully monitored hack sites was about twice as high as the rate experienced at bridge eyries that were monitored on a part-time basis.

DEC and Peregrine Fund personnel voiced the hope that the peregrines would lay their second batch of eggs in a more suitable space on the Throgs, obviating the need to intercede. However, Dolores and I were of the firm opinion that, true to form, the female would place her second set of eggs in the same cavity or in a similarly unsuitable one.

Other News

Hospital. The news from the other peregrine nesting sites continued to be extremely positive. There were three eggs at the New York Hospital/Cornell Medical Center. It was exhilarating to learn that a new nesting site was progressing through the first stages of its establishment. The fact that it was located on a building in Manhattan was the icing on the cake. After all, there were thousands of buildings in the New York metropolitan region.

Tappan Zee. Observations at the Tappan Zee Bridge indicated that the female was sitting on eggs in the west tower nest box. Its opening faced south and the nearest viewing point from land was about half a mile distant. Ted and I went to the site and observed a peregrine carrying prey to the upper reaches of the west tower. The anticipated addition of a second new peregrine nesting location was cause for great elation. There were now four working nests to monitor and enjoy.

Throgs. Kathy's next call set my adrenaline surging. The four eggs that had been taken from the Throgs were fertile. Any successful hatchlings were slated to be released in North Carolina. The Peregrine Fund's reintroduction program mission was to reestablish peregrine nesting with special emphasis placed on those locales where they had historically nested prior to their near extirpation and where they had not yet returned on their own.

Even more exciting news was that a second clutch of four eggs had been laid at the Throgs. However, as we had predicted, the eggs were in a cavity very similar to the first one and, again because the space was perilous, the eggs had been removed. But this time, two dummy eggs had been substituted for the peregrines' eggs. There were two reasons for the placing of the dummy eggs. First, the artifice of substituting two ordinary hen eggs had the goal of keeping the peregrines in the incubation mode. Peregrines cannot differentiate between their own eggs and others and are unable to count. The other purpose was to discourage them from laying a third clutch. As long as the peregrines had eggs, they would not lay again. I was advised that DEC and The Peregrine Fund had agreed to foster one or two chicks, from the laboratory, back to this prolific pair if the conditions at the eyrie were deemed to be reasonably satisfactory.

Understandably, Dolores, Ted, and I, and others who had followed the situation at the Throgs, were extremely disturbed by this unexpected turn of events. Our wonderful peregrines had managed to produce eight eggs and now were sitting on two hen eggs. It seemed horrible to us that human interference, designed to enhance the nesting success of peregrines as a species, would result in depriving these two magnificent creatures of the joy of rearing their own progeny. We tried to console ourselves with thoughts of the unpalatable alternative, which was not to intercede and thereby almost certainly doom any hatchlings. A positive thought that helped some of us through this time of turmoil was that the eight eggs that had been taken might result in eight healthy young peregrines gaining independence at another location.

The Peregrine Fund had a similar agreement with the State of New Jersey and took five eggs from two New Jersey bridges. Of the total of thirteen eggs donated by these three bridges, all were fertile and twelve chicks hatched. All twelve youngsters matured to release age. Everyone eagerly awaits the time when there will be sufficient numbers of peregrines so that these interventions are no longer necessary.

Hospital. Between May 15 and June 26, I made thirteen visits to the New York Hospital nesting site. My observations were made from Roosevelt Island about 250 yards across the East River from the nest ledge. While this viewing location was farther from the eyrie than those used by other observers, it had three very distinct advantages. The most important consideration was for the birds themselves. By stationing myself across the river, I did not interfere with their normal activity pattern, which was not the case with some of the viewing positions from within the building itself. The second advantage was that because my observation post was directly east of the nest box, it allowed me to see into the nest box itself. The third benefit was the unhindered view of three sides of the hospital building and most of the surrounding area. I was able to follow the peregrines when they were aloft to a much greater degree than were observers in closer viewing locations whose views were blocked by buildings.

My May 15 visit was shared by Dave Gardner, who had become a staunch peregrine devotee and student. From Roosevelt Island, we observed the adult male alight on the nest ledge. He had a prey item in his talons, which the female quickly took. She retreated into the nest box to feed the two chicks that had hatched three days earlier. The third egg, which had not hatched, was not viable. The two chicks developed normally and dispersed satisfactorily. New York City's newest peregrine nesting site was a success.

Tappan Zee. At the Tappan Zee Bridge, one chick was observed in the west tower nest box. Dolores and I went to the site on June 3. We peered through our 60X magnification telescope, straining our eyes to see through the light fog hanging over the Hudson River. We were elated to find three healthy looking chicks being fed by the adult female. We gloried in the knowledge that there were two additional peregrine eyries in the New York City metropolitan region that had produced chicks. We boldly predicted that there would be many more new peregrine nests established. After all, there were more bridges available and thousands of buildings. We drove away thinking how fortunate we were; we were sure that, almost assuredly, we were the first humans to have seen the three nestlings at the Tappan Zee.

Fostering

As the middle of June approached, we became increasingly concerned that the Throgs peregrines would cease their incubation activity. More than six weeks had elapsed since their second clutch of four eggs had been removed and the dummy eggs substituted. Chicks hatch approximately thirty-three days after the last egg in a clutch is laid. At some point, the peregrines would surely perceive that the incubation phase had gone beyond any reasonable time frame. If they stopped incubating the dummy eggs, it would become impossible to foster a chick to them for rearing because it would be highly unlikely that they would accept and care for a chick once they had terminated their nesting cycle.

Peregrines, as is the case with most birds, cannot determine time accurately. They will continue to sit on their eggs, or as in this case a pair of dummy eggs, well beyond the normal period required for hatching. Also they have a powerful propensity to feed and nurture any chicks that are in their nest. These factors would permit the placement of a two-week-old chick simultaneously with the removal of the dummy eggs and with the reasonable expectation that the chick would be accepted. If the chick were to be rejected, close monitoring of the eyrie would enable the timely removal of the chick so that its life could be saved.

I conferred with DEC concerning the fostering of a chick to the Throgs peregrines. We agreed that this might be feasible if the birds were still sitting on the dummy eggs and the condition of the eyrie area seemed reasonably safe. I was, therefore, entrusted as a sort of unofficial official to make a personal inspection of the eyrie on the afternoon of June 14. While waiting for TBTA transportation to the eyrie area, several maintenance workers engaged me in conversation, eagerly recounting their experiences with the peregrines. Most of their stories centered on the peregrines' aggressive defense of their eyrie and the close calls they had had when the peregrines had flown at them, missing them by mere inches. They also informed me that the pair seemed to have established a routine at the nest. The male flew to the nest each day at 9:30 A.M. and again at 2:30 P.M. He visited his mate or replaced her on the eggs. They were very taken with this pattern of behavior and obviously had developed a fostering attitude toward the birds.

At the eyrie, as I stepped onto the catwalk, Rio screamed at me as he flew past my head. I ignored him in the hope that he would merely use his aggressive flying techniques and vocalizations to try to thwart me rather than slashing me with his razor-sharp talons. It was dim as I peered into the nest cavity. The female was sitting quietly as if she were trying to blend into her surroundings. We made eye contact for only a few seconds before I broke it off and departed quickly in respect for her delicate condition; she had been sitting on this third set of eggs for forty-five days. I had accomplished my mission: I had determined that the adults were still in the incubation phase, which meant that it was possible to foster a chick to them. Although the nest cavity did not contain sufficient development space, a two-week-old chick would be safe for a short time. The plan was to place a foster chick in the spot now occupied by the dummy eggs and relocate it later to a spacious box that would be installed near the current cavity.

I rushed home to report to DEC that the breeding season at the Throgs could still be salvaged for both the peregrines and their human spectators. But the peregrines' instinctual procreative drive demanded that the next phase of the reproductive cycle, the nurturing of chicks, be put into gear. Time was of the essence because even the high peregrine patience quotient has its limitations. We humans, who were bound to the land with only eyesight that can soar with the peregrines, craved the sight of the hundreds of hunting forays that would be necessary to provide food for the rapidly growing young.

To me, monitoring multiple peregrine nesting locations is very gratifying. This year, 1988, was the first breeding season with four productive nests that I could visit and about which I received reports. It seemed that whenever there was bad news regarding one site or a lull in the action, another pair of peregrines was able to provide a lift. It was wonderful to have this balance in our peregrine fortunes, especially considering the abysmal 1987 season. The good news came when DEC advised us that the three chicks at the Tappan Zee nest had fledged. Dolores and I had observed the chicks in their nest box several weeks earlier and now they were on the wing. We really felt we were participants in the entire process.

On June 26, I saw both adult peregrines at the Throgs aloft at the same time. The female conducted several obviously serious hunting expeditions. There was a strong northwest wind blowing, which often incites the peregrines to take to the air even if only for the mere pleasure of enjoying the power of it. I was very concerned because this behavior signaled the abandonment of the incubation phase, in which case it would be too late to foster a chick. On the other hand, this behavior could also have signified that the female had a nestling. We had observed during prior breeding seasons that when the female had unhatched eggs, she would not leave the nest space for lengthy periods. She would take some exercise but only enough to keep herself in reasonable condition. Hunting for herself was out of the question during the incubation period; her mate had that responsibility entirely. About a week after all the chicks were hatched, the female would allow herself gradually lengthening periods away from the nest. Chicks need to be almost constantly brooded for about the first week after hatching because their thermal regulation systems are not as yet developed. The suspense we experienced now was exciting but not appreciated because it was generated from a lack of facts about creatures we had grown to love.

The following day, Peter Nye, director of the Endangered Species Unit, informed me that a ten-day-old male chick had been placed in the peregrines' nest the previous morning. That report explained the female's sudden burst of behavior the previous afternoon. Not only was she released from her need to attend to the eggs but also she had a chick which did not require help with thermal regulation during the warm June weather. The chick was not one of their own but the peregrines did not know it and we humans, who had watched and waited for such a long time, were just happy to have another opportunity to observe the development of a peregrine chick.

The circumstances that surrounded the placement of the chick were extraordinary. DEC's Kathy O'Brien and Marty Gilroy, and Jim Weaver of The Peregrine Fund, found the male sitting on the dummy eggs. He was obviously torn between his normal instinct to flee from the three large threatening creatures and his conflicting drive to remain and protect his eggs. He bravely chose to stay with the eggs. Amazingly, Jim reached down into the cavity and was able to take the male in hand. This tenacious behavior, on the part of the bird and of the man, allowed Jim to read his band. He was Rio, the same individual who had been rescued on March 16, 1986, at the Throgs and had been released at the Bronx-Whitestone Bridge two weeks later. It corroborated our earlier supposition that Rio had been replaced by another male during his two-week rehabilitation period. Furthermore, it proved our contention that he drove out the male who had replaced him. This series of events provided proof that there were peregrines waiting in the wings, available to replace any breeding adults that might be lost. The female was close enough to the three interlopers to allow them to observe that her right leg band was upside down. This identified her as the original 1983 breeding season female.

On July 5, I assisted Kathy and Marty in relocating the foster chick to a nest box. First, however, we attempted to enlarge the existing nest. Marty brought a platform which he planned to attach to the front opening of the nest cavity. It was hoped that this modification would obviate the need to physically move the chick, an activity which is always fraught with some danger. Marty had previously measured the nest cavity and had fabricated a custom-fitted platform.

The first step was a trial fitting of the platform, at a similar cavity away from the eyrie, to avoid disturbing the peregrines. The fit appeared to be satisfactory and we continued on to the eyrie. As soon as we entered onto the catwalk, the female voiced a tremendous, penetrating cacking sound from within the cavity. Several seconds later, Rio flew in to join the defense of their eyrie. We were surrounded by two angry, screaming peregrines. Rio flew at us menacingly, coming within inches of our heads. Although we knew that he was capable of slicing into us, we trusted that he would not. Peregrines usually fly very close to human interlopers and sometimes make contact but rarely cause meaningful injury. The female then emerged from her cavity and placed herself halfway between us and her chick. She continued to vocalize loudly while Rio flew at us repeatedly and displayed the most aggressive aerial tactics he could muster, short of slashing us.

Marty and Kathy advanced to the nest cavity while I remained about twenty yards behind and tried to read the female's leg band. Marty was not able to attach the platform to the steel girders because the dissimilar surfaces were difficult to work with and the position was extremely precarious. He decided that the problems confronting us were overwhelming and, in the interest of reducing the stress on the birds, it would be better to withdraw from the eyrie immediately and return with a box. We returned with an open box designed to be installed on a flat surface. The box was several inches high and was filled with sand. The negative feature of this change in plans was that the chick would have to be handled and thereby stressed. However, there did not seem to be any better course of action.

The adult peregrines again greeted us with their defensive tactics. We hated to see their high level of disturbance but we knew our intervention was absolutely necessary for the chick's safety. Inwardly, I exulted in being able to get so close to the peregrines and to experience their unfettered ferocity. I think the three of us are the type of people who could not spend as much time and thought on the peregrines as we do if there weren't something very special in the way we feel in our interactions with them.

Marty fastened the box to the top of a steel gusset that was located several feet from the original nest. The position of the box was excellent for three reasons. First, the gusset was larger than the box and thus provided additional space for the chick to explore safely. True, once on the gusset the chick could possibly go off the edge directly down to the water below; but chicks generally do not lose their footing. Second, there were several steel beams leading from the gusset to serve as pathways, enabling the chick to get to the nearby catwalks. The third advantage was that the interior of the box was visible to observers from a distance, which would mean less disturbance to the peregrines.

While Marty and Kathy labored to attach the box, I had very limited success in trying to read the female's leg band due to the incessant trembling of the bridge. I rested the scope on a large bag of sand to dampen and minimize the tremor transmitted to the scope. Still, I was able to decipher only a few numerals; but those numbers did match those of the 1983 resident female's band, which was indeed upside down as was that of the original female. There was no doubt that she was the one and only reigning female at the Throgs.

We installed several signboards along the catwalks, warning anyone approaching the eyrie that there were nesting peregrines in the area and that they should stay clear. When everything was in place, Marty reached down into the nest cavity and removed the protesting eighteen-day-old male chick. He was white-downed and appeared plump and healthy. He was extremely feisty and not only did he yell robustly but also he tried to escape from Marty's grip. As soon as Marty placed him in the box, he bolted straight outward. Kathy alertly grabbed him before he could go over the edge to certain death below. I thought to myself that this relocation procedure had come perilously close to causing the loss of the chick but quickly realized that Marty and Kathy were very experienced in handling peregrine chicks under adverse conditions. What seemed to be a close call was merely routine action to seasoned raptor handlers.

Kathy carefully put the youngster down in the center of the box twice more but held her hands lightly around his body. Both times he immediately squirmed and looked for the shortest way out to freedom. He did not want to be held nor did he want any part of these humans. The wildness he exhibited was an appropriate reaction to the extraordinary circumstances in which he found himself. Though his attitude was extremely promising for his long-term survival, it presented a short-term problem for us. It was obvious that he would go over the edge if he were merely placed in the box. Marty removed two of the warning signs and attached them to one corner of the box, thereby creating a blind corner. When the chick was placed into this corner, he relaxed and showed no interest in leaving. The chick could not see around the boards and evidently felt secure, akin to a horse with blinders.

We departed silently, hoping that the chick would stay safely in his new home and that his adoptive parents would nurture him. A discussion with one of the TBTA workers unearthed the fact that he had seen two brown, mottled eggs on the Verrazano/Narrows Bridge several weeks earlier. He pinpointed their exact location, which enabled their later recovery, establishing the fact that a nesting attempt had been made. The worker also delivered a lengthy monolog about the aggressive attacks he and his coworkers had experienced when their work assignments took them into the peregrines' region of the bridge. They had had many close calls and greatly respected the peregrines' ferocity, especially when defending their eyrie. As I commiserated with him regarding his fear of being slashed, I detected that he had developed a fondness for the wild creatures. After all, both he and the peregrines made their living on the Throgs.

At the Throgs, after we had moved the nestling, my friend and fellow peregrine watcher Dave Gardner, from his beach vantage point, observed Rio deplume prey and deliver it to the nest. That was the surest sign that the adults were feeding the chick, that the relocation had been successful.

Tappan Zee, Police, and Liberty Plaza

Dolores and I went to the Tappan Zee Bridge on July 7 with great anticipation. The three chicks which we had observed in early June had fledged. The most notable event at the Tappan Zee this first breeding season was a fledgling's fall into the Hudson River. Luckily, this near disaster was witnessed by workers on a maintenance vessel moored at the bridge. They scooped up the hapless peregrine, which later was returned to the upper reaches of the bridge.

When Dolores and I arrived at the Tappan Zee, we found one of the youngsters on the wing. Our spirits rose even higher, a few moments later, when a second fledgling joined its sibling. We searched for the third fledgling, but to no avail. Then for an hour Dolores and I were enthralled by the aerial antics of the two fledglings. They disported themselves as two young healthy peregrines should, with great flying routines and the exuberance that newly fledged creatures feel in the early days following their leaving of their nest. Flying in tandem, zooming at each other and veering off at the last possible instant to avoid colliding, and grasping each other's talons were some of the highlights of their repertoire. The third fledgling did not appear on that visit, nor was it ever seen again. Peregrine fledglings seem to have a strong propensity to repeat their errors. The most likely scenario here was that the fledgling that had ended up in the water below the bridge earlier in the season had again made a mistake. This time it had cost it its life.

Several days later, at the Throgs, Dolores and I were at home and heard the clear sound of peregrine alarm calls. We rushed out onto our terrace and were astonished to see a dozen New York City police officers on the top of the Queens tower while others were making their way up a cable. The female dove at the officers repeatedly and vocalized at her usual high pitch. We wondered what the officers could be thinking about this screaming wild creature that obviously was troubled by their presence. We were concerned about the safety of the officers as well as that of the peregrines. An officer could possibly have lost his footing if the bird were to distract him. They utilized safety ropes but a misstep, nevertheless, could cause them to suffer an injury. It was even conceivable that an officer might shoot an attacking bird in self-defense. I phoned the Throgs office and was advised that the police were conducting a training exercise for emergency service personnel. I described my safety concerns and was connected with the police official in charge of the training session. The official assured me that the officers would only be using the cable and the tower and that he would instruct them to ignore the peregrines. I returned to my observations and was amused as I watched the female single-handedly try to dislodge the many humans who were perched on the structure that she considered her inviolable territory. I could enjoy the spectacle now that I felt confident that there was no appreciable danger to the peregrines. The police descended the cable in groups of two. At one point, the female alighted on a handcable and faced two oncoming officers. She tried to stare them down but the men kept advancing toward her and when they were ten yards from her, she finally gave way and flew off. After all of the officers were gone, she returned to the eyrie.

During July, another potential nesting site came to light in New York City. Steve Walter, an intrepid birder and hawk watcher, called me to report that he had been regularly observing a pair of adult peregrines frequenting 1 Liberty Plaza, a building in Manhattan's financial district. He had also observed them from his fourteenth floor office at 2 Rector Street. We anticipated that the peregrine nesting expansion in the New York City metropolitan region was in its early stages and the coming years would provide many excellent opportunities to observe and study them.

The Fosterling

At the Throgs, on July 16, Ted LeViness glimpsed two peregrines in flight and thought that one might have been a fledgling. Two days later, at 7:00 P.M., I discovered a fledgling on the main pier. This was the first definitive observation of a fledged chick for the 1988 season at the Throgs. I wondered whether he had flown to the pier or had merely fluttered down to it. I was concerned about his flying ability because, according to my calculations, he was less than five weeks old. I watched the youngster until darkness set in at 9:00 P.M. There was sufficient light projected from the roadway and the decorative illumination of the cables to enable me to observe the fledgling bed down on the bare concrete of the pier while leaning his body against a pair of electrical conduits. Apparently even this insignificant structure provided some feeling of protection and solace.

My feelings regarding this youngster varied from elation at the upcoming prospect of watching him develop to independence to concern for his future survival. A single youngster at a nest site seems to be at a disadvantage because it does not have siblings with whom to share flying, eating, sleeping, and the general cavorting in which youngsters engage. Of course, the adult birds provide much of the interaction and sharing required by a developing fledgling but it is not quite the same as when there are at least two young. Youngsters will sleep together, practice their flying and hunting together, and share all their activities. The adults do not sleep with the young, especially when the young bed down for the night in an exposed or odd location. The ever-hungry fledglings become increasingly aggressive toward their parents, especially when they appear with a prey item. The adults eventually tire of their youthful exuberance and attempt to avoid their own young for segments of each day. More and more they deliver the prey they capture to the fledglings and immediately fly to a nearby location where they can monitor their young but avoid direct interaction.

My concern for this youngster prompted me to leave my bed early enough the next morning to share the sunrise with him. At 5:20 I saw him stirring in the exact spot in which he had gone to sleep the previous night. Sunrise came at 5:41 and I had no doubt at all that the other creatures who were witness to it enjoyed it in their own way. At 7:00 A.M., the fledgling's breakfast was delivered by the female. In the early evening of that same day, I found the fledgling on the Queens anchorage, which established the fact that the youngster was capable of flying. His current location was at the same height level above the water as was his previous location on the pier; he must have flown across the watery expanse. The fledgling again spent the night on the pier, and all of the following day. One evening, later, I monitored the fledgling from 5:00 P.M. through 8:00 P.M. He received no meals during that period but did defecate at least four times, leaving no question about his having eaten sufficient food. At nightfall, the youngster decided to take to wing, which prompted the female to intercede to prevent his straying from the safety of the Throgs. She flew past him and herded him back to a good roosting spot for the night, the top ledge of the north side of the Queens anchorage. The youngster demonstrated his flying mastery by flying with consistent, measured wingbeats and by executing a very skillful landing. If I had not known this was the youngster, I would not have been able to distinguish his flying from that of the adults.

The next evening, I observed bird remains on the northwest corner of the anchorage ledge. I could not identify the remains and I became alarmed because I was also unable to find the fledgling. I had to check the dead creature and clear up the mystery or I could not rest. While

I pondered the problem, a young man in a rowboat paddled up to the pier that I was using as an observation point. I engaged him to row me out to the anchorage and, as we approached it, the fledgling suddenly flew in over our rowboat. I was jubilant to see that he was alive and well. Apparently unnerved at seeing us there, he aborted his intended landing on the ledge and flew upward, making repeated, unsuccessful landing attempts along the flat face of the anchorage. He kept putting his talons to the blank wall expecting to find another ledge.

Then we heard the loud distress calls of the adult peregrines as they zoomed onto the scene. They were apprehensive at seeing us so close to him but, I think, the sight of his flailing at the wall was more upsetting to them. I know it was disturbing to me. It would have been a comical scene if the potential danger of the water below had not been a factor. The female's vocalizations changed from alarm to a "follow me" type of call. The fledgling dropped away from the wall and flew down to within several inches of the water. Although he had complete control of his flight trajectory, my heart was in my mouth as he beat his sickle-shaped wings so close to the water. I thought that they must surely make contact with the water and that he might go in. Why did he have to fly that close to the water? Peregrines do not like to go into salt water, or even to touch it. Why did he tempt fate by flying unnecessarily close to it? Evidently the female had the same reaction as I did. She sped to his side and actually forced him to move upward and onto the main pier.

We continued on in the rowboat to the anchorage, where the boatman and I climbed up onto the ledge, only several inches wide and cluttered with debris; walking upon it was difficult. One missed step could have produced an unwanted saltwater bath. The female swooped down at and called loudly. The intensity of her aggressiveness increased as we worked our way closer to the carcass. When we saw that it was a beheaded pigeon, we beat a swift retreat under the continued vigilance of the peregrines.

The following afternoon, Rio carried half of a headless passerine to and fro between the side piers as if he were looking for the fledgling. Then he sat with his mate for more than an hour before he consumed the prey. Later, the female was on one end of a pier while a pigeon perched at the other end out of her sight. Rio assessed the situation immediately and flushed the pigeon off the pier, whereupon the female pursued it avidly but unsuccessfully.

The next morning, Ted LeViness and I observed the adults bringing food to the fledgling on the Cryder House roof. It was a safe place because there was nothing dangerous on it and its access doors were kept locked. In fact, I had previously discussed with DEC the possibility of installing a nest box there. We decided to go up on the roof to observe the youngster and his physical condition. Also, we wanted to inspect the roof to ascertain if there was a suitable location where a nest box might be installed in a future season. We slowly made our way across the roof and did not see the fledgling until we were only several feet behind him. The youngster then must have felt our presence as he turned his head and looked at us. He still failed to react, except to show surprise not quite bordering on consternation. At that moment, the female arrived, screaming in alarm and urging the youngster to fly from his perch and escape. He hesitated for a few more seconds and then at last understood what he was supposed to do. He flew off and she herded him to the south side of Cryder House, where he alighted on a parapet railing.

Ted and I inspected the roof but avoided its south end because we did not want to disturb the youngster again and possibly flush him. Rio arrived and joined his mate in a series of almost constant diving attacks at us, accompanied by shrill vocalizations. These tactics were calculated to make any but the most intrepid interloper leave the area. Of course, to Ted and me their flying routines and oral offerings were visual and auditory delights. Some of their passes at us were so close that we were able to feel the rush of the air from their wings. We felt as if we were interacting with them in a healthy way, although the peregrines did not appreciate our presence on the roof. In fact, Cryder House maintenance staff had remarked that whenever any of them had entered onto the roof during the past two days, they had been attacked by the adults. The entire roof became the peregrines' exclusive territory when one of their young ventured upon it.

The fledgling was in excellent physical condition and his flying ability seemed adequate in all respects. The roof had several spots that would have been suitable for a nest box. We returned to the beach and observed the adults hunt and carry prey items to the Cryder roof. An interesting observation during this period was the harassment of the female peregrine by an immature American kestrel. She was carrying prey when the kestrel made several passes at her. A short time later, Rio was observed diving at the kestrel. These interspecies conflicts, happily, rarely lead to an injury to either of the protagonists. We had a wonderful day of observations and were so physically close to our peregrine family that we really felt as if they were family.

Early in the morning of the next day, July 24, the youngster was still on Cryder House. Both adults flew with him in a manner that strongly suggested that they wanted him to return to the Throgs. In one instance, the youngster flew halfway to the bridge, only to return to the roof. He showed no intention of leaving his new home base. The adults shifted gears and went into the hunting mode. Spirited attacks were launched at several passing birds. Rio snared one and immediately flew up to the Cryder House roof; but, instead of alighting or passing off the prey item to the youngster, he repeatedly called to him in an attempt to lure him from the roof with the food. Rio's efforts were to no avail. Finally, he dropped the prey onto the roof and flew off to the Throgs alone. A short time later, the female again fed the fledgling on the roof, where he remained for the entire afternoon.

It had become apparent to us that a lone fledgling tends to progress slower because there is no age-related playmate. This fledgling displayed normal flying skills but showed much less enthusiasm for flying than the other fledglings we had observed at this and other sites. The presence of other young birds provided considerable motivation to fly more frequently and to engage in high-spirited antics. Also, parents, whether human or peregrine, exhibit a similar reluctance to participate in youthful pranks and energy-draining physical activities.

Several evenings later, all three peregrines were together on the Throgs. As night descended, the youngster chose to bed down in a very odd spot. At the point where the cables that support the roadway pass through the towers, a housing, called a shroud, nestles the cable. Although the cable is perfectly round and attached at an angle, the shroud's upper surface is almost flat. The fledgling went to sleep on this small space, quite confidently.

On the morning of July 27, Ted observed the peregrines hunting, including several forays near Cryder House. On this particular day, I named our Throgs fledgling "Phil." This first naming of a peregrine at the Throgs was a long time in coming. Since 1983, when we had first started observing the peregrines at the Throgs, none of them had ever been given a name by any of the many observers. For myself, I felt it was somewhat presumptive to name a wild creature that did not even know I existed. However, there was ample precedent for giving peregrines names. Rio had been named, as were his hackmates, when he was selected for a controlled release in Boston, Massachusetts. Young peregrines released by The Peregrine Fund are routinely assigned names in addition to being identified by the numbers on their identification bands. Also, the peregrine watchers at other nesting sites in New York City had been giving names to the adult peregrines and chicks.

I decided Phil was an appropriate name because he filled a tremendous need that the adult peregrines had to complete their breeding cycle. He also filled some needs of quite a few adult humans. I began to consider that the adult female, our most important and most senior family member, still did not have a name despite the fact that her mate and foster fledgling now had names.

The fledgling was now generally more active than the adults but they had to cater to his almost insatiable demands for food and attention. We were treated to many close views of the youngster as he flew past our terrace. He had rich, brown feathers and radiated health and power. We never tired of looking at him or searching for him. The creature's beauty, youth, and potential are hauntingly attractive to those of us who had become peregrine devotees. This is beyond explanation to those who do not experience that surge of adrenalin when beholding such a magnificent raptor.

One afternoon, Rio delivered a kill to Phil and after allowing Phil to feed on it for a short time, Rio joined in and they fed on the bird simultaneously. Phil dove several times at a dove at the water's edge. He started chasing prey more frequently. He captured a large insect and ate it. During this period, Kathy O'Brien and Marty Gilroy inspected the Throgs and upgraded the nest box by cleaning it and arranging the substrate within it.

Dolores and I traveled to California on August 9 for a two-week vacation. On August 15, we were at the picturesque Morro Bay Rock at the shoreline of the Pacific Ocean. This famous landmark was home to a nesting pair of peregrines. As luck would have it, I briefly saw one of the peregrines as it dove from the top of the Rock and disappeared around to the seaward side.

Upon our return to New York, Ted LeViness advised us that he had last seen Phil on August 11. That observation turned out to be the last known sighting of Phil. He had been placed at the Throgs on June 26 at the age of ten days and had been on the wing for twenty-five days when he was last seen. We wished him well and hoped that he would survive to maturity and create his own family.

In the ensuing months, the adults were observed regularly but our time spent watching them was greatly reduced with the dispersal of Phil. On the afternoon of December 10, we heard the piercing, loud alarm calling of the adult peregrines, which easily penetrated our apartment. This was both strange and welcome to us. The peregrines are usually silent at this time of the year unless there is something special happening. We observed both peregrines diving repeatedly at a red-tailed hawk, which flew the entire length of the Throgs. It was a treat to see some action and hear those wild voices again.

A few days later, we noticed a pigeon flailing strongly in the water near the anchorage. Try as it might, it could not get airborne. The peregrines undoubtedly had injured it during an attack, which would have driven it into the water. The female peregrine circled the pigeon, whose strength was waning and who was at the mercy of the water currents below and the hovering peregrine above. The female alighted on top of a group of three piles, allowing her to watch her prey. Rio joined her on this platform, which we had never seen them use during our six years of observations.

They waited patiently for the pigeon to succumb and, as soon as the pigeon dropped its head into the water and stopped moving, the female made a pass at it. Twice she tried, unsuccessfully, to pluck it out of the water. Then she deftly snatched it in her talons and flew to the north side of the anchorage with Rio following closely behind. We thought about how lucky we were to have been able to share this episode with them. We almost envied them the fresh, warm, salty meal that they would share and enjoy. These two peregrines had become very special to us for many reasons. The first that leaps to mind is their extreme fidelity to one another throughout the year. The breeding season brings all wild creatures together for the one overriding natural drive to procreate. Even those animals that lead solitary existences throughout most of the year join their mates during the breeding period. We observe the Throgs peregrines throughout the entire year. They spend hour after hour perched close to one another or within direct view of each other. We see them in the meanest cold and snows of winter. We see them during the summer doldrums when there is not the slightest movement of air for them to use and their youngsters have dispersed. We find them hunkering under cover during rainy periods. At other times, they prefer sitting out in the rain. They hold their feathers very tightly to keep the water from penetrating through their outer feathers. This is not a bathing session but something they enjoy nevertheless. A sign of fidelity.

1988 Update

The Verrazano-Narrows Bridge again failed to produce young in 1988. The two eggs laid did not hatch and were retrieved by Marty Gilroy on August 21. He installed a covered nest box in the hope that the peregrines would use it rather than the unsuitable niches they frequently chose.

On October 26, the remains of a female peregrine were found on the Verrazano-Narrows Bridge. Her band identified her as having been released in 1981 in Philadelphia. Because her physical characteristics did not match those of the breeding female of that 1988 season, she was not thought to be the breeding female. Then why was she found there and what had killed her? Even more inexplicable was the fact that this was the third adult female peregrine that had been discovered dead on the Verrazano-Narrows Bridge since 1985. One possible explanation involved the ingestion of a poisonous substance that was in the bridge area and had found its way into the peregrines' food chain. It was a very troubling mystery.

The New York Hospital/Cornell Medical Center peregrine nesting season was a resounding success, especially for an initial nesting attempt. Two of the three eggs laid were fertile. The two resulting chicks fledged and dispersed satisfactorily. They were on the wing for at least two full months before they left the Hospital vicinity.

The Tappan Zee Bridge provided a second new peregrine nesting location that was extremely successful. All three eggs were fertile.

Three chicks fledged but only two were observed at the conclusion of the season. The two fledglings had been flying for more than two months when they were last seen at the Tappan Zee.

Yes, 1988 was a most remarkable peregrine year in the New York City region. Expansion was the watchword. Two new nesting sites were established which had produced a total of four chicks that developed satisfactorily to independence. Additionally, there was another adult pair of peregrines that were regularly observed in lower Manhattan. The Throgs pair provided eight fertile eggs for The Peregrine Fund's reintroduction program besides raising a fostered chick to dispersal. The future for peregrines looked exceedingly bright, not only in the New York City area but throughout the nation.

On December 22, Dolores and I observed both peregrines at the Throgs. We said good-bye because we planned to drive to Florida the next morning. Dolores had a Christmas vacation and I had recently retired. We left the next morning and suffered a disastrous automobile accident only several miles from our home. Dolores was severely injured, requiring extensive surgery and a five-month rehabilitation period. We were homebound for the winter with our peregrine neighbors.

7

Hands On

(1989)

Dolores and I were at home in New York City for the entire winter of 1989 because of the injuries she had suffered in our December, 1988, auto accident. We saw the adult peregrines at the Throgs Neck Bridge almost daily but our first noteworthy observation occurred on February 19. We heard the peregrines' alarm calling and through our apartment window we could see both adults diving at a pine tree. It was difficult to see the object of their attention but by using our scope I found a red-tailed hawk perched unconcernedly on an upper branch. It did not flinch even when the peregrines came within inches of it on some of their diving passes. Finally, it lumbered off, with Rio continuing to harass it until they both flew out of my range of vision.

On February 25, with the temperature at fifteen degrees Fahrenheit and fifteen miles an hour northwest winds, one adult was perched on the Bronx tower, the other on the Queens tower. Rio and his mate began to frequent the area where they had nested last season. We hoped that they would nest in this area because they had been successful there four times and this location provided good viewing for us.

During February, the accumulated debris in various cavities at both towers of the Throgs was removed to discourage the peregrines from laying eggs in those cramped quarters. Because peregrines do not usually lay their eggs on bare metal, it was hoped that this would prompt them to utilize the nest box which had been installed during the 1988 nesting season. Personally, I doubted that the peregrines would cooperate in this plan. The female had displayed a penchant for

102

placing her eggs in very snug cavities that would prove to be too small and dangerous for her nestlings as they grew.

Toward the end of March, the adults copulated frequently and perched very close to one another for long periods of time. On March 25, Rio caught a bird and took it to his mate. This food-presenting element of courtship behavior augured well for the upcoming season. When Rio spotted a red-tailed hawk flying high over Cryder House, he quickly rose to the occasion. Spiraling skyward, Rio intercepted the hawk and escorted it out of his territory. There was no real need for Rio to have challenged this raptor since it was traveling high and obviously posed no threat. But the territorial defense instincts of most birds, raptors or not, dictate that they must act aggressively toward any other predatory creature that passes through their territory. This attitude is especially strong during the breeding season. The size and species of the transgressor, its distance from the nest, and other seemingly pertinent factors do not always greatly influence this mode of behavior. Nesters repulse interlopers even when, by doing so, they may needlessly endanger themselves.

Half an hour later, we again heard loud peregrine calls. We could not see what was alarming our friends but by following Rio with our binoculars on his rising trajectory, we finally observed a high-flying peregrine. Again Rio challenged the interloping raptor, although there was no real purpose. On the other hand, a nonresident peregrine was always a welcome sight to us. It hopefully signified that the peregrine population in the New York City metropolitan region might at long last be self-sustaining, with nonbreeding birds in the region available to replace lost breeders.

Kathy O'Brien inspected the Throgs eyrie and observed the female sitting near the nest box. Although she was unable to find any eggs, the overall conditions were promising for another successful season. Kathy removed debris and castings from the box during her visit.

Newer Sites

We were also beginning to receive welcome reports from other established nesting sites as well as from potentially new locations in our metropolitan region. On March 1 at the Verrazano-Narrows Bridge, Chris Nadareski (City of New York, Parks and Recreation, Natural Resources Group) checked the nest box which had been placed under the roadway near the Brooklyn tower in 1988. He discovered a pair of old, faded eggs near the nest box. On subsequent site visits, he and Kathy both observed the peregrines copulate.

The situation at the New York Hospital/Cornell Medical Center was similarly encouraging. Barry Freed, an inveterate peregrine watcher at the hospital, observed copulation attempts as early as February 16. This pair had been present on their territory all winter, as was the case with the other known pairs in New York City. In March, a second, banded adult male joined the resident pair. Both males carried food to the female. There were no observations of the female copulating with the newcomer before the eggs were laid. By the end of April, the original male was no longer seen in the area. The new male was identified by his band numbers as having been hacked from Owl's Head, New Hampshire, in 1987.

A cover had been installed on the hospital nest box before the start of the second breeding season to provide additional protection. Ironically, it became more difficult to make observations of activity within the box because the cover obscured viewing except from the east. Observers at the hospital were innovative and used a mirror attached to the end of a pole to see into the box. On March 17, a peregrine was observed in the box and copulation was witnessed on March 26.

John Askildsen, president of the Saw Mill River Audubon Society, reported that he had regularly observed one and sometimes two adult peregrines at the Tappan Zee Bridge throughout the winter. Additional observations at the bridge were very promising, with courtship flights on March 14 and copulation on March 27. These were very good signs that the adults were on their territory and preparing for their second consecutive breeding season.

In mid-March, John called me to report that he had seen an immature peregrine in the vicinity of Riverside Drive and 118th Street. The truly amazing feature of this sighting was that he had spotted the bird from his seat on a train traveling southward along the east bank of the Hudson River. I usually did not investigate one-time sightings of single peregrines, especially immatures, unless there was reason to believe that there might be a nesting possibility at the location. Since this particular observation did not seem significant to me at the time, I did not follow up on it. As a volunteer, I could not possibly investigate every such report, nor was I obliged to. But how could I have guessed that John's report would later prove to have been more than just an isolated peregrine sighting?

By late April, reports of peregrine pairs at three potentially new locations gave rise to renewed hopes that 1989 would be a year of continued nesting expansion. A new peregrine nesting location was discovered in upper Manhattan at the magnificent Riverside Church, which overlooks Riverside Park and the Hudson River at 120th through 122nd streets. The church's inspiring architecture dominates all of the other structures in the neighborhood. Early in January of 1989, Professor Fred Warburton of Columbia University observed a peregrine in the area surrounding the university and the church. Three weeks later, he saw a second peregrine in the vicinity. Evidently the birds were using the church as their headquarters. These sightings did not come to the attention of DEC until April 24. Consequently, observations did not begin in earnest until after that date. The chance March observation made by John Askildsen was undoubtedly that of one of the church pair because that male also sported the subadult plumage of a one year old. I began to think that any peregrine sighting, no matter how inconsequential it may appear to be at the time, may lead to an important find.

Another pair of adult peregrines were being observed regularly in the lower Manhattan financial district, mostly at 1 Liberty Plaza. Adult peregrines had been observed in that general vicinity during 1987 and 1988. One Liberty Plaza did not seem structurally suited for a peregrine eyrie nor did it appear that the installation of a nest box would enhance its possibilities because of ongoing exterior repairs. Consequently, an alternative site was selected, the Irving Trust Building at 1 Wall Street. Building personnel constructed a box designed by DEC and attached it to a wall structure on the roof. The peregrines did not use the box but some of their feathers were found nearby, indicating that they had at least frequented the area.

The third potential site was at the East River Arch Bridge. This 1,017-foot-long steel-truss railroad bridge connects Queens County and Ward's Island at a particularly dangerous section of the East River known as "Hell Gate." The treacherous currents in these waters are caused by the rushing of tidal water through a curving, irregular river channel and have claimed many vessels during the centuries, hence the name Hell Gate for the area and, familiarly, for the bridge. The Triborough Bridge is several hundred yards to the south of the bridge. It is a suspension bridge and serves three of the five counties within New York City: Queens, New York (Manhattan), and the Bronx.

Peregrine sightings had been reported in the vicinity of the Triborough Bridge in 1985 and 1986, but no breeding activity had been observed. In 1989, a pair of peregrines was observed at the Hell Gate Bridge on March 17. Following several more sightings, it was decided to try to assist them because neither the Triborough nor the Hell Gate bridge seemed to provide secure nesting opportunities. The Hell Gate, at first glance, appeared to be a perfect location because it is situated almost entirely over the East River, has its own supply of pigeons, and adjacent land areas teem with prey. The railroad traffic across the span would certainly be less disturbing than the constant and noisier vehicular stream which peregrines experienced at other bridges. However, the fresh graffiti on the structure, even on its highest point, told the sad tale of urban vandalism. It was logical to assume that youngsters who would venture into such dangerous conditions and climb such heights merely to deface property would surely find great sport in disturbing, if not destroying, a peregrine eyrie.

DEC installed a nest box on the roof of the tallest building at the Manhattan Psychiatric Center on Ward's Island. The two important advantages to be gained if the peregrines were to choose this site were that the building was owned and operated by the State of New York and would provide a high degree of safety for the nest box, and that there would be the bonus of the substantial "built-in" monitoring by the maintenance staff at the State Psychiatric Center.

Personal Contract. Dolores and I had been observing peregrines for seven consecutive seasons. My own involvement and monitoring had expanded beyond our mutual efforts to cover some of the other nesting sites in the New York City area. In recognition of my efforts, Barbara Loucks offered me a personal service contract with DEC to formalize some of the responsibilities that I would be assigned. I accepted the contract with great pleasure as an affirmation of the value of my monitoring and that of Dolores, Ted LeViness, and others.

This contract relationship was renewed for the subsequent three breeding seasons, 1990–1992.

At the Throgs, during the early days of April, there were several periods when the female was not seen for a few consecutive days. Each such absence aroused our hopes that she might be sitting on eggs but she reappeared with enough regularity to dispel those hopes.

I conferred with Barbara about the uncertainties raised by our observations and we decided that an inspection of the Throgs was warranted in order to search for eggs or any other telltale signs of nesting activity. On April 13, I was honored to be asked to perform a thorough inspection and found absolutely nothing. The peregrines did not show themselves during my entire visit. The only redeeming feature of this uneventful visit was that I was spared the danger of their frenetic attacks, which, in fact, are more raucous than dangerous as it is rare indeed that a peregrine will attack a human with intent to "kill." I inspected the area halfway to the Bronx tower and also checked the south side of the Queens tower, all to no avail. A bridge worker informed me, however, that just four days earlier he had been strongly attacked by both peregrines when he had approached the nest box area. Although I left the Throgs without any definite evidence of nesting, I knew that it was very possible that Rio happened not to be in the vicinity while I was there and that the female might be sitting tight in a well-hidden spot. There were so many dark, small cavities among the myriad of steel beams that she could easily have eluded discovery. I hoped that she would nest in a safe, spacious cavity but I would not find fault with the female if she were to pick a very secluded cavity after the ordeal she had experienced during the 1988 season. In fact, Dolores and I both anticipated that that was exactly what she would do.

Dr. Cade

The following day was very special for Ted LeViness and me. Dr. Tom Cade, founder of The Peregrine Fund, Inc. had invited me to accompany him on a tour of peregrine nesting sites in New York City. Dr. Cade sojourned in New York City for several days. His main order of business was to accept the prestigious Arthur A. Allen Award, which is presented periodically to those individuals making outstanding contributions in ornithology while integrating the activities of professionals and amateurs. Dr. Cade was to receive the award in recognition of his leadership and for his orchestration of the activities of amateur and professional ornithologists and falconers in their combined efforts to reintroduce the peregrine falcon in the eastern United States.

Ted and I met Dr. Cade, and Dr. Aronian of the New York Hospital/Cornell Medical Center, at the hospital. We made an inspection tour of that site and then proceeded to three other locations. The recent hospital news had been wonderful; there were three eggs in the nest box. Ted and I arrived at the site early and started our observations from ground level. We saw the female alight on the nest ledge; she was soon followed by the male. As we watched, they mated. Peregrines are known to copulate even after having successfully laid their eggs. Of course, peering upward twenty-four stories, we were not certain that actual copulation had been achieved, but it really did not matter to either the participants in this event or the audience. The birds were cementing their pair bond and the watchers were enjoying the sharing.

Barry Freed joined us and we proceeded to a slightly ajar window at the nest ledge which providing us with a view of a part of the ledge. The female soon came to the window and glared menacingly at us. Interposing her body between us and her eggs, her message was very clear: we would have to get by her if we tried to go to her eggs. We had no such intention but we appreciated her defense tactic. To see into the nest box, Dr. Cade used the mirror-on-the-stick device. The instant he projected it onto the ledge, the bird hit it. But Dr. Cade was able to ascertain that there were three eggs in the box and that the male was sitting on them. We took some photographs of the female from our advantageous position.

When we moved to the roof of the building, Dr. Cade surveyed the scene with an intensity that demonstrated his unflagging interest and pleasure in the peregrines' return. We craned our necks over the roof parapet to peer down at the adults at the nest box. They took to flight a few times, providing us with additional visual delights. Interestingly, from the hospital roof, we could see two of the other new potential peregrine nesting sites. The Triborough and Hell Gate bridges were easily observable, less than two miles distant. In fact, if a peregrine were to be perched in a reasonably prominent spot on either of those bridges, it would have been observable. The third location, the Riverside Church, was partially within our line of sight. The time was coming, if it had not already arrived, when someone positioned on a tall structure almost anywhere in Manhattan would be able to have at least three peregrine nests within sight.

Dr. Cade, Dr. Aronian, Ted, and I then drove to the nearby Hell Gate Bridge. We scanned the entire structure, concentrating on its upper beams where a peregrine would be most likely to place its eyrie. Almost immediately, Dr. Cade cried out that he had a peregrine in his sight and that it appeared to be in a posture that strongly suggested it was on eggs. We were jubilant at this discovery. Inwardly, I was extremely elated that it was Dr. Cade who had first spotted the bird. It seemed most fitting that he be the one to do so because he had done so much for the species. Although he was to receive an award for his peregrine work the following day, his discovery of an eyrie was an extra special award that obviously was very gratifying to him. Dr. Cade beamed like someone new to peregrines, although he had seen thousands of them and had been at so many sites. His love affair with discovery and peregrines had not been jaded. Personally, I looked forward to many more years of peregrine finding and watching and could not conceive of tiring of that pursuit.

The Hell Gate peregrine was sitting near an opening on the underside of a steel beam at the very top of the structure. The steel beams are hollow with a lattice work design for most of their length. They are, however, four sided for several feet at each of their ends. The ends are butted up against the adjacent beam in an unbroken line that runs from one end of the bridge to the other. The bridge curves over its entire thousand-foot length but at the top of the span the arc is so minimal that the floor of the cavity, where the peregrines were nesting, is actually flat. As we watched the sitting peregrine, its mate flew onto the scene to complete the picture. At this point, Bob DeCandido (founder of the Pelham Bay Park Hawk Watch) joined our party at the Hell Gate.

To follow up our two very satisfying site visits, we proceeded to my apartment to observe the peregrines at the Throgs. Dolores then finally met Dr. Cade, after having started the whole process, both for herself and for me, by writing to him in 1983. Little did she realize then to what new horizons that one letter would eventually lead us. We observed the peregrines for an hour and everyone was eager to go to the next site.

We decided to observe the peregrines that were frequenting the financial district. Chris Nadareski had been monitoring the pair there regularly. He made arrangements for us to inspect the nest box that had been installed on the roof of the fifty-four-story building at 1 Wall Street. The box abutted a utility structure but was easily approachable. It appeared untouched and I, for one, did not expect otherwise. Peregrine eyries, whether located in natural or urban settings, are not placed on the top of the structure but almost always on the highest ledge below the top. We observed a single adult peregrine flying intermittently for half an hour. It was possible that we were actually seeing two different birds, each one flying alone at different times.

What a great day it had been! We had seen seven, or very possibly eight, peregrines at four sites. The efforts of so many dedicated workers and the sums of money invested were bearing fruit. The fact that many of today's eyries are not at historic locations is not important to the long-term outlook. The world has changed drastically since the eastern peregrines were extirpated. The peregrines will have to adapt to the current conditions if they are to reestablish themselves as a self-sustaining species without human intervention.

The Palisades

During the middle days of April at the Throgs, the female was seen much less frequently than the male. One day, a lone subadult peregrine was seen briefly flying about the Throgs. On another occasion, Rio repeatedly dove at crows that were nesting in a tree adjacent to Cryder House. His furious attack was not provoked; the crows never approached the Throgs. Of all of the peregrine attacks against crows that I had witnessed, not one had been started because a crow had strayed beyond the boundary of its own territory. The peregrines seemed to have a natural antipathy for the crows and that appeared to be sufficient provocation for an attack.

On April 27, Bob DeCandido and I invested several hours observing that section of the sheer cliffs of the Palisades that lies between the

110

Tappan Zee Bridge and the George Washington Bridge. These rugged cliffs had supported peregrine eyries in the past and we harbored the hope that the current increase in the peregrine population might develop a pair that would again attempt to nest on these historic cliffs. We started our survey at the northernmost section of this region and our last viewing site was in a New Jersey park, several hundred yards north of the George Washington Bridge. There, only several feet above the edge of the Hudson River, the sheer Palisades cliffs towered over us. We felt rather insignificant as we scanned the imposing cliffs with the wide expanse of the Hudson River at our backs.

After futilely searching the cliffs, we turned our attention to the bridge. A bird was perched atop the New Jersey tower. Its erect, regal posture and "precarious" perch position on the very top edge of the tower structure immediately signaled to us that it was a peregrine. Excitedly we waited for the bird to display some behavior that might provide us with a clue to its situation at the bridge. We fully realized the possibility that this was one of the peregrines from the Riverside because we could see the church, a mere two and one-half miles distant.

First the bird unsuccessfully pursued a passerine and then flew to a perch below the roadway. It seemed to be familiar with the bridge structure. I noted that all of the peregrine visitors observed at the Throgs had frequented its upper reaches. This peregrine then returned to its former perch atop the tower and sat motionless for half an hour. Just as our concentration began to flag, the bird vaulted from its perch and sped upward. We could see nothing above the rising peregrine and Bob offhandedly remarked that it must have sighted a raptor high in the sky beyond the normal range of human vision. Each of us kept our binoculars trained on the ever-rising bird. That is what we thought until I realized that we were standing back to back and our angles of view were diverging. I was watching a peregrine flying north high above the Hudson River, undoubtedly using it as a guideway on its migratory trip to its breeding territory, while at the same time Bob was still eyeing the "bridge bird."

This event was very stimulating to us because it gave rise to the plausible theory that the bridge bird was defending its territory rather than merely frequenting the bridge. This event, coupled with the hunting episode and the bird's obvious familiarity with the bridge, indicated the distinct possibility that the George Washington Bridge was hosting a peregrine. We left the site with the bird on the tower and our hopes rising for the peregrines' return to a historic breeding region, the Palisades. The news of our observations was immediately disseminated to DEC and the growing numbers of peregrine watchers in the New York City area. Many follow-up visits were made to the site and a few sporadic sightings were garnered, and then none at all.

Fortunes at the Throgs

At the Throgs, Kathy O'Brien performed a thorough inspection on April 28. She found fresh peregrine droppings but was unable to find the adults or any eggs. She made loud noises, trying to attract the attention of a hidden bird, but to no avail. This was a repeat result of the inspection that I had made two weeks earlier. This total lack of defense of their eyrie area by the peregrines was puzzling. We hoped that it was due to the female's "sitting tight" out of sight and Rio simply not being in the immediate vicinity.

One morning Rio called loudly as he again attacked the crows at their nest tree. But this time there was a difference in the crows' response. Each time Rio made a pass, the crows chased after him as he sailed by, only to turn tail and scatter to cover when Rio reversed his direction. Evidently the crows were willing to confront their dangerous enemy, to a greater extent, now that they had young of their own to defend. Happily, there was no damage inflicted to either species. The increasing frequency and vitality shown by Rio in his aggression toward the crows indicated that he was in the nesting mode.

During the second week of May, Rio and his mate engaged in startling interactive flying sequences near their nest box. They flew at each other in a demonstration of their aerial prowess that was a thrill to witness. They also flew in unison, in very tight formations, showing their skill in a totally different way. These joint flying sessions were undoubtedly calculated to further cement their pair bond. I would like to comment that this obviously pleasurable activity was a demonstration of the pair's love and affection for one another, but such an unscientific description would be labeled as anthropomorphic. However, I'm the one who has seen them sit side by side, hour after hour, day following day, for the many months until the next breeding season activities start. Their fidelity to each other is always a revelation to those of us who are lucky enough to see it often enough to taste the essence of it. Time is a factor not easily understood in situations such as this unless meaningful portions of it are invested by the observer.

Early one evening, I found a one-year-old female peregrine visitor perched atop the Queens tower. Suddenly she executed a power dive at a pigeon flying several feet above the water. Her tremendous burst of speed was to no avail as the pigeon was able to escape by dodging the pass and flying into a group of trees. A healthy pigeon is a tremendously skillful flyer and more times than not is able to evade the first pass of the slashing talons of the pursuing peregrine. Its less-than-sleek outward appearance belies its prodigious flying ability. The thwarted peregrine, using the brisk wind, flew to the Bronx tower and circled above it about a dozen times. Finally, she alighted on the north side of the tower where I could no longer see her. I watched for half an hour, during which time the resident adults did not show themselves. My continued observations until nightfall went unrewarded as I no longer saw the visitor nor the resident peregrines.

On another afternoon, both adults attacked the nesting crows but the female quickly returned to the nest box area. She acted as if she had eggs or young to minister to. The next morning, Rio pursued two blue jays very avidly, missed his first approach, but easily snared one on his second attempt. Carrying his prize up to the Throgs, he was joined by the female before he alighted. I could see him perched there until darkness set in more than two hours later. The morning after that, Rio attacked a pigeon but missed it on his first pass. He used his downward speed momentum to enable him to zoom up and over his intended victim. He then quickly flipped over, dove down again at his prey, and captured it. Rio carried the pigeon up to the Throgs and alighted approximately twenty yards from the nest box. He immediately began to deplume his catch. Only several minutes had passed when the female emerged from the nest box area, flew to Rio, took the carcass, and returned to the eyrie.

By the fourth week of May, our observations at the Throgs began to confirm the distinct possibility that chicks had hatched. The female was deserting the nest box area more frequently and sharing with Rio more of the crow harassment duties. She would fly from her perch to intercept Rio when he returned to the Throgs with prey. I advised DEC that the peregrines were displaying a definite behavioral change that signaled a post-hatching condition. I was asked to perform another Throgs inspection to determine the nesting status.

On May 22, I made my second inspection of the Throgs. Even before I was able to enter onto the catwalk, the female raised the alarm; she was quickly joined by Rio. They both called loudly but did not defend the nest box itself. On a visit during the past season, when there had been a chick in the box, the female had positioned herself between the box and us. This time, they were defending an area somewhat to the east and north of the nest box. As I walked along the catwalk, their cries grew more strident. I was sure that I was approaching their eggs, or, more likely, their chicks. During some of his screaming attacks, Rio missed me by mere inches. On one pass, I actually felt the rush of air from Rio's beating wings on my face. They took turns coming at me; Rio was more persistent in his flying attacks while the female challenged me by putting her body in my path.

When I had walked almost to the end of the catwalk, the virulence of their combined attack efforts seemed to climb to fever pitch. I experienced an ever-so-slight sensation which caused me to reach up to my head. I found that my cloth hat was no longer on my head. When I looked ahead, I saw the female flying eastward, away from the Throgs, clutching my hat in her talons. She had picked the hat from my head with such deftness that I cringed at the thought of what damage she could have inflicted on me if she had had the slightest desire to do so. She flew about fifty yards from the Throgs, turned to look back at me, and opened her talons, releasing my hat to the water below. She wore an unmistakable look of disdain.

This hat caper reminded me of a similar incident that had been recounted by Fritz Reillmann at the 1987 Raptor Research Conference. In his case, however, the peregrine had slashed his forehead and presented the hat to her chicks in the nest.

I did not relish disturbing the adults but experience had clearly taught me that without intelligent human intervention, chicks are lost that could otherwise have been saved. I continued my search without finding the nest cavity. The brave defenders harried me continuously as I scanned likely cavities from many vantage points. At one turn, they perched, side by side, on the catwalk railing and faced me down. It became obvious that the spot which they had selected was not one readily visible from the catwalks or other normally accessible locations. I retreated under fire, sure that they were defending a well-concealed nest.

The following days produced observations that continued to confirm the premise that there were growing chicks in the eyrie. The female increased her participation in hunting and in harassing the local crows, activities which Rio had almost exclusively tended to during the period of her confinement. She returned to the eyrie area much more often than did Rio. This is the usual pattern. The females themselves feed their chicks during the chick's development in the nest.

Both adults were observed much more frequently now because they had hungry chicks to feed and crows and other predatory birds to chase from their territory. There were very intense moments with superb flying stunts. It was interesting to note that when the peregrines collaborated on a crow attack, there was absolutely no defense by the crows. They hunkered down and flew only to avoid the peregrines' onslaught. When only one peregrine attacked, however, the crows usually flew after it as they would have done against any other raptor that invaded their territory. On one occasion, Rio was diving at and chasing crows with particular abandon. Dolores and I were standing on our terrace witnessing the spectacle with rapt attention. On one turn, Rio came within several feet of us. We clearly heard the sound of the air rushing past his furiously beating wings as he sped by us. That ordinary event in a peregrine's average day was an incident that again brought home to us how lucky we were to have peregrines as neighbors.

One evening, Rio made a kill and flew to the south side of the anchorage as if he were searching for an out-of-the-way spot on which to enjoy a quiet meal. We sometimes took the liberty of trying to read the intentions of our peregrine neighbors because we had spent so many hours observing them during seven seasons that we often could analyze their behavior correctly. Rio alighted on the first pier, where he was soon joined by his mate. She did not hesitate, but immediately took the prey from Rio and flew to the nest box area. This behavior almost certainly indicated that she was feeding chicks. There were many other observations of food being taken into the eyrie. We noted that the crow hatchlings, meanwhile, had fledged from their nest and had dispersed to other trees adjacent to the nest tree.

The peregrines continued to act aggressively toward any large creature that came into their view. Great black-backed gulls were harried fairly regularly. Usually these very large gulls were avoided by the peregrines because their size and strength would make them a very formidable opponent. Black-backs will even challenge peregrines when the situation demands it. For example, I observed a peregrine attack, disable, and drive a pigeon into the water near the Cryder House boat pier. The peregrine alighted on a set of pilings near the pigeon to await the proper moment to retrieve it. Its unusual perch position, however, quickly attracted the attention of a great black-backed gull. The gull immediately flew directly toward the peregrine and acted as if it would land right on top it. This displacement approach is a common technique used by many birds to demonstrate superiority over the perched bird. The gull's effort was successful. The peregrine hastily retreated toward the Throgs with the gull following close behind. The gull chased the peregrine almost all the way to the Throgs before returning to collect its prize.

I discussed the peregrines' pattern of behavior with DEC and we decided that another inspection was needed. Determined to find the nest, I resolved to invest as many hours as might be necessary in making observations from ground level prior to the actual inspection in order to pinpoint its location. During the morning of the appointed inspection day, a series of such observations revealed that the birds always returned to one particular beam. I felt very sure that I would be able to find the nest when I went up onto the Throgs later that day.

Ted LeViness accompanied me on the inspection so that, while I peered into cavities searching for the nest, he could fend off the peregrine attack team, and also watch for clues to its location. Ted's presence was poignant because, since 1983, he had invested thousands of hours in observing the peregrines at the Throgs and at other sites. No one had logged more observation time at the Throgs than had Ted, myself included. Yet this was his first eyrie inspection. His feelings were understandably at a high anxiety level. Ted had read extensively about peregrines and had observed them on their fall migrations for many years. Since they had been extirpated from the eastern United States, it had never occurred to him that he might one day be able to observe them in a natural setting close to his home. When in 1983 he had the good fortune of being able observe nesting peregrines at the Throgs, a mere seventeen miles away from his home, it was a much-appreciated gift. Now, in 1989, he was going to inspect, at close range, the eyrie of a female peregrine that he had been observing for seven consecutive breeding seasons. I couldn't help but think that sometimes devotion is rewarded.

Fortunately, when we stepped onto the catwalk, the adults were not nearby. We rushed along the catwalk to a vantage point where I would be able to see the nest beam. The second I focused my binocular on the cavity, two chicks raised their lovely white heads to greet me. If they hadn't done so, they could not have been seen. Our elation was immediately interrupted by the screaming female, who had flown onto the scene with the obvious intention of defending her chicks.

Everyone, peregrines and humans alike, calmed down after a moment. Ted and I made our way to the end of the catwalk to gain access to the nest cavity. The only position affording an unhindered view of the cavity was from the beam itself. Ted got down on his hands and knees and peered into the dark of the beam. He shouted that there were four chicks and that they all appeared to be healthy. I replaced him at the opening and briefly ogled the youngsters. The odor that greeted our nostrils, from the cavity, would normally have been considered extremely offensive but to us it was a special perfume.

We departed quickly with great satisfaction in our successful mission. The only negative factor was the realization that the chicks would have to be moved to a larger, safer nest. The beam in which they were ensconced was about five feet long but only one and a half feet in height and width. They could not possibly have developed properly in such confined quarters. Furthermore, their first movement out of the cavity could result in a fall to the water below since there was no platform structure at its opening except for the beam itself.

The adults returned to their normal activities. Peregrines are exceedingly resilient to disturbances at their eyries because of their strong propensity to continue with the nesting cycle to its natural conclusion. That same evening, I saw Rio flying toward the nest with a kill. The female rocketed down from her perch atop the tower, vocalizing loudly. She wanted the carcass and she wanted it immediately. Rio kept flying, prompting the female to dive at him again.

Realizing that her aggressive behavior was making no impact, she tail-chased him directly into the eyrie. He deposited the food and flew right up to the top of the tower, where he cleaned his beak.

As the month of May drew to a close, I contemplated the wonderful sights and sounds that I had been fortunate enough to enjoy, both from remote observation points and from my personal inspections of the Throgs. Naming our extraordinarily productive adult female seemed to be appropriate at this point. It was awkward to continue calling such an old friend "the female" while first-season adults and fledglings were given names at other peregrine nest sites and her mate Rio had a name. I dubbed her the "Queen," recognizing her as the most senior breeding female in the New York City metropolitan region, the most productive with twenty-eight eggs to her credit, and a Queens County resident. We looked forward to the remainder of the breeding season with great enthusiasm.

Other Sites Updated

While the Throgs site had been receiving so much attention, the Verrazano-Narrows Bridge had not been neglected. On April 27, Kathy O'Brien and Chris Nadareski inspected it and found the female sitting on four eggs near the Staten Island tower. Kathy reinspected the site on May 10 and observed the female sitting on a live chick only a few days old. The female flushed, enabling Kathy to see that there was also a dead chick and an unhatched egg. The fourth egg was missing.

One week later, Kathy found that the nest held just the one live chick and the unhatched egg. The chick was sitting up well but had a grimy substance on the top of its head. Because of the chick's unsatisfactory condition and the need for a foster chick at the Wall Street location in New York City, Kathy removed it and the unhatched egg. The Verrazano site had again failed to successfully fledge young. For five breeding seasons, 1985 through 1989, only one chick had fledged there and that one had disappeared early. Additionally, three adult females had been found dead on the bridge. The Verrazano certainly seemed to have a problem that thwarted peregrine nesting success.

But as the once-proud Brooklyn Dodgers baseball team used to proclaim each lost season, "Wait till next year."

The Hospital. The New York Hospital/Cornell Medical Center peregrine progress reports gave every indication that this site would be successful for its second breeding season. Of interest was Barry Freed's reading of the adult male's band, which identified it as having been hacked from Owl's Head, New Hampshire, in 1987. This corroborated the theory that the peregrines that are released in the northeastern section of the United States tend to travel southward along the coast and that when they find attractive nesting locations in urban areas, usually at bridges or tall buildings, they establish territories.

At the hospital, the first chick hatched by May 17 and the other two emerged shortly thereafter. The two males and a female were banded on June 8 by The Peregrine Fund's Marty Gilroy and DEC's Kathy O'Brien. As soon as Marty's face appeared at the nest ledge window, the female became highly aggressive and ran menacingly toward it. Her intent to attack was abundantly clear from her striking blows on the window. She had displayed this behavior on previous occasions when observers had approached the nest ledge trying to see into the nest box. At one point, Marty was able to grasp one of her legs but had to let it go because both adults attacked him, hit his head, and raked his arm. Who could blame them for exhibiting such ferocity when confronted with such a large, frightening creature near their young? These were wild peregrines who could not possibly fathom any relationship with humans at any level.

Marty managed to gather in the chicks and, with Kathy's assistance, banded them and took some blood samples. Kathy measured their tail feather growth and, in the process, found that the female chick was infested with lice. Marty dusted all the chicks with a commercial pet bird-lice powder. The entire operation was completed in about forty-five minutes.

Both male nestlings had fledged by June 24. On that fateful day, one of the youngsters demonstrated dramatically that there were dangerous conditions at every nesting locale and that observers can be very important to the their survival. One of the males had attempted to alight on the top of the New York Hospital's thirty-story-high smokestack. Almost predictably, he missed his landing and fluttered down into the stack. Barry and his wife Rita Freed were among a group of observers at the hospital who witnessed this event. If these intrepid peregrine watchers had not been on the scene and had not been alert, the youngster would most certainly have perished. He would have simply disappeared and no one would have had a clue as to the cause of his demise.

Barry and Rita rushed to the hospital authorities and feverishly worked to obtain permission to gain access to the equipment at the bottom of the smokestack. Time was of the essence because the gases and ash materials in a working smokestack are lethal. When the access door at the bottom of the stack was opened, the ash-covered youngster was still very much alive. They rushed him to a nearby animal hospital, where he was cleaned and placed in an oxygen tent. Two days later, he was returned to the nest ledge, after having been named, appropriately, "Phoenix." The female nestling fledged on the same day.

Several evenings later, Dolores, Dave Gardner, and I went to the hospital to meet Barry and Rita Freed and observe the peregrines, at close range, from within the building itself. Dr. John Aronian joined our group, as did my friend Tom Renner, another peregrine watcher. Barry informed us that only two days after Phoenix had been placed on the nest ledge, he was again observed perched on top of the smokestack that had almost claimed his young life. This was another example of the propensity shown by peregrine youngsters to return to danger areas and repeat their mistakes. Oddly, that same evening, all three fledglings were seen on the smokestack.

While we were there, a building maintenance man notified us that a fledgling had been discovered wandering in a corridor adjacent to the rooftop tennis court. Dr. Aronian grabbed a large towel, and, went to the roof and gathered her into it. It was a female banded "K25K;" she was destined to play an important role as an adult. She was released from the roof while Red-Red, the adult female, circled overhead.

Red-Red alighted on a ledge just above the nest ledge clutching a large pigeon in her talons. She was very perturbed when she saw us peering down at her. She glared at us menacingly and vocalized her displeasure as if she were ordering us to get off her property. I sympathized with her but was at the same time mesmerized by the sight. Red-Red began to deplume and tear the pigeon apart despite our prying eyes. We were close enough to see the seeds from the pigeon's stomach strewn about the ledge. She fed on it intermittently but was unable to finish her meal because K25K arrived and appropriated the prey. Red-Red flew to the smokestack. Phoenix and the other young male were on the nest ledge with the adult male, so we had the entire family in view. Reluctantly, we departed because darkness was falling. It is difficult to explain how warm I felt as I put this visit with the peregrines into my memory bank. The youngsters continued to be observed regularly throughout the summer until they dispersed satisfactorily.

Tappan Zee. The peregrines at the Tappan Zee had fledged three young in 1988, their first breeding season there. At least two of the young had developed to the point that when they disappeared from the site it appeared that they had acquired their necessary survival skills. We hoped that the adults would be able to repeat their excellent performance in 1989 but our observations indicated otherwise. Dolores and I went to the Tappan Zee on May 19 and found the female in the west tower nest box. We observed the small white head of a chick in the box. We watched for almost two hours, trying to find another nestling, but we failed in that attempt. It was impossible for us to see very far into the box from our ground-level viewing site, and a chick could easily have been hidden from our view. While the female fed the chick, the male flew into view and we enjoyed seeing the three peregrines together. When the feeding was ended, the female joined her mate on the top rail of the bridge and then both flew off. Within a few minutes, the female dutifully returned to her nestling. The Tappan Zee site had again produced young, albeit only one.

I returned to the Tappan Zee four days later on an intermittently rainy day. Again both adults and their chick were at the eyrie but no other nestling was visible, dashing my hope that there was more than one. The chick defecated out of the open end of the box rather than within the box as it had done during my previous visit. During this four-day interval, it had "learned" not to befoul its own nest. I left the site with mixed feelings, but having one healthy chick was obviously better than having none.

One week later, on May 30, the Tappan Zee chick had grown considerably and sported some dark feathers. When I returned to the site on the afternoon of June 16, the chick was on a beam below the nest box. It alternately hopped and wing-flapped back and forth on the narrow surface. Its vigorous and untiring movements demonstrated its muscular strength and stamina but I worried because it did not seem to show the coordination needed in such unforgiving circumstances. If it were to fall, it could easily end up on the roadway to an almost sure death. I again left the location with mixed emotions. It was a great thrill for me to see a well-developed youngster who had very probably fledged within hours of my arrival, but the dangerous conditions that surrounded it were frightening. My fears were eased when I remembered that at least two of the three fledglings from the 1988 nesting season had survived to dispersal under virtually identical conditions.

Unfortunately, my fears proved to be prophetic. The youngster was taken from the roadway the very next day. Luckily, it was unhurt and was being cared for by a raptor rehabilitator. Barbara Loucks of DEC asked me to place the fledgling, if possible, in or near the nest box. Failing that, I was to put the bird in the most suitable location on the bridge structure according to the circumstances.

As we spoke, the thought crossed my mind that this fledgling might stand a better chance of survival if it were placed with the young at the Throgs. It had given up its safe height advantage and descended to a heavily used roadway. This error in judgment, if one can use that term when describing a bird's behavior, was likely to recur. Unlike the Tappan Zee eyrie, the Throgs eyrie was below the roadway and there were large landing platforms below it. Another advantage at the Throgs site was that there the youngster would have the benefit of the company of other fledglings.

But the fledgling was delivered to the Tappan Zee by a DEC conservation officer, who handed me the young, wild peregrine in a pet cage. A maintenance worker and I climbed onto the personnel platform of a gigantic cherry picker and were slowly lifted upward. The wind was whistling through the bridge structure at fifteen to twenty-five miles an hour with occasional higher gusts. Our perch swayed in the wind as we gained elevation. The cherry picker could not reach the height level of the nest box so I chose a large steel plate a few yards below it. When we reached the target spot, I placed the cage so that when I opened its lid the peregrine hopped right on to the plate. The placement was perfect. The cherry picker telescoped downward and the youngster vocalized lustily. We were very fortunate that neither of the adult peregrines had appeared while we were engaged in this procedure. Before we had moved ten feet downward, the fledgling had already wandered out onto the narrow beam. It seemed to me that the chick had a reasonable chance to survive because, below this beam, there were several additional structural beam levels that would serve as landing opportunities above the roadway. The chick also had better coordination than it had had when I first observed it, obviously a consequence of its being several days older.

The adult male then alighted close to the fledgling and quizzically checked it, which was understandable since he had not seen his wayward fledgling for three days. I left the bridge with a distinct sense of accomplishment. The fledgling was back home, a parent was with it, and it had another chance to survive.

I drove to a marina, north of the Tappan Zee, which site provided the nearest land-based viewing location of the Tappan Zee. I wanted to ascertain whether the youngster would be accepted by the adult male and whether he would maintain his position on the bridge. I did not have to wait long, for, within forty minutes, the male arrived with a fresh kill and deposited it on the platform where I had placed the fledgling. The youngster quickly scampered across the beam to the prey, mantled it, and began to feed. The adult left and I followed suit. There was no question in my mind that the fledgling had been accepted and would be cared for.

The bridge workers had spontaneously volunteered to monitor the peregrines and to call me if a problem were to arise. I hoped that I would not hear from them. Sadly, the bad news was delivered to me, six days later, by Kathy O'Brien. The fledgling had been found dead on the roadway. We had tried to help but sometimes the built-in propensities of a creature spell its own doom. Peregrines that cannot avoid the many dangerous conditions that they encounter in their everyday lives will not live to adulthood and will not perpetuate their kind. This evolutionary process known as natural selection develops a successful breeding stock of birds that has demonstrated its superiority by adapting to and surviving in adverse and changing environments.

8

Riverside Church

(1989 - continued)

The Riverside Church site was experiencing a very eventful breeding season. DEC invested a significant amount of time in assisting the peregrines there. On April 24, Kathy O'Brien conferred with Riverside's maintenance director, Tony Holton, who had seen an adult bird sitting on two eggs the day before. The next day, both the eggs and the bird were gone from the north-facing twenty-first-floor window ledge. The eggs had been placed directly in front of a window that opened outward, and it was probable that someone had opened the window, inadvertently pushing the eggs farther out on the ledge. The wind or an adult's movement may have resulted in their falling off the ledge. Later, two egg-yolk splashes and a shell fragment were observed on the ledge below the nest ledge.

To prevent any more mishaps of this type, Kathy applied a mixture of sand and marble chips, the best substrate materials she could obtain at the site, to the north and west twenty-first-floor ledges. This would prevent the eggs from rolling, allow any water to drain away, and provide a cushioning bed. While Kathy and Tony were engaged in this work, the adult female alighted nearby and stared at them intently for twenty minutes. She was unbanded, unlike her one-year-old mate who wore a black band on each leg. It was unfortunate that the DEC representative did not get the opportunity to read his bands.

Tony observed scrapes in the gravel bed soon after they had placed it on the ledges and saw one egg on a west ledge. On May 17, Kathy returned to Riverside with Marty Gilroy of The Peregrine Fund and they found four eggs. Some of the gravel was very rough, so they augmented it with sand and smaller gravel. When Marty opened the nest-ledge window, he was met by the female; but she retreated to the outer edge of the ledge where she remained throughout the operation. Marty picked up the eggs and handed them to Kathy, who held them while he and Tony piled a layer of finer material over the coarser gravel and made a depression in it. The team placed three eggs into the depression. The fourth egg, which was dented and leaked fluid, had no chance of hatching naturally so it was taken to the lab in the slight hope that it could be saved; further examination disclosed that it was not viable.

Tony's consistent monitoring of the eyrie was instrumental in providing the timely reports that helped DEC provide assistance to the peregrines. Later, when he reported that broken egg fragments were on the ledge below the nest and that the nest substrate was in disarray, Kathy inspected the site and found that the nest had been dug back down to the coarser gravel, thereby exposing the unsuitable sharper materials. The female sat steadfastly on the eggs. Kathy decided to upgrade the nest by placing more of the smaller gravel and sand on the ledge and installing boards at the outer edge.

When Kathy went out onto the foot-and-a-half-wide ledge, the female moved off the eggs but perched close by. Kathy picked up the two remaining eggs and, as Tony worked feverishly to install the boards, the female silently glowered at Kathy and the pile of gravel. The job took a little longer than expected, prompting Kathy to sit on the ledge with one egg cupped in each hand under her jacket. The female even tried to walk up onto the gravel despite Kathy's presence. While Kathy waited for Tony to finish his work, she observed the male flying overhead; he was carrying prey. When Tony was ready to affix the boards, he had to push back the female with a board to gain access to the attachment spot. Finally, he positioned the boards, reworked the substrate, and made a depression in it. As Kathy reached forward to put the eggs into the depression, the female saw them and immediately hopped over the board and positioned herself over the egg before Kathy had actually put it down. She stood on it for a second with one foot as she stared at Kathy. Kathy had to put the second egg down under her body because she was already sitting. Kathy also pushed the gravel up to prevent the eggs from rolling away. The female settled in on the eggs and, thankfully, the remainder of the incubation phase progressed uneventfully.

Tony observed two chicks on June 13. Two weeks later, Ted LeViness, Bob DeCandido, and I went to Riverside and observed the peregrines from a tenth-floor balcony directly below the nest ledge. We had an unobstructed view to the west and were able to see the adults leave and return to their eyrie. After the male captured a passerine and carried it to the eyrie, a shower of feathers wafted down on our heads. The male hunted successfully again, arriving at the eyrie with a large bird that showed much yellow, very likely an exotic escapee.

Kathy, Marty, and Chris Nadareski met at Riverside on July 3 to band the nestlings and install a nest box. After Marty had taken the chicks inside the room adjacent to the nest ledge, he captured the adult female with a hand net. Her reputation for holding her ground on the nest ledge had prompted Marty to take the net. The team hooded her, but she still fought strongly enough to warrant restraining her further; they placed her in a coat sleeve. They then placed a black, anodized band on each leg of the adult female and took a blood sample from her. They double-banded the two nineteen- to twenty-day-old female chicks, dusted them for lice, and took blood samples from each. One chick's right leg band was covered with green tape to help the site observers differentiate between the two chicks.

The nest ledge substrate was removed to allow for the installation of a nest box. Three large eggshell fragments were found and taken. After the box was in place, Marty covered its bottom with smooth, round gravel. Several perch poles were attached to the box and adjacent walls. The female was released via the north window and the chicks were put in the box in the west window. As soon as the team had exited the building, they spotted the female flying up into the nest. The male was not observed throughout this entire procedure.

On July 8, Ted and I went to the Riverside site and enjoyed watching both adults hunt. The male stooped to the Riverside Park canopy several times but came up empty. The female hunted over the Hudson River and once journeyed all the way to the New Jersey shore. We enjoyed the flying displays, knowing full well that these were really serious food-gathering forays. Watching peregrines diving, soaring, or performing aerial maneuvers was thrilling to inveterate peregrine watchers such as we. Finally, the female snared a pigeon and was joined by her mate as she returned to the eyrie with the nestlings' next warm meal.

On July 22, I spent four hours observing at the Riverside site. The adults hunted successfully and the chicks engaged in vigorous wingflapping. The chicks were just about ready to leave the nest ledge on their maiden flights. On my drive home, I was spotted a peregrine perched on the top rail of the Hell Gate bridge.

Early the next morning, the chick that wore the green-taped band fledged and was named "Kelly" by the local peregrine watchers. She spent most of her first day out of the nest on a ledge one story below the nest. There were other raptors in the neighborhood besides the peregrine family. A pair of American kestrels was observed on the nearby Interfaith Center, and occasionally the kestrels and peregrines interacted; no serious results were observed.

On a sunny, balmy ninety-degree day, Dolores and I, and several other peregrine watchers, were on Riverside Drive gazing upward at the fledged youngster. We must have presented quite a sight with our faces, scopes, and binoculars all pointed skyward. A Channel 4 television cameraman was videotaping the participants of a celebrity walkathon. As they streamed past our viewing point, his curiosity prompted him to ask what we were doing. On being informed of the peregrine nesting drama taking place at the Riverside, he immediately grasped the newsworthiness of the situation. He rushed back to his office to inform his management of the interesting story.

Channel 4 returned to the Riverside site on each of the following three days, represented by reporter Ben Farnsworth and a full camera/audio crew. Their primary goal was to film the second chick as it left the eyrie for the first time. They paid their dues by suffering through the hot, humid hours with nothing but the hope that the bird would cooperate and fly close enough to their camera to enable them to obtain some decent footage. On Wednesday morning when the second chick fledged, the camera crew was stationed on the Interfaith Building, one block south of Riverside. The fledgling could have flown in several directions but, as luck would have it, she flew straight toward the camera. Their wait was rewarded with excellent material, which appeared on the evening newscast.

During this period, there were many anxious hours devoted by

127

many anxious watchers to monitoring the Riverside eyrie. Although Kelly had been observed regularly since she fledged, no one had seen her receive a meal for about two days. Kathy and some other observers at the site had become concerned because Kelly could suffer dehydration if she were not eating sufficiently during this period of hot, sunny weather. With no access to other sources of drinking water, the fledgling was wholly dependent on its food intake for its liquid needs. Kathy, therefore, placed three chicken breasts, disguised with pigeon feathers, in a spot visible to Kelly. She showed interest in the offering but seemed unsure as to how to fly down to it. Early the next morning, Kelly received a meal on the top of Grant's Tomb. While this allayed the fears of the worried peregrine watchers, I never doubted that the fledgling was being properly fed. After having studied nesting peregrines for seven breeding seasons at several different sites, I had for some time come to the conclusion that a healthy pair of mated adults will not fail to nourish a youngster unless there are extraordinary circumstances preventing them from so doing. The activity pattern at Riverside had been perfectly normal in every way and I had confidence in the peregrines' instinctual drive to nurture their young.

The second fledgling, dubbed "Katie," was not observed for the remainder of the day after her morning debut nor for most of the following day. Again, there was "panic in the streets" as some watchers feared that the newest fledgling might be lost or in trouble. There were untold numbers of places where the youngster could be perched, out of sight. In the end, though, her absence prompted no course of action. We could not search the city. I trusted that she was all right because it was unlikely that she would fly far from Riverside. Fledglings tend to stay close to their eyrie during the initial period after fledging. Peregrine parents monitor their youngsters carefully and feed them wherever they are.

Because of the high level of anxiety of some of the peregrine watchers, Dolores and I went to Riverside in the late afternoon. We found the adult female perched on the top spire of Riverside and both fledglings on Grant's Tomb. We telephoned the news to those worried individuals whose blood pressure readings had undoubtedly risen to unhealthy levels. The adult female delivered a fresh pigeon to her young, who shared the meal with a demonstration of sisterly affection that etched itself into our memories. Kelly and Katie fed from the carcass simultaneously without a sign of aggression toward one another. There was no pushing or shoving. The only cloud in this otherwise sunny situation was the continuing observations that Kelly seemed to be favoring her right leg, although this condition did not seem to hinder her.

I returned to Riverside the following afternoon to find the adults on the north side of the church gazing down at their youngsters on Grant's Tomb. Katie took to wing and was immediately joined by the adult female, who zoomed downward with an attitude suggesting that she wanted Katie to return to the safety of Grant's Tomb. After a short flying session, Katie alighted very close to Kelly and the adults conducted some unsuccessful hunting forays. The fledglings touched beaks in a way that could only be described as a kiss. The peregrines were a constant source of inspiration to me.

I made a few more visits to Riverside over the next week and saw the fledglings each time. After the breeding season, we received word that Kelly had been trapped on October 7 and released in Old Lyme, Connecticut. She had traveled more than 100 miles and was in excellent condition.

Wall Street. A pair of peregrines continued to appear in the Wall Street area of the financial district throughout the spring season. On May 15, two peregrine eggs were spotted on the thirty-fifth floor of 40 Wall Street. This location was two blocks east of the nest box that had been installed on 1 Wall Street in March. Kathy viewed the site the next day. She observed a thoroughly soaked peregrine on the nest ledge in a heavy rain. A second bird flew in and settled on the eggs for a while, but then merely stood over them. Kathy, from her vantage point six stories above the nest ledge, saw that the eggs were lying on broken mortar and brick fragments. The exterior of the building was undergoing a major refurbishing and this was creating the debris that was falling onto the eighteen-inch-wide nest ledge. This project was slated to continue for another year and some of the very jagged substrate materials would probably damage the eggs once the peregrines started to incubate them in earnest. Up to that point, the peregrines appeared to have been brooding rather than incubating the eggs. (Incubation, you will recall, is not initiated until the last one or two eggs of a clutch are laid in order to obtain synchronous hatching. Brooding keeps the eggs from freezing but embryonic development does not commence until the birds incubate the eggs by sitting on them regularly.) An additional danger at the nest ledge was the ease with which the eggs could roll off.

The following day, Kathy and Marty Gilroy observed three eggs and watched the adults copulate twice, which led them to speculate that a fourth egg might be laid within two days. The male had a band on each leg and the female wore only a right leg band. Because of the unsatisfactory nest conditions, Kathy and Marty decided to relocate the eyrie. They selected the nearby 48 Wall Street building because the peregrines roosted there regularly and it had some excellent ledges. With this new, safer location in the offing, Kathy returned to the Verrazano nesting site to retrieve the sole chick surviving there, which was not in satisfactory condition, for placement in the Wall Street site. Hopefully, this would entice the peregrine pair to adopt the chick and bond them to the territory.

Kathy and Marty were only partially successful in removing the encrusted material from the chick's feathers. On May 25, the chick was fed quail meat, then was placed in the nest box at 48 Wall. Although the adults were in the vicinity earlier, they were not observed during the rest of the day. Their absence indicated that they were not going to adopt the fostered chick. At 5:30 P.M., the chick was removed and shipped to The Peregrine Fund facility in Boise. It was eventually hacked with other young at a site in Maine and fledged successfully, thus providing the only bright light in this story, this being the only chick to survive from the two sites, Wall Street and Verrazano-Narrows. It is interesting to note that a male hackmate of this chick was struck and killed by an airplane at JFK Airport on August 21.

Hell Gate. Although the Hell Gate bridge site conditions had held great promise when we inspected it in mid-April, the peregrines there failed to produce young. I made twenty-two site visits between April 15 and July 9. Twelve of the visits produced no sightings of peregrines but I continued to monitor the area regularly because many of my visits had been too short to be conclusive. I hoped that I had missed them because I'd made my observations at times when they happened to be out of sight, but the telltale signs of nesting failure grew clearer as the season wore on.

On my first visit, I could not find a peregrine. On the second, I observed one flying actively and making what I interpreted to be a territorial perimeter flight. The third visit was encouraging because the female was sitting in the same spot which we had previously identified as the possible nest location, and because the male was flying above the bridge. The next four visits were inconclusive because, during these times, only one bird was visible. On one occasion, however, the bird that I had observed was in the nest. On May 4, Chris Nadareski observed both adults at the Hell Gate. Unfortunately, this was to be the last time that season that both adults would be observed at the site at the same time.

My last fifteen site visits were for the most part unrewarding. I observed only one peregrine on each of two visits. By the middle of May, I regularly found crows perching on the bridge with impunity. No nesting bird can tolerate a crow during the breeding season. This attitude is universal from the smallest sparrow to the largest raptor. Peregrines are particularly hostile to crows and these crows' repeated unchallenged presence at the Hell Gate structure was a sure sign that the peregrines were not nesting.

I returned to the Hell Gate site on the afternoon of June 18 and had the pleasure of watching an adult male peregrine hunt for forty-five minutes. He used both the Triborough and Hell Gate bridges for hunting perches and pursued pigeons and smaller birds very avidly. I could not determine whether or not he was the male that we had observed at the bridge earlier. He very easily could have been the resident male from the nearby New York Hospital site.

New Adventures at the Throgs

June at the Throgs was an exciting time because the adults hunted many times each day to satisfy the insatiable demands of their four growing chicks. Nestlings, at this stage in their feather development, need to consume prey equivalent their own body weight daily. Furthermore, the increased energy expenditure of the adults caused by their many hunting forays also raises their nutritional requirements. A typical day of observations would yield an average of seven kills. Pigeons and doves comprised about half of the prey items and the remainder were passerines.

We saw collaborative hunts in which the peregrines enjoyed a decidedly higher capture rate than when attacking singly. On one hunt, the Queen dove down at a pigeon flying close to the water and snared it on her first attempt. Another time, she performed the classic peregrine kill. Stooping on an unwary pigeon, she raked it as she streaked through and turned quickly to snatch it before the injured creature could even begin to take evasive action. Several times we saw a peregrine fly toward a pigeon and merely grab it. The victim made no attempt to escape and the predator employed no tactical effort other than that of apparently approaching the quarry unnoticed from a favorable angle.

Other interesting hunt scenarios developed when Bronx pigeon fanciers released their birds from rooftop coops to enable them to take their exercise. The birds sometimes flew into the peregrines' prime hunting airspace. Often, when a tightly formed flock of pigeons approached the Bronx tower of the Throgs and noticed the peregrines, they turned and flew away as one, without incident. Sometimes the peregrines zoomed through a large flock without making contact. It seems that the adage "there is safety in numbers" is true for flocking birds. It is easier for a predator to capture a lone bird than to pick one from a large group. Many different species of bird utilize this flocking behavior when confronted by a predator against which they have no defense except to flee. The sheer number of possible targets seems to cause the attacker to fail to select any one target. The strategy works very often because the pursuer is deterred from his usual gambit of concentrating on one individual and chasing it until it is either captured or escapes. At other times, the peregrines successfully attacked flocks but we could not determine the winning factor in any particular instance. On the other hand, when a pigeon panicked and left the safety of the flock, and was pursued and caught, the reason was obvious.

Early one evening, as the Queen and Rio were perched on the Queens tower, an almost completely white pigeon flew onto the scene. Their exhilaration was evident as they lifted off the tower to catch supper. White coloration in some prey species produces a visual flash pattern which seems to produce a much higher interest level than does that of the normal coloration of that species. The peregrines' vigorous pursuit forced this quarry to seek sanctuary in a favorite pigeon roosting area on the south side of the anchorage. Queen and Rio both flew into this rather cramped space twice to try to flush out their game. The Queen alighted on a beam athwart the front of this area while Rio went to the first pier. The Queen then went deeper into the area, trying to force the pigeon to fly so that Rio would have a good chance to catch it out in the open. She succeeded in getting the pigeon to leave the safety of the roost but, when it flew away, it wisely hugged the anchorage walls so closely that Rio and Queen did not pursue it. Ten minutes later, Rio captured a large pigeon near the bottom of the anchorage. He had great trouble in gaining altitude despite his vigorous wingbeating. Rio gave up on his original destination and alighted on the north side of the anchorage ledge. Although we could not see him, we knew that he had started to deplume the prey the instant he sat down on the ledge because we could see the pigeon feathers wafting down to the water below.

June 7 was moving day for the chicks at the Throgs. Kathy O'Brien and I, with the assistance of Triborough Bridge and Tunnel Authority personnel, planned to move the chicks into a nest box. The importance of this operation was not overlooked by the Fourth Estate. The *New York Times* and the *Long Island Newsday* newspapers each sent a photographer to record this event for inclusion with written articles that they planned to publish. Kathy had assembled the following equipment for this project: a prefabricated nest box, sand, crushed stone, tools, hard hats, a long-handled fisherman's type of net, a safety belt, rope, and some other items.

The moment we descended to the catwalk, Queen and Rio sounded their alarm calls and flew at us. Their attack level was moderate because we were still about seventy-five feet away from their chicks. We assembled the nest box and moved to the spot where it was to be installed. This action brought renewed attacks, with increased vigor, because we had reduced our distance from the chicks by half. We clamped the box securely to a large gusset, filled it with sand and stone, and embellished it with two perch poles for the adults. The gusset's location provided the chicks with easy access to the catwalk.

At this point, I was wearing my bicycle helmet and one of the photographers and Kathy were helmeted as well. As we made our way to the nest cavity, the adults raged at us with greater and greater ferocity. Rio flew at us continuously while Queen, from very close perches, cacked at us as loudly as she could. Kathy donned a safety belt and secured it to a beam. She then went out onto the nest beam and positioned herself facing the nest opening. I stood on a more substantial beam over the nest cavity. I had a small airline type of animal carrier in which we would place the nestlings for the short trip to their new home.

Kathy peered into the nest cavity and beamed when she saw that all four chicks were alive and well. Her plan was very simple. She would insert the net into the nest beam, snag a chick, and pull it out. This was much easier said than done. The net's metal frame was larger than the opening and, even after it was modified, it could only fit into the cavity diagonally. The nestlings were very mobile and easily eluded the net. An electrical conduit partially blocked the opening, forcing Kathy to grope blindly for the chicks.

After many failed attempts, we attached a noose to the end of a stick. The idea was for Kathy to carefully move the noose back and forth in the nest until she snared a chick. A single talon would do. Kathy moved the noose every which way without success. Then she yelled, "I've got one." Slowly she pulled the nestling forward. To her great dismay, she saw that the noose was around the chick's neck. I urged her to continue to pull out the youngster, as gently as possible, because there was no other course of action available. As soon as the chick was within reach, I easily removed the rope from its neck, as it was quite loose. The chick was fine and voicing its displeasure loudly. Placing it into the cage, I felt the warmth of its body through my light gloves.

Kathy decided that the noose-extraction method was too dangerous. We reverted to the net technique after modifying its frame into a "U" shape. Kathy deftly snagged two more chicks. When I put the second and third chicks into the small cage, they fidgeted and, because of their close confinement, grasped each other. The twenty-four talons the chicks possessed among them were bound to bind into each other and did. With one hand gloved and the other ungloved for greater dexterity, I gently pried loose each talon individually. Pulling a talon the wrong way could injure the chicks' feathers or bodies. Because there was no space for the fourth chick in the transfer cage, I quickly took the first three chicks to the newly installed box. Despite placing them carefully in their capacious new quarters, their closeness in the transfer cage had caused them to grab at each other again. The three were lightly bound into each other. I separated them again. Three screaming peregrines in a box, one in a box beam, and two adults yelling in the open made for a noisy but wonderful aggregation. I sat in the open end of the box to insure that none of the chicks left it. Kathy extricated the fourth chick and as soon as we placed it in the nest box, we gathered up our gear and departed.

It had taken almost three hours to accomplish this difficult move. It rained the entire time and only the chicks remained dry and warm. The adults hit one photographer's helmet twice and parted the other one's hair. My helmet was hit hard twice and Rio's wing brushed my ear. Such are the vicissitudes that peregriners must suffer in the performance of their work. The operation was a complete success, although observations of the eyrie from land were prevented by a thick fog that rolled in and remained all that afternoon.

It was wonderful to contemplate that as a result of our relocation efforts, all four youngsters were ensconced in a safe and spacious box. Their chances for a satisfactory fledging and dispersal were now very good. I was elated to have had the opportunity of assisting in a hands-on way in such an important project. Having held each chick's warm little body in my hand had been a thrill. Prying their talons from their sisters, placing their little bodies in the nest box, and sitting with them during those anxious moments until the relocation was completed made for pleasant memories. Hearing the strident calls of both the young and the adults, feeling Rio's wing on my face, and having my helmet struck by him were all part of the symphony. I was in my element, the falcon watcher's dream.

The next morning, a dense fog again obscured the Throgs until 9:00 A.M. Rio hunted from noon until 2:00 P.M., when he and the Queen suddenly alarm called and flew near the eyrie in a very agitated manner. This behavior would have worried me if Kathy had not advised me that the chicks were going to be banded that day. In fact, I was able to see Kathy and Marty scurrying low along the catwalk as they were leaving the nest box area. Conditions quickly returned to normal, as evidenced by the Queen's incessant hunting during the remainder of the day. The next few days at the Throgs were ordinary. Hunting started before 7:00 A.M. on the first of those days when the Queen hit a pigeon and then a dove but failed to capture either of them. Rio joined his mate in the next hunt but he also failed. Then they hunted at the Bronx tower, where the Queen missed her first attempt to capture a pigeon but was successful on her next attack, the first capture of prey for the day. One hour later, Rio caught a dove and tried to deliver it to the young himself; the Queen intercepted him and took the catch from his talons. She alighted on the anchorage and deplumed the bird prior to taking it up to the nestlings. The third kill of the morning was a blue jay which Rio took directly to the nest. Rio made the fourth kill by 10:15 A.M., an unidentified passerine.

The fifth kill of the day, at 4:20 P.M., was the result of Rio's and Queen's joint efforts. The Queen fed on this pigeon until she had consumed most of it and then delivered the remainder of it to her chicks. Rio was obviously hungry and very much wanted some of this last kill. It was late in the day and he had not yet eaten. He had hunted most of the morning and afternoon but now redoubled his efforts. Rio's frustration was unmistakable as he pursued prey with uncharacteristic abandon. He pursued every bird in sight, without waiting for the quarry to be in a reasonably favorable attack position. He hunted repeatedly with no success. The fifteen miles an hour northwest winds invigorated both Rio and Queen. They used the wind to perform their breathtaking aerial maneuvers and at times perched close to one another on top of the Queens tower. Rio hunted consistently but caught nothing. At 7:50 P.M., the Queen flew on a beeline toward the Bronx tower. She had spotted a lone pigeon flying south from the Bronx. Neither the Queen nor her victim changed course. The Queen just seized the bird and flew with it to the Throgs, making the capture seem so easy after Rio's many failed attempts. Rio arrived quickly at his mate's side and she flew off, leaving the meal for him. He "dug in" and ate continuously for twenty-two minutes. This day's observations clearly demonstrated the female's complete control of the feeding schedule not only of the chicks but also of her mate.

The following day's observations covered the period from 4:45 A.M. to 11:10 A.M., during which five successful hunts were made. The prey captured included two doves, one pigeon, one blue jay, and an unidentified passerine. One unsuccessful joint hunt was conducted against a flock of pigeons. This attack initially seemed promising when one of the flock was singled out and separated from its group, but the speedster was able to elude its pursuers. In a later, successful hunt, Rio injured and drove a dove into the water near the anchorage. He deftly picked it out of the water and took it up to the eyrie. In midmorning, the Queen snared a pigeon and left it with Rio for his consumption. That same morning, the Queen had shown her increasingly defensive posture as her young were growing. She dove on a great black-backed gull and actually hit it lightly. Usually these large aggressive gulls are avoided by the peregrines because they are extremely dangerous.

June 16 was the first day that I was able to observe a chick from our apartment terrace. It was in the catwalk area near the box and I watched it for an hour and a half during the early evening. The next morning, a Sunday, I joined the large contingent of peregrine watchers who had assembled at the beach area. The adult peregrines were hunting vigorously and at least one pigeon was snared by 8:00 A.M. At 9:20 A.M., we were treated to the sight of this fledgling and its parents flying side by side. This was the first known fledging of this season. I use the word known because it was very possible that another of the four nestlings could have fledged earlier without having been observed. The fledgling flanked by its parents flew toward the north side of the anchorage. We hoped that she would land high up on the anchorage on an extremely spacious ledge just below the roadway. But her trajectory indicated that it was more likely that she would alight on the large ramp, near the bottom of the anchorage, located several feet above the high-tide level. The ramp area is potentially perilous because the fledgling would have had to maintain a level flight on her next trip or go into the water. Flying down from the top of the anchorage, the youngster would have the advantage of two good landing locations: the ramp directly below the ledge and the main pier of the Queens tower.

I had a nagging worry concerning this first fledgling. According to my calculations, and based on Marty's estimated age of the chicks, the June 17 fledgling was closer to five weeks of age than to six weeks. There is an enormous difference in that one week at that stage of a chick's development. The sixth week at the eyrie gives the nestling a significantly longer period of time to develop its flight muscles and overall coordination. I feared that this fledgling had come out too soon for its own good.

Within ten minutes from the time the fledgling had taken its maiden flight, the Queen snared a pigeon and delivered it to her

137

youngster on the anchorage. During the remainder of that day, three more pigeons were caught. The following morning, Rio snared a pigeon during a collaborative hunt and took it directly to the north side of the anchorage. I could hear the fledgling vocalizing in response to the food delivery. This was an encouraging sign but my observations were at a disadvantage because I could not see the north side of the anchorage. A pigeon and a dove were also caught that morning. The dove displayed extraordinary flying ability and almost eluded Rio, who had to dive at it repeatedly until he was able to hit it just before it gained sanctuary in some trees. The hunt was an exhibition that everyone who saw it enjoyed, except the dove, and even it must have appreciated the action until the very end.

Our concern for the fledgling grew as the first post-nestling day drew to an end. We had not seen the bird fly during the entire day and that was not an encouraging sign.

The second post-nestling day was more disheartening than the first because the one kill observed during the two-hour observation period was carried to the three chicks at the nest. There was no activity at the anchorage where the fledgling was last seen. We despaired that it might be lost. Although there was no sign of activity on the part of the other nestlings, it appeared that they were being given food. That seemed to corroborate the premise that they were not yet ready to leave the nest, and, if they were not ready to fly, then perhaps neither was the early fledgling. Usually peregrine chicks hatch within a day or two of one another and are ready to fledge at similar intervals and males tend to leave the nest before females do; but these nestlings were all females and should have been ready at approximately the same time.

Queenie

There were no further sightings of the fledgling and we all but gave up on it. Our hopes now centered on the other nestlings because the adults continued to bring food to the eyrie. The following morning fog made it impossible to see anything at the Throgs until 12:15 P.M., when I had the glorious sight of two chicks near the tower. They sat close to one another and they looked healthy. I named both the youngsters

"Queenie" after their mother and because we could not tell them apart. During the many hours I watched them that day, the adults visited them frequently and took food to them. The young would lay side by side for long periods of time. One poked its head under its sister's wing and the other put its head on its sister's shoulder. They had only small spots of down left on their heads.

These scenes were very gratifying to observe but the absence of the other two chicks was very ominous to me because, in addition to the early fledgling that had been accepted as lost, I believed that the fourth chick was most probably also gone. Chicks usually stay together for at least part of the day and I had only seen two chicks in over seven hours of observations. Some of the other peregrine devotees, at the Throgs site, felt that I was premature in my feelings of doom but I could see no reasonable cause for a chick not to show itself at all. Regardless of my personal feelings, the facts would soon come out and I could only hope that I would be proven wrong.

On the twenty-third day of June, six days after the missing chick had fledged, the Queenies did not show themselves until late in the afternoon. When they finally appeared, one of them positioned herself at the very end of a steel beam and peered outward into space. She seemed to be ready to go. I had seen that look before. She was about six weeks old and it was prime time for her debut. She did not leave her eyrie just then but I knew her big move was imminent and decided to keep a vigil until dark. One Queenie engaged in bouts of heavy wingflapping at the very edge of the outer beam.

Uninterrupted peregrine watching can be fantastically rewarding, especially if you arc a student of behavior as I am; and I was rewarded. I observed Rio perched on the southeast corner of the anchorage ledge, an unusual spot for him to occupy unless he had a specific reason to be there. At this exact moment, the Queen delivered a prey item to the Queenie that I had in view. Interestingly, Rio was looking over his shoulder as if he were gazing at a fledgling. I certainly hoped that that might be so.

Queenie was eating quite contentedly when the Queen returned to her side. The youngster immediately rushed her mother and shouldered her off the Throgs. The Queen returned twice more and received the identical response from her ungrateful youngster. Finally, on her next attempt, the Queen took possession of the carcass and fed

139

on it with her offspring still close by. Rio left the anchorage ledge after having been there for twenty-four minutes. Queenie again shouldered her mother off the edge and regained the carcass. The Queen came back and reclaimed the remains a second time. After five minutes of incessant begging by Queenie, the Queen relented and delicately fed her, beak to beak, just as she had done earlier in the chick's development when she had been incapable of feeding herself. This scene was something so special that I almost felt that I was intruding despite the fact that the participants could not possibly have known of or been affected by my observations. Still, I felt privileged to have witnessed this part of the Queenie's growing up and wouldn't have missed it for the world.

The Queen moved a short distance away from Queenie, who vigorously flapped her wings. She looked as if she were ready to go at any moment. I became increasingly nervous about her fledging at this time of the day; it was almost 8:00 P.M. and sunset was only half an hour away. Queenie then did a hop-flight several feet inward and out of my sight. Two minutes later, Queenie at last took her maiden flight. She looped down and then up under the nest box area with the Queen flying at her side. It was very apparent that the Queen was trying to shepherd the fledgling back to the safety of the eyrie. Nightfall was not a good time to leave the nest for the first time. However, the fledgling had to have her way and continued flying directly toward the north end of the anchorage. The Queen flew alongside the entire way and then returned to the eyrie alone. I hoped that the youngster would remain on the anchorage for the night.

At 5:35 the following morning, a Queenie was sitting on the Queens tower pier. I could not tell whether it was the one that had fledged last evening or her sister. I assumed that the early fledgling was lost and that the other unseen nestling was also gone. After observing for an hour, Ted LeViness and I went to the United States Coast Guard station at nearby Fort Totten to try to arrange for the use of a vessel that would take us out under the Throgs so that we could make an inspection of those structures that are not visible from land. We especially wanted to search for the missing fledgling that had flown directly to the anchorage a week earlier. We planned to assist any bird that might need it. If we were to find a dead chick, then we would at least have that knowledge, and its body, for examination.

The Coast Guard was very cooperative and scheduled our trip for 10:00 A.M. Ted and I returned to our observations at the Throgs and were elated to see a second youngster flying strongly from the Queens anchorage to the Bronx tower, so there were at least two healthy fledglings on the wing for the 1989 breeding season. Throughout the morning, the adults, in addition to hunting, attacked almost every large creature that strayed to within several hundred yards of the Throgs. Special attention was given to birds that invaded the area from the Queens tower to its anchorage. Herring gulls, great black-backed gulls, and crows were the prime targets. The peregrines choreographed their attacks to appear as vicious as possible to intimidate the interlopers into fleeing. Having two defenseless fledglings on the wing girded the adult peregrines into this frenzy of territorial defense. The Queen and Rio could have easily inflicted grave damage to many unsuspecting large birds but very rarely did so. In most instances, they did not make contact. In those cases when they did touch the enemy, they usually refrained from slashing them. The adults adjusted their defense perimeter, and enemy species identification, in relation to the development stage of their chicks.

To review, when chicks fledge, large predatory gulls, such as the great black-backed and herring, are deemed a menace to the young because the young are accessible to them. Unfledged nestlings are not in danger from these gulls and therefore the adults, in this case peregrines, tend to ignore them during that phase of the nestling's development. It was interesting to note that some of the targeted predatory birds at the Throgs site, in particular the crows, were themselves residents of the area. It must have been a puzzle to them to be attacked in their own territory, especially when they had been tolerated previously.

Ted, Dave Gardner, and I went to the Coast Guard station and were assigned a handsome forty-one-foot vessel and a crew of three for our inspection tour. We inspected the Throgs anchorages, main piers, pier fenders, and undersides. We found nothing noteworthy but appreciated the chance to view the nest box and bridge structures from a wholly different perspective, which would help us to better interpret future observations.

I couldn't help but think that if this inspection had been made one week earlier, on the day that the chick flew to the anchorage, or on the following day, the outcome might have been different. There might have been a chance to save the chick. As it turned out, the chick was lost and we did not know the reason except that it had apparently left the nest about a week too early.

The afternoon's peregrine activities at the Throgs were mostly territorial defense efforts. The most thrilling altercation of the day was the violent attack of an osprey flying over the East River close to the Bronx shore toward the Throgs, despite the fact that the osprey presented no threat to their youngsters. Rio and the Queen hit the osprey, forcing it to lose altitude. Undaunted, it continued flying low over the water, attracting a second, much harder strike. The osprey flipped over and plunged into the water out of sight. At first, I thought that the force of the peregrines' strike had turned the larger raptor over and that it had been badly injured. However, when the osprey emerged from the water and flew apparently unhurt, I realized that it had flipped itself over to confront its adversaries with its talons, which are both its offensive and defensive weapons. The osprey flew westward from the Throgs and then must have remembered its original destination because it turned and resumed flying toward the Throgs. The peregrines did not attack again and the osprey winged on to Long Island Sound.

Rio harassed a great egret and then took on a group of crows. These encounters were punctuated by some thrilling aerial maneuvers. Rio's appetite must have been invigorated by these activities because he then commenced a series of hunts directed against pigeons. He even resorted to the technique of trying to flush pigeons from their favorite roosting spot on the anchorage. He seemed unfocused and did not succeed in any of these attempts. When a great black-backed gull happened to fly by, both adults went at it so ferociously that the gull was able to escape their wrath only by plunging into the water.

The other interesting behavioral observation of that day concerned Queenie. Perched on the first pier, she jumped off and was on a perfect trajectory to land at the 1983 eyrie. Both adults intercepted her just as she was about to alight. Their interference caused Queenie to miss her landing and to flutter downward toward the water. She kept grabbing at the featureless wall of the anchorage but with nothing there to provide a toehold, she continued to lose altitude until I could no longer see her. I kept watching the area, expecting to see her fly up and away from the water. I was getting panicky as the seconds ticked by and she did not reappear, remembering the two previous times when fledglings had ended up in the water. I rushed down to the beach to check the area where I had last seen her. Dave Gardner was there and had witnessed the same sequence of events as I, but with the addition of Queenie's strong recovery and flight to safety on another pier. I wished that I had had more faith in the youngster's flying ability but it had not looked very promising from the vantage point of our terrace.

The following evening, Rio delivered a pigeon to Queenie on the third pier. She fed for half an hour on the fresh kill without depluming it. She ate slowly, in a very relaxed manner. Rio returned to the pier and tried to feed on the remains but was repeatedly shouldered off the pier by Queenie. Finally, Rio managed to seize the remains and took it to the fourth pier. The Queen and Queenie followed Rio there and, after some shuffling about, Rio departed, leaving his mate in charge of the remains. The Queen fed herself for a short period and then gave her youngster very small tidbits, just as if she were a new hatchling rather than the full-sized flying machine she had become. They stood shoulder to shoulder; Queenie did not try to bully her mother as was her tendency of late. This one pigeon carcass had been their center of attention and for over one hour had become their bone of contention. The fact that there was a vast supply of pigeons available all around them did not seem to enter into the equation.

In this, my seventh season of watching the peregrines at the Throgs, each new day still brought the expectation of seeing the peregrines doing the myriad of things that I had seen them do before. But every so often a new and entirely unexpected behavior is played out. Early one morning, a squirrel was scampering about on the roof of the Hammerstein Mansion. The Queen dove down and made seven passes at it. It ran for cover several times but did not seem to take the attacks seriously. I checked with all the peregrine watchers at the site and established that this was the first report of a land mammal being harassed that was not on the Throgs itself.

Less than an hour later, a one-year-old male peregrine flew through the area. He was at a high altitude and went unchallenged or possibly unnoticed by the resident peregrines. Then the Queen flew through a flock of twenty-five pigeons but failed to snare one. Half an hour later, the Queen captured a pigeon and took it to the eyrie. Within two minutes, she flew out with the carcass and Queenie, in midflight, tried to take it from her.

That evening, Queenie used a unique spot for a perch, a suspender gatherer. Suspenders are steel cables which hang down from the large weight-bearing cables and hold up the roadway. They are hung in sets of four and are held in position by gatherers. The Queen did not approve of this perch and tried to lure her offspring into the air by flying close to her and tempting her with prey. These tactics did not work. But the second Queenie, who had observed the procedures with her sister, was attracted by the prospect of being fed and alighted nearby on the weight-bearing cable. The Queen then landed next to the youngster on the cable and after a minute released the prey item. When neither of the fledglings responded by flying after it, the Queen dove down and snatched the carcass before it reached the water. The Queenie on the cable followed her mother down immediately and they flew away together. The Queenie on the suspender gatherer then took refuge under the Throgs roadway.

As each nightfall approached, the Queen tried to position her youngsters in a safe area on the Throgs. Many of her late evening gambits demonstrated her fear of leaving her young in an unsuitable location. For example, one evening as the light was fading fast, a male fledgling started to fly due east away from the Throgs. The Queen observed this from her tower perch and stooped on a beeline to him. At great speed, she intercepted him and stopped him by putting her body in his way. She then shepherded him back toward the Throgs, where he alighted on a main cable. When she positioned herself several yards from him on the cable, he flew into the eyrie area.

The last few days of June provided no dramatic incidents as the youngsters honed their flying skills and increasingly mimicked their parents. When the Queenies alighted on the top of the Queens tower, it marked the first time we had observed them using one of their parents' favorite resting locations that also served as a hunting vantage point. As they sat on the highest point in their territory, the Queen arrived with a prey item and fed them.

The Wind. During a day of strong northwest winds, the Queenies followed the adults up the Cryder House "wall of wind." We could

144

hear their calls as they rose higher and higher. This was a demonstration of their continuing mastery of sophisticated flying techniques. Landing appears simple but it requires an approach plan and physical coordination. The wind, if any, has to be gauged and taken into account. The final approach is usually made from below the intended landing point so that a soft touchdown can be accomplished by the braking action of spread wing and tail feathers. Fledglings improve their landing technique with each one that they perform but the early ones are awkward. Often, after a beautiful flight, beginners miss their landing entirely, which can prove to be very dangerous in watery and smokestack environments.

Northwest winds elicit spirited flying sessions from many birds. During the fall migration, which in the eastern portion of the United States runs from September through November, the greatest numbers of migrants are observed on days with northwest winds. This well-documented phenomenon applies not only to raptors but also to passerines. While most raptors will not migrate during rainy periods or against adverse prevailing winds, peregrines are known to fly regardless of weather conditions. When northwest winds blow strongly, however, the peregrine migration movement swells to a crescendo. Birds in their own territory will respond not only to brisk northwest winds but also to other strong winds, regardless of direction, such as those associated with storms; and they will use its force to move in the most unorthodox trajectories. The peregrines at the Throgs site regularly climb the Cryder House northwest wall of wind to attain the same altitude as the top of Cryder House, where they often hold perfectly motionless, except for slight primary feather adjustments, for a brief time before they crest the roof. Once above the roof, they usually zoom back toward their home on the Throgs to complete the circuit. Sometimes they make this round trip several times within an hour. There is no question that this activity is purely for their own pleasure. It is difficult to describe certain kinds of animal behavior without becoming anthropomorphic, but there is ample evidence that many creatures perform acts which can only be thought to be pleasurable to them.

The Throgs area is home to many birds in addition to the peregrines and they, too, succumb to the siren call of the wind. I have seen pigeons fly up into the face of gale-force, gusting winds and actually fling their bodies into the unseen aerial maelstrom, which carries them away at unflyable angles before they are able to regain their composure and fly under their own power. Herring gulls will purposefully move into the most violent wind currents to be borne away at much greater speeds than they could ever hope to attain by any other means. I have seen smaller birds venture into the windy skies with no possible gain other than the need to have the natural forces exert their will.

This period brought the first observations of the young crabbing with one another. Crabbing involves two raptors intertwining their talons during an antagonistic interaction or play activity. Although usually engaged in by youngsters, courtship also may include crabbing. It is always stimulating to see a pair of young, healthy animals interacting in a playful but skillful way that at the same time hones their survival capacity. While the youngsters played, the Queen was busy attacking a great black-backed gull and then a black-crowned night heron.

9

The Queenies

July's weather was average for New York City: hot and humid. It was the best time of the year for peregrine watchers. Two fledglings were on the wing reveling in their newfound freedom and skills and the Queen and Rio hunted frequently to satisfy their youngsters' robust hunger. One Sunday morning, an assemblage of peregrine watchers was treated to a unique observation. A crow had wandered over the water beneath the Throgs. The Queen pursued it and quickly snared it, actually flying several yards with the creature in her talons before releasing it near the pier fender. The crow took sanctuary within the fender and was not seen again. We had never observed a peregrine catch a crow, let alone fly with it and then release it alive.

The energetic Queenies often enjoyed crabbing but they were animated by any activity that involved flying coupled with a chase. Their crabbing game appeared to be somewhat perilous when the Queenies spiraled downward with locked talons, but they always disengaged in time to fly off gracefully. The tower pier and its protective fender caught their attention; it was a roost for multitudes of pigeons. The youngsters would playfully chase after pigeons but when the pigeons turned sharply, the fledglings would disinterestedly break off the game. The fledglings also liked to sit on the Cryder House roof surveying their territory, the only one they had ever known. In a short few weeks, they would have to leave and every day and night would be filled with unknown perils. They would encounter unfamiliar circumstances and their first mistake could be their last one. It was an unpleasant thought and I rapidly returned to the joyful sights of the day.

The adults favored the Throgs to the exclusion of all other structures. Whenever a youngster alighted on Cryder House, it was usually summoned by the Queen, who tried to lure it back to the Throgs. In one instance, a Queenie alighted on the terrace railing of apartment 15A. She was so close to us we were able to read her band number (K29K). We loved seeing the rich brown colors of her juvenile plumage and the beautiful blue hue of her cere. Early that evening, a Queenie was perched on a handcable alongside the Queen. Dolores and I watched like proud parents as she repeatedly took off and landed, apparently practicing her landing technique—and doing very well.

A day's activities would not be quite complete without some territorial defense action. The white pelican is a very large bird rarely seen in the New York City area. When one made its appearance at the Throgs, the adult peregrines paid their respects by diving at it as aggressively as they would have if it were a raptorial peregrine eater rather than a fish consumer. Even one of the Queenies displayed a territorial defense attitude. Leaping from her perch on the first pier, the fledgling executed two adultlike precision dives at a great egret that was fishing from the barge. Her second dive caused the egret to move when it realized the potential danger in such superb flying technique. It was a feast for my eyes and for the eyes of other watchers.

July Fourth was celebrated as Independence Day for America and for the fledgling peregrines but for many of the avian creatures that ventured into the peregrines' territory there was no picnic. By 8:00 A.M., a pigeon had been pursued to the point where its life depended on its clinging to some barnacles exposed at low tide on the anchorage. The Queen peered down at what she hoped would be her next meal, and the Queenies were nearby demanding to be fed. She flew at the desperate quarry and tried vainly to flush the pigeon from its precarious hold. Each time, the pigeon released its hold, but it wisely did not fly and regained its hold. Eventually, the Queen lost interest and left; but the pigeon did not leave its haven for over an hour.

The Queen and Rio hunted avidly, trying to quiet the insistent hunger calls of their young. The fledglings followed their parents on some hunting expeditions and, while their unvarnished flying ability began to rival that of their parents, their lack of experience was still very evident. They still relied on their parents for food and were several weeks away from true independence. The Queenies still enjoyed crabbing with each other and seemed to revel in diving on any and all flying objects. One stooped at a double-crested cormorant with such great accuracy that the quarry was forced to go into a crash dive that resulted in an uncharacteristic splash. Cormorants normally dive for their below-water fishing with a smooth entry that barely leaves a ripple on the water's surface. This cormorant surfaced, half a minute later, and immediately looked upward as if to say, "What was that?" And then there were the times when a potential meal was ignored. A Queenie was perched on a handcable one time when three pigeons flew by and apparently recognized her predatory form. They flew around her as if they were perplexed as to which direction to fly. Oddly, one pigeon alighted on the cable only several yards from the fledgling. There was no reaction from Queenie and peace reigned.

Early the next morning, the Queenies were on the main pier face to face, touching beaks. A moving sight indeed. Then the Queen executed a seemingly easy capture of a pigeon and took the prize to the anchorage, where the youngsters joined her and took possession of the meal. Later, the Queen dove at a great black-backed gull and a Queenie half-heartedly chased a pigeon while her sister pursued pigeons at the fender, though, occasionally, it seemed that the fledgling was seriously trying to catch the pigeon.

An hour later, the Queen, carrying prey remains, and her fledglings flew to the Cryder House roof. Dolores and I heard much alarm calling coming from the roof. We investigated and found both youngsters on the north parapet. One wisely took off as soon as she spotted us but the other let us approach to within twenty-five yards. Suddenly the Queen came diving down at us, all the while calling loudly. Queenie flew off and joined her sister in circling about 500 yards to the west. The Queen continued to voice her unhappiness with our presence on the roof, even though the youngsters had departed. She kept circling and vocalizing above us but did not dive at us. At the north end of the roof there was a half-eaten pigeon on the terrace overhang of the penthouse apartment. As we retreated from the roof, the Queen was still circling overhead and admonishing us.

An hour later, a neighbor excitedly informed me that he had seen the Queen capture a pigeon close to his west-facing nineteenth-floor window. The amazement and joy that he had experienced was unquestionably very moving at the moment the event had taken place and he still savored the dramatic scene as he vividly recounted it to me. He was not motivated enough, however, to try to seek that experience again. I find it perplexing that many people who are granted a glimpse of the extraordinary, whether it be beauty or skill or a combination of these qualities, do not seek out the experience after they have appreciated the special essence of the incident they had chanced upon. Peregrine watchers are a select group and it is impossible to foretell who will become a devotee and who will feel, "Is that all there is?"

The ensuing days were filled with the wonderful flying antics of the Queenies. On one occasion, we heard the air rushing past their feathers as they zoomed close by our terrace. The chase became an integral part of their daily activity pattern and was very important in the development of their hunting prowess. One morning the youngsters collaborated in chasing a double-crested cormorant. The bird quickly realized that it could not evade the pursuing youngsters in the air and plunged into the water. In another instance, a Queenie dove at a black-crowned night heron with great precision. It hit the hapless heron and forced it to take refuge in the water.

When there was nothing in the area to attract the fledglings' attention, they would frequently fly about aimlessly. I once clocked them flying very strongly for five minutes without any evidence of a slowing in their wingbeats. One Queenie dove down from the Cryder House roof directly at a pigeon that was feeding along the water's edge. The pigeon flushed into flight at this attack but his number wasn't up this time as Queenie changed targets and chased several great black-backed gulls. In another instance, a Queenie unexpectedly passed by a pigeon that was flying in the opposite direction. She did a complete 360-degree roll without slackening her speed, seemingly to have another look at the bird without changing course. Many gulls rest and preen on Little Bay. The Queenies enjoyed diving at the gulls sitting in the water, as well as those aloft, practicing flying skills. They never hit the gulls but they seemed to become even more energized when a harassed bird took evasive action.

The fledglings often chose perches that their parents did not use, or approve of. The parallels with some human families were evident. The Queenies alighted on the LeHavre Buildings' roof parapet railings, especially the building located between Cryder House and the

Hammerstein Estate. The Cryder House roof remained a frequently used area for the young but became less disreputable to the adults. Either they had tired of the constant battle with the young or they were allowing them more independence, or both. One Queenie alighted on the terrace railing of apartment 9K, adjacent to mine, just twenty-five feet away.

The adults were almost always monitoring the activities of their young and were always on their territory. For example, a Queenie "attacked" a great black-backed gull which quickly counterattacked and pursued the youngster. Rio zoomed onto the battlefield and defended his progeny. His insistent diving strategy soon drove the gull from the area. Later, the Queen snatched a pigeon from an enormous flock that had been exercising near the Bronx tower. As she flew toward the Queens tower with her prey, the fledglings intercepted her. They tail-chased her to the Queens anchorage, where they undoubtedly received their meal. On July 9, the Queen captured a pigeon and was returning to the Queens end of the bridge when a Queenie approached her and took possession of the prey directly from her talons. We had witnessed our first in-flight prey transfer for the 1989 season. The interaction was accompanied by vocalizations from both birds. The youngsters were developing their skills, on a timetable, that augured well for their timely and successful dispersal. Dolores and I observed the fledglings through August 14.

The sights and sounds of four peregrines at the beautiful Throgs setting amid the surrounding water was a joyous scene. Where else could one watch an adult female peregrine nimbly jump off her perch on top of the Queens tower and fly on a straight line, as if she were attached to a taut string, over Little Bay toward the wilds of Fort Totten and Little Neck Bay? As we watched the Queen do this, she spiraled upward for several minutes, describing rather circumscribed counter-clockwise circles. After rising to an altitude of about 500 feet, she reversed her direction to clockwise circles. Suddenly Rio entered into her orbits and as the mates circled in unison, they were joined by one of their youngsters. Three peregrines soaring together was spiritually uplifting not only for the peregrines but also for the observer.

Belted kingfishers are handsome birds sporting a white band around their necks and white underparts. Their white flash pattern, as they fly, is attractive to peregrines. One kingfisher that happened by the Throgs was avidly pursued by the Queen. The bird literally flew for its life and escaped to fish another day. On another occasion, the Queen stooped at a flock of fifteen pigeons, from her perch on the tower, and seized one. She flew into the Throgs structure with the very-much-alive bird, having failed to administer the usual killing neck bite. When she reappeared with the now inert prey, she was immediately pursued by a hungry Queenie. Later, a Queenie flew out over Little Bay and stooped at a great egret. Emboldened by the lack of response from its much larger "adversary," it went on a binge of playful diving at pigeons and gulls. It was joined by its sister and together they pestered many birds until the feeling passed or they tired. One sultry afternoon brought heavy rain, lightning, and peals of thunder, accompanied by gusty winds. The fledglings flew about in this cauldron of forces with the knowledge passed down through the eons of peregrine history. And we humans watched in appreciation, undoubtedly as our ancestors had always done when observing other animals performing their special feats.

As July marched on, we could see the Queenies developing the skills that they would need to survive when they left the protection of their parents. Their bouts of pigeon chasing around the main pier began to closely resemble serious hunting attempts. We looked forward to witnessing the young capture prey on their own as a vital prelude to their successful dispersal. One morning, a Queenie alighted on the roof of the LeHavre building directly across from our terrace where, for a full ten minutes, we enjoyed ogling her at sixty power. The changes that marked her metamorphosis into the avian predator that she had to become to survive were evident. Her youthful demeanor was now overshadowed by the enormous, dark eyes that transmitted the falcon fierceness that is characteristic of her breed. She sat bolt upright, like adults are wont to do. The hunter's mien was the foremost visage that emanated from this beautiful youngster.

Fledglings learn to hunt whether or not they have the benefit of adult role models. Released youngsters learn to hunt for themselves although there are no adults to emulate at the site. At the Throgs, the fledglings had had the experience of having observed many hunts and of being included in some of them. I would like to characterize some hunts and prey-related interactions as training exercises but the weight of scientific opinion considers them inborn reactions to the developmental stages through which the young progress. An example of "training" behavior was typified by the following sequence of events. The Queen sped toward a large flock of pigeons and when she stooped at them, the Queenies joined her in her pursuit. Snaring a pigeon, the Queen flew a short distance and then released the bird. I had witnessed more than a hundred captures by my seventh season of peregrine watching and I had never observed a firmly held pigeon escape the peregrines' taloned grip. She must have tried to incite the youngsters to pursue the pigeon. Rio was within sight of this exercise but did not join in.

The next day, the Queen again snared a pigeon, held it for a few wingbeats, and released it. The young were in the area and I surmised that it was an attempt to goad them into the hunting mode and eventually into making a kill. Fledglings love to chase birds, almost as soon as they leave the nest, but they do not identify the birds flying about them as food until they make their first kill. Once a fledgling makes its first kill, it seems to learn the lesson for all time.

Increasingly, whenever the Queen initiated a hunt, one or both of the fledglings would try to "help." Usually, when one Queenie started to chase a bird, the other one joined her. A particularly sophisticated attack involved a pigeon that was winging its way over Little Bay. Queenie flew swiftly, inches above the water, until she overtook the bird; then she abruptly rose twenty feet to attain its flight level and have a go at it. The pigeon never saw its pursuer. Queenie's sister joined in the foray but the quarry escaped, despite receiving a slight hit. They were close to making a kill and it was merely a matter of time until they succeeded in capturing prey for themselves.

The Queenies continued to "hawk" insects, although they had progressed to more advanced levels of hunting. Once when the Queen dove down at a pigeon and hit it lightly, one Queenie was encouraged to join in the attack, but this was a failed effort. The next hunting session was far more productive. Queen snared a pigeon and was immediately beset by both young. She dropped her catch into the water and they all took turns trying to retrieve it. Queen gave up the project first and one Queenie soon followed suit. However, the other Queenie persisted much longer before she, too, finally lost interest, after almost ten minutes of nonstop flying. One hour later, the Queen and her young were together as the Queen caught a pigeon. She dropped it into the water. After a few minutes, the victim regained its composure and was able to lift itself out of the water—only to be hit by the Queen again. This was followed by an even stronger strike, delivered by Queenie.

Fifteen minutes later, the Queen and a fledgling were pursuing a passerine. The Queen hit it slightly and Queenie grabbed it. This was the first observed capture by a fledgling for the season. It was very satisfying to see the youngster take that most important step on the road to independence.

I was on the Fort Totten side of Little Bay one afternoon when I saw a raptor flying low over Little Bay Park. It alternately flapped and glided over the field in a manner similar to a northern harrier. As it flew toward me, I observed that it was one of the Queenies. She flew above me and then by a mixed stand of trees in which there were a score of crows. They did not react but a screaming passerine flew upward to challenge Queenie, who was obviously upset sufficiently by this little daredevil to change her course. She flew over Fort Totten and I laughed at the thought that she might be seeking the army's protection.

During the last half of July, the peregrines hunted and dispelled unwanted intruders. The youngsters were much more inclined to attack large birds than were their parents, as if it were more of a game for them than anything else. The adults could be expected to slacken their defensive efforts in view of the superb flying skills that the young had attained. The fledglings continued to harass black-crowned night herons and once brazenly molested a great blue heron that stood more than four feet high. The Cryder House pier railing was occasionally used by the young as a convenient perch from which to conduct their boisterous forays against herring and great black-backed gulls sitting in the water.

It was interesting to see how the fledglings seemed to share everything with a minimum of squabbling while they thought nothing of cold-shouldering their mother whenever food was involved. They pursued Rio almost as though he were prey, whether he was carrying prey that they wanted or whether they were trying to induce him to provide a meal for them. The parents almost became just another flying creature that they could harass; and these particular creatures could even outfly them which, I am sure, added to the allure of chasing them. In one instance, I saw Queenie fly at Rio, which caused him to speed away to the Bronx tower. She instantly turned her attention to the Queen, who also quickly flew to the Bronx tower, where she perched next to her mate. As much as the adults were driven to indulge their young, it was time for the fledglings to be weaned from parental dependence.

One evening an immature duck was paddling on the water fifty yards offshore. The Queenies could not resist the temptation to stoop at it, although there was no capture opportunity involved. They repeatedly harassed the young duck until it utilized its normal foraging technique and dove. However, each time the duck surfaced, the Queenies renewed their attack. Finally, the duck paddled to the beach, waddled up the sand, and hid behind a washed-up piece of lumber. This ploy worked perfectly as the young peregrines instantly lost interest in their now landbased game. Two minutes later, Queenie carried a very small prey item. Her sister gave chase and they both alighted. The prey was still alive in Queenie's talons and it was almost certain that she had caught the bird herself. She fed on the bird with her sister looking on. The fledglings had come a long way; but still had a longer way to go.

Even carcasses sometimes seemed to have a life of their own. Queenie fed on one for fifty-six minutes and then the Queen arrived and stepped onto the remains. Before she could begin feeding on it, the second Queenie zoomed in and took possession of it. She had picked at the dregs for only several minutes when Rio flew in, sidled up to her, cautiously tore a leg off the now ridiculously small carcass, and flew off with his "prize." Queenie continued to pick at the remaining piece until I could no longer see it. That one prey item had been a family possession for at least one and a half hours. I think that the sharing of the prey item was the controlling factor in this playlet. All the players were extremely well fed and there was no need to husband food in the manner they had acted out. I also had the suspicion that the adults somehow realized that their family was very close to the time when the young would strike out on their own and this food sharing activity would no longer be possible. At any rate, it provided fantastic behavioral watching opportunities for me and I never took these for granted. The peregrines might abandon the Throgs site for any one of many reasons.

July ended with several interesting observations. The Queen and her young were chasing a pigeon and just when it appeared that they were about to seize it, the pigeon dove through bushes and alighted on the Cryder House lawn. It wisely took cover in the thickest area of the plantings. Two members of the attack force flew away but one Queenie circled low over the lawn. She searched for the bird very seriously for a few minutes before giving up. This protracted search and show of obstinacy indicated that the youngster had acquired some additional hunting tactics that were important to its survival. Another hunt waged jointly by the adults ended very oddly. The fledglings were trailing behind their parents as they pursued a dove. The Queen delivered a disabling strike to the quarry, which plummeted into the water. As the adults circled their victim preparatory to extricating it from the water, a small boat arrived at the scene. When the boat stopped alongside the dove, the adults left. However, the youngsters kept circling the area. The boatman took the dove from the water with a fish net and steamed away. One fledgling also departed but the other one continued searching for the dove for several more minutes, showing admirable tenacity if not perspicacity.

In an unrelated incident, Rio was lazily gliding past the anchorage when the Queenies vocalized and took to the air, prompting Rio to start working his wings and fly toward the Bronx. The Queenies always relished a chase and cranked up to maximum power. Rio became a gray streak as he zoomed toward the Bronx with the Queenies in hot pursuit. Only the peregrines themselves might know if the younger but larger daughters could have matched their father's speed. I don't think any youngster could rival Rio's flying ability, whether it relates to flapping flight speed or aerial technique.

August 5 was the last day that Dolores and I observed both Queenies at the Throgs. One dispersed but the other stayed on through August 20. We missed the youngsters when they left the area but we were elated that they had amply demonstrated that their development was complete. They had a reasonable chance to survive on their own and that was all that we could hope for. We remembered the last observations of the young with fond reverie. The Queen, Rio, and both Queenies were airborne at the same time, a sight to gladden any heart. The Queenies would break off from a session of crabbing to make a short dive at Rio. I sensed that they still went at him from habit more than need. As the season drew to a close, the Queenies would sit together, sometimes for a minute, sometimes for an hour. It did not seem to matter as long as they could share something, time, a kill, a perch, a hunt, or whatever peregrines can divine. Seeing the fledglings together on top of the Queens tower was always good for a spiritual lift.

On the last day the Queenies were together, they seemed more than ever in tune with one another. They collaborated on hunts with their mother as well as with each other. One attack put a pigeon in the water. While one fledgling circled over the distressed quarry, the other perched nearby, watching the victor and the victim. The pigeon took too long to expire and the youngsters lost interest; the sisters flew away together.

After the first Queenie left the Throgs area, the quantity and quality of our observations decreased markedly. The Queenie that lingered had no playmate and did not engage in the antics that had characterized their relationship. We observed her occasionally but the precipitous decline in her activity pattern was, obviously, directly related to her sister's disappearance.

We continued to observe both the Queen and Rio at the Throgs through the entire winter. This overwintering of the adults was a continuation of the trend that had been established during the six previous seasons at the Throgs. In fact, I had no doubt that the Queen had not spent a night away from the Throgs since she had taken up residence there in 1983. Observations at the other peregrine nesting sites in the New York City metropolitan region indicated that the adults there also remained on their territory during the period between the conclusion of one breeding season and the start of the next.

157

10

Migrations and Movements

(1989 - 1990)

Migration 1989

Having noted that New York City peregrines had shown a distinct predilection for remaining on their territorial nesting grounds all year round, it must be noted, however, that most peregrines do migrate southward from their breeding territories. Raptor enumerators at hundreds of hawk watches in the United States were reporting increased numbers of peregrines as well as ospreys and bald eagles in recent years, due to the beneficial effects of the enactment of pesticide controls and the establishment of reintroduction programs.

Dave Gardner, my hawk-watching friend Bill Van Meter, and I traveled to the Cape May, New Jersey, hawk watch on October 3, 1989, hoping to witness an outstanding migration flight. The weather was perfect; a cold front had just moved through the area and the wind was shifting to the northwest. We had stopped at the Brigantine Wildlife Refuge and arrived at the hawk watch in the late morning. As we stepped out of our car, a friend called out, "You've missed over sixty peregrines this morning." Looking up, we were pleasantly amazed to see raptors everywhere. There were three peregrines within sight over the parking lot. Not concerned with what we may have missed but happy with the prospect of seeing vast multitudes of falcons and hawks, we rushed to the viewing platform. By the close of the day, a

158

daily record of 157 peregrines had been tallied. A record 1,023 ospreys went through in the day's total raptor count of 3,111.

Returning to the concrete wilds of New York City, we learned that a pair of peregrines had been reported frequenting the 42nd Street vicinity in midtown Manhattan, near Grand Central Station. Their favorite perching spots were on the Lincoln Building at 60 East 42nd Street. Several knowledgeable observers had reported seeing peregrines in the area going back to 1987 and 1988. On July 21, Kathy O'Brien observed a peregrine carrying a pigeon as it flew over 42nd Street near the Lincoln Building. Kathy also observed a second adult peregrine perched near the first one. It was eating a pigeon, apparently the one that had just been taken in.

Kathy determined that the peregrines did not have young. The female wore two dark leg bands but the male's legs were not observed. It was too late in the nesting season to assist the peregrines with a nest box. It seemed likely, however, that they had established their territory and would attempt to nest the next season. It was even possible that they had tried to nest this year but had failed. A midtown peregrine nesting site would add a special flavor to the Grand Central Station area.

The Outerbridge Crossing, a bridge connecting Staten Island and New Jersey, was another site that hosted a pair of adult peregrines that was not known to have produced young. Reports of peregrines at the bridge dated back to 1985 when a pair was observed for a period. In subsequent years, there were unconfirmed reports of single birds. In 1989, an adult pair was on its bridge territory throughout the entire breeding season and into the fall. Despite frequent observations by Chris Nadareski and others, no breeding behavior was noted. It was not established, then, that migrating birds were finding homes in the area.

In the early fall, Dolores and I met Heinz Meng at a renaissance festival in which he had demonstrated falconry techniques. He asked me to provide him with a recapitulation of the 1989 peregrine nesting activities in the New York City region for use in the many presentations he makes for the general public. After I had prepared the nesting summary and mailed it to him, it occurred to me that other raptor enthusiasts might enjoy receiving such information. I established *NYCAERIES* (New York City and Environs Raptor Involved and

Enthusiasts Society), a raptor newsletter. The first one-page issue was mailed to thirty persons. Within two years, the newsletter had attracted over ninety paid subscribers ($10 per year) and blossomed to a ten-page document detailing migration hawk counting and many other raptor topics in addition to peregrine coverage. Unfortunately, the workload required to produce a high quality newsletter became too burdensome and *NYCAERIES* was regretfully discontinued after three years in print. (This was migration of a different kind.)

Migration 1990

Peregrine watchers in the New York City area, then, are clearly not relegated for the six months or so from the dispersal of the fledglings until the next breeding season to watching resident peregrines sitting quietly on their territory with an occasional hunting episode or aggressive expulsion of an interloper. There is that wonderful phenomenon called migration. From early September through early December, hundreds of thousands of raptors work their way south along various well-known flyways on the North American continent. Fortunately, New York City is situated on and close to several of these consistently used migratory routes. Stationed along these routes are hawk watchers who identify and enumerate the numbers of each species passing through.

There are seven established hawk watches within an hours' drive of New York City and two of them are conducted from locations within the city itself. Each season, more and more people are engaged in helping count the migrating raptors; many others just enjoy the sight of them.

Migration movements are greatly influenced by the weather. The most favorable conditions are produced when a cold weather front moves through and the winds change to a prevailing northwest, a phenomenon noted at both coastal and inland hawk watches. The concentration of birds is even more pronounced when poor flying conditions, such as rain or adverse winds, precede the front. The raptors have long distances to travel and energy conservation is crucial. Some birds migrate thousands of miles from the upper North

American continent to South America. Favorable winds and thermal air currents enable them to traverse long distances with the least energy expenditure. Peregrines are unique even when on their migratory journey. While the highest peregrine counts are garnered in conjunction with favorable weather, these magnificent birds also travel on adverse wind days and during rainy periods when almost no other bird will venture forth. It is a stirring event to see a peregrine on migration. Picture the traveler approaching the hawk watch location on the usual flight path. The first feature that differentiates peregrines from the other birds is their tendency to flap their wings with a measured, consistent cadence. One gets the feeling that peregrines do not care very much about the prevailing wind. They seem to just want to keep moving. Peregrines are observed not to miss a single wingbeat while flying a straight line past a hawk watch.

The majority of peregrines migrating through the New York metropolitan region, by the way, are members of the *tundrius* race and are lighter complexioned than the local resident peregrines.

An observer that discovers a raptor flying directly out over a large body of water or coming in to land from water would do well to look for the identifying factors of a peregrine. Almost all migrating raptors will avoid flying over large bodies of water, even if it requires them to fight the prevailing wind or backtrack and give up some of their hard-won progress. Peregrines, on the other hand, fly over water regularly and have been known to cross the ocean. They exhibit an unmistakable confidence in their ability to fly over any obstacle.

This almost universal raptorial aversion to flying over water contributes to a funneling effect which is a boon to hawk watchers because it concentrates raptors on flyways. For example, when the hawks traveling along the east coast arrive at the Cape May, New Jersey, peninsula, they are confronted with water on all sides. Many hesitate when they see the water ahead and either turn to the inland side or work their way back to the first contiguous land area that will allow them to continue on their southerly course.

Other birds are also migrating at the same time, of course, and some raptors avail themselves of this cornucopia of prey. In most years, the highest single-day count of migrating peregrines occurs during the first week of October at most hawk watch locations; 1990 was no exception. At the Fire Island Hawk Watch, forty-nine pere-grines were observed on October 2 of the 243 season's total. This was their record daily high peregrine count since the official hawk watch was started in 1983.

The new daily and seasonal records for peregrines, experienced at many hawk watches in 1989 and 1990, was a clear signal that the peregrine population was expanding as a result of the reduction of the use of injurious pesticides and the reintroduction programs being carried out in the United States, Canada, and other countries. For example, Tony Tierno, a long-time peregrine-watcher on Long Island, observed an immature female peregrine at that island's Cedar Beach on September 15. This southward migrating bird had a silver-colored band on one leg and a red band on its other leg. The red band identified it as bird that had been hacked from a site in Canada.

September 17, 1990, was one of those special days in the annals of hawk watching. The wind was blowing briskly from the northwest after a cold front had moved through the New York City metropolitan region and lower New England the previous day. Conditions seemed perfect for a heavy flight; historically, September 17 was a big flight day and the weather scenario was the kind that usually produced the best flights. Also, I received word that over 10,000 raptors, most of which were broadwinged hawks, had moved through the Boston area. It seemed likely we could not miss seeing thousands of raptors if we went to the proper location. Consequently, Dave Gardner, hawk-watching friends Bob Kurtz and Frank LaVia, and I went to the Quaker Ridge Hawk Watch in Greenwich, Connecticut, because it seemed to be the most promising location. More than 30,000 raptors, predominantly broadwings, were counted there on September 14, 1986.

By 1:00 P.M., approximately 1,300 hawks had been tallied, but we felt sure that the count should have been ten times greater. A knowl-edgeable hawk watcher arrived and told us that he had seen hawks in vast numbers over Route 1. That explained the low numbers we were seeing at our inland location. The birds were traveling on a more easterly route because the strong winds were pushing them toward the water barrier of Long Island Sound.

We drove to the Read Sanctuary in Rye, New York, and parked in a large, open field about seventy-five yards from the water. When we gazed skyward, we were astonished to discover that there were hundreds of raptors overhead, mostly broadwinged hawks, streaming past our observation site. We scanned this skein of raptors and found that there was an unbroken line of them extending as far as we could see. There were thousands of birds. We started counting the migrators, although this was not an established hawk watch because there was no one else there who had been appointed to do the counting.

We had an unhindered vista and, as we looked upward in any direction other than above the water, we saw groups of raptors ranging in numbers from several up to 700. This was the classic broadwinged hawk method of moving south; soar upward on thermal updrafts until the lift ebbs and then glide as far as possible in the travel direction. Because the rising air currents are frequently well circumscribed, the hawks tend to gather together in ever-increasing numbers where the lift is most pronounced. We tallied 9,500 hawks between 1:20 P.M. and 5:00 P.M. when the movement slowed to a trickle. An average of 3,000 hawks per hour passed our observation point and that was exclusive of the many we had missed because they were out of sight due their altitude, or were above the clouds. On that same day, Bob DeCandido, of the Pelham Bay Park Hawk Watch, enumerated 15,459 broadwings passing there of the total of 15,625 raptors that he observed. It was wonderful to be able to see so many free-wheeling hawks in the sky at the same time. It gave one the feeling that the world was still healthy if it could support so many truly wild creatures.

The 1990 Raptor Research Foundation's annual conference was held in late October in Allentown, Pennsylvania. Ted, Dave, Tony, and I attended the conference, the theme of which was "The Missing Solution: Cultivating the Masses." Several papers focused on methods for educating the public in addition to the usual wide array of more scientific topics covered. No sessions were scheduled one day to allow for an all-day excursion to observe the raptor migration at the nearby Hawk Mountain Sanctuary. Now, that's education.

11

Trouble

(1990 at the Throgs Neck Bridge)

Dolores and I returned to New York on January 28 after vacationing in Florida. Immediately on entering our apartment, I went to the terrace and was greeted by the sight of one of our peregrines perched on a handcable. "There's no place like home," I sighed; home is where the peregrines are. Our friend and fellow falcon watcher Dave Gardner updated us on the status of the birds at the Throgs. The news couldn't have been better; that very morning, he had observed the adults hunting. During the following weeks, I saw the Queen and Rio almost daily and, usually, together.

By the second week in March, the Queen and Rio began to frequent the nest box area. We hoped that they might lay their eggs in the box because it would be safe for their eggs and chicks and there would be no need for our intervention.

On March 18, I rolled out my bicycle to make observation visits at four potential peregrine nesting sites, the Hell Gate/Triborough bridges, Riverside Church, 42nd Street, and New York Hospital. I found no peregrines at the first site and proceeded to my second destination, using the Queensboro Bridge to cross the East River into Manhattan. I scanned the Queensboro's ornate towers and superstructure on the off chance that a peregrine might be perched there. Although the Queensboro had not been a nesting site, the peregrines from the nearby New York Hospital had occasionally been observed on it. I then pedaled through Central Park to the beautiful Riverside Church, where I also failed to see any peregrines. Undaunted, I sped downtown to 42nd Street to search for the peregrines that frequently perched on the Lincoln and other buildings in the area. Peering upward from street level to likely perching spots thirty to sixty stories above was very difficult; and again I found no peregrines. I headed to my fourth destination, the New York Hospital. This site had produced young for two consecutive years. I was familiar with the peregrines' favorite perches and it was relatively easy to scan the nest building and adjacent structures. I found one adult but that was all. When I returned home, a peregrine was perched on the Throgs. Where else but in New York City could one check five peregrine sites in three and a half hours by bicycle?

Toward the end of March, the Queen was conspicuously absent and Rio was observed regularly. We were sure that she had laid her eggs and that there was a strong possibility she had used the nest box.

Each April, the New England Chapter of the Hawk Migration Association of North America (HMANA) convenes in a city located in the northeast. Dave, Ted LeViness, Tony Tierno, Dolores, and I attended the meeting, held in Holyoke, Massachusetts. We learned that a pair of peregrines had nested on a building in nearby Springfield the previous season. A video camera had been installed at the eyrie and the activity at the nest was broadcast live over a local cable station. The live broadcasts developed a devoted cadre of viewers, one of whom noticed that a chick was not eating and called the station. They examined the nestling and found a bone lodged in its throat, preventing it from ingesting food. The problem was remedied and the chick developed satisfactorily. A video monitor at the HMANA conference played the last season's tapes.

I always look forward to raptor conferences with great anticipation because, in addition to the information disseminated and the intellectual stimulation, there are people to meet and acquaintanceships to renew. For me, the high point at this conference was meeting the two individuals who had known the Queen and Rio before I had first seen them. Imagine! A young peregrine banded by a woman in a nest in the wilds of Franconia Notch, New Hampshire, in 1981 (Queen), and a male nestling (Rio), hacked by a man in Boston, Massachusetts, in 1984, had found each other in New York City and were now producing young. Not only was I able to relate the details of their exploits at the Throgs to that woman and to that man, the banders, but also we had Dave's wonderful photos to show them.

Their expressions of satisfaction were a delight to share. I hoped that someday I would have the thrill of learning of a fledgling from the Throgs having established itself as a breeding adult.

We drove to Springfield to observe the peregrines on the Bank of New England building. From the highway, the BNE building loomed ahead of us and even before we exited, we observed a peregrine soaring toward us. How fortunate it was to have the bird present itself when we were prepared for a long vigil at the site and possibly even failure in our quest. Many were the times when we had spent hours at a site and observed nothing or had had merely a glimpse of a bird. It was a treat to enter into a new city and be greeted so elegantly. We took up a viewing position on the street across from the BNE building and viewed the nest box on the twentieth floor ledge just below the top of the building. We observed a peregrine on the nest ledge and watched it conduct several unsuccessful sorties.

Inspections. On April 14, Dave, Ted, and I inspected the Throgs eyrie to try to determine the current nesting status. At first, we could neither hear nor see a peregrine. However, we were able to view the nest box into which the four female chicks had been transplanted in 1989 and another nest cavity from a prior season. I was closest to the boxes and observed a peregrine in the large 1989 box. How gratifying it was that our peregrines had egged in the safest spot possible. The peregrine did not see me at first because its view was severely hindered. I occupied just one sliver of space in a wide expanse and there were many intervening beams blocking its view. I could not determine whether it was the Queen or Rio who was in the box because I saw only a fragment of the bird. The peregrine then spotted us and immediately gave the alarm call. It was Rio. In less than a minute, the Queen arrived, vocalizing loudly. We knew it was the Queen because of her size and two prominent brood patches.

They screamed at us in unison, with a shrill that was music to our ears. The Queen's call was a little louder and deeper. We would have liked to have stayed longer to determine how many eggs were being incubated but we did not want to stress them unduly or allow our presence to cause them to move off the eggs. When we returned to the roadway, Queen circled overhead and continued to voice her displeasure at our trespass. Shortly, Rio appeared aloft and Ted quickly pointed out that the eggs had to be uncovered because both adults were away from the nest. He rushed back to the nest and returned with the news that there were four eggs. Our mission was accomplished. Some days are created especially for those that can savor the flavor. The Throgs peregrines were off to a great start for the 1990 season. The Queen was in her eighth season and her eggs were in a safe nest, which she had selected. The fact that I had been involved in providing the nest box made the unfolding drama even more special.

Then only Rio appeared out and about, until April 23 when the Queen started to increasingly absent herself from the nest. We hoped that the reason she was out and about was that she had growing chicks that did not need her constant attention. On May 7, the Queen and Rio were away from the box for a full twenty minutes, another signal that they had chicks. I conferred with Barbara Loucks and we agreed that an inspection of the eyrie was needed. This was to be a carefully conducted visual inspection only. It was crucial that the nestlings not be disturbed lest they be panicked into leaving their nest box.

On May 12, Dave Gardner and I went to the Throgs and took up a position where we were able to view the chicks without being seen. At first glance, it looked like there was one large, strange creature in the box but, with further scrutiny, we could see that the chicks were huddled together. Since they did not cry out, or move, Dave and I slowly crept to a better vantage point, where we could see that there were four chicks. Three were sitting upright and one was lying down. Each one was in contact with at least one of its nestmates. Dave voiced concern about the prone chick but I assured him that nestlings often lay in that position. All their eyes were open and bright but they held absolutely still. We departed with great anticipation for the upcoming weeks and months that hopefully would be filled with numerous hunts and the successful fledging of the young.

On May 20, Chris Nadareski and Marty Gilroy went to the Throgs Neck and Verrazano-Narrows bridges and found two male and two female nestlings at each site. After banding the nestlings, they removed one female from each clutch and shipped them off to The Peregrine Fund facility in Boise. The reason was the continued poor success rate at bridges compared with the rates experienced at building and hack sites. The 1989 breeding season results had again corroborated this trend; only one chick survived at the Verrazano and even it was not in satisfactory condition when it was removed. The Throgs peregrines managed to see two of their four young through to dispersal. Hack sites usually attain a successful overall dispersal rate of at least 70 percent. Locally, the New York Hospital building site was able to have all three of its young develop to independence. Only time will tell if those trends will continue and the interventions at the bridges are accomplishing their goals.

Attack Birds. During the last weekend of May, Dolores and I watched Rio attacking pigeons at their roosting area on the anchorage, where they rest, preen, and court. Rio's arrival would fluster some of them into flight. He would try to grab one and, if his attempt was unsuccessful, which was the case more times than not, he would patiently wait for another opportunity. In one instance, Rio alighted on a ledge and when a pigeon flew, he made a half-hearted approach toward it, changed his mind, and returned to the ledge. He then hopped toward another pigeon, footed it, and held tight to his victim as he rode his victim rodeo style for a few minutes. There was no urgency to kill his prey as is the case when flying with a flailing victim's added weight and drag. Finally, he administered the fatal neck bite and settled down to some serious feeding.

The blue jay, you might recall, is one of the peregrines' favorite prey, as it is a poor flyer and displays a distinctive white flash pattern on its wings, irresistible to peregrines. Jays also have a unfortunate habit of flying over water where the lack of cover gives a peregrine an excellent advantage. One morning at the Throgs, we observed a blue jay kill being taken to the eyrie. The peregrines were in a hunting mood and shortly conducted another successful foray, again claiming a blue jay. The next capture was exciting because we were able to observe the preliminaries. "Eagle-eyed" Tony Tierno spied a blue jay while it was still flying over the Bronx. It was headed toward the water and Tony ventured that if it were to continue on its course, the peregrines would surely intercept it. His prediction proved to be exactly right. As the jay approached the Queens tower, Rio dove at it; he was joined by the Queen. They stooped at it alternately but Rio was the prime attacker. The quarry was driven downward and Rio finally hit it into the water. The jay, though injured, was still very much alive and as feisty as the breed is noted to be. When Rio flew by slowly to try to pluck the jay from the water, it valiantly reached up to defend itself.

After several circling passes, Rio easily took the ill-fated jay from the water and delivered it to the nest.

The following morning, we saw the peregrines attack a flock of pigeons. The female appeared to merely pluck one of them out of the group before they had time to react. Usually pigeons see the peregrines early enough and take evasive action. Despite continuous observing, we saw no other prey item taken until four hours later, when Rio returned with a small, dark carcass, probably a starling.

The first day of June produced the first observation of a chick on the Throgs for the 1990 season. From our apartment terrace, we could see the chick very clearly on the westerly catwalk. It was an important sighting because it meant that the chick had made its way along several intersecting catwalks.

Six hours of observations on Saturday produced only one notable sighting: a collaborative capture of a robin. Sunday was filled with almost continuous hunting forays. The first kill was somewhat unusual. The many pigeons which roost on the Queens pier usually flutter down to it along the tower legs. The peregrines rarely pursue these rapidly falling birds. In this instance, though, the peregrine descended with the pigeons and captured one.

The next kill was an entirely different matter. A sparrow was pursued by both adults. Fabulous diving tactics were lavished on this quarry before Rio bound into his little victim. Watching these two dramatic hunters use their prodigious skills to capture one small bird caused me to feel that their efforts seemed too grandiose in relation to the size of the prize. But a small meal is better than none. Animals are programed to take prey as it becomes available because the next opportunity could be uncomfortably delayed. Also, though the bird or animal doesn't know it, varying the prey intake reduces the chances of the predator ingesting a substantial amount of poison from one prey species.

The next hunting foray involved both adults and their most favored prey, a pigeon. They took turns diving at it and drove it lower and lower toward the water. When all three birds flew behind the anchorage and no bird returned, we surmised that the pigeon had been caught. Twenty minutes later, the peregrines flew into view and one carried a small carcass up to the nest. Evidently they had shared a meal before taking the leftovers to their young.

169

We had been observing peregrines for eight years now, and one thing had became clear: no two sightings would ever be exactly alike. To us, the variety of events in the peregrines' everyday existence always provided a new experience. For example, Rio streaked from a perch on a cable toward a robin on the anchorage ledge. The robin cowered down to avoid his grasping talons. Each time Rio made a pass, the robin hunkered down and moved quickly from side to side, sometimes retreating into a declivity or behind some debris. Its dodging efforts were working well but Rio was persistent and he alighted close to the robin. The two birds eyed each another, neither one moving. Rio tried to gather in the robin in one foot but it was too agile. Rio made a few more flying passes at the robin and, finally, lost interest and left. We wondered what the robin was doing on the anchorage away from his normally safer, grassy habitat. We philosophized that some birds must "think" that the grass is greener on the other side.

The next day, Rio and the Queen collaborated by combining several swift dives to snare a hapless pigeon. The Queen performed the catch and carry. She alighted on the Throgs with the pigeon still thrashing in her grasp. She quickly ended its misery with a routine neck bite. She started depluming the bird and I left her to dine in private.

After a period of damp weather with little or no wind, a weather front moved through and brought fresh westerly winds. The adults reveled in its consistent force. The Throgs anchorage stood stolidly in the path of the wind as it rushed eastward across the water. The flow was deflected, creating an updraft upon which the peregrines rode as on an elevator. It was a delight to watch them enjoy the freedom of unlimited motion without having to flap their wings. Again and again, they rode the "elevator" up and soared over the Throgs. On a few occasions, they half-heartedly pursued pigeons. They apparently enjoyed the air more than the prospect of a meal. In one instance, they followed a pigeon into its roosting area on the anchorage. They tried to flush out some pigeons but they wisely hunkered down and stayed put. The peregrines were too exuberant and didn't have the patience needed to roust the pigeons. They resumed riding updrafts and playing in the wind.

Fledgling. At 6:00 A.M. the following day, to my extreme delight, I spotted a fledgling atop the Queens tower. The first fledgling of the season had debuted and I was almost assuredly the first human to lay eyes on him. I refer to this bird as him because males ordinarily fledge before females and there were two males and one female remaining at the nest after the one female chick had been removed. He sat very calmly for a short time and then walked about the top of the tower. According to my calculations, he was almost seven weeks old.

An hour later, I saw a nestling on the catwalk at the same spot where I had made the two previous sightings. The nestling still had considerable down on its head. I was somewhat concerned because I hadn't yet seen the third nestling. Usually when there are two or more chicks in a brood, they will stay together much of the time. That evening, I saw the adults flying around Cryder House. Dolores and I thought it was likely that the fledgling was on our roof and the adults were monitoring him. We went up to the roof entrance hallway and found the Queen perched on a parapet looking inward. We felt sure her youngster was there. She noticed us and commenced cacking loudly. As usual, when her young were on the roof, it became her territory, and she defended it as she would have defended her eyrie. We left quickly to avoid disturbing her.

The next day, the fledgling alighted with great skill on the Throgs cables and on a Cryder House parapet railing. Obviously he had had several days of practice to attain such adroitness. Once, he actually went into a short stoop-like dive when a pigeon flew near him. The unique factor this season was that a fledgling had managed to remain undetected for such a long time.

I enjoyed watching the fledgling "earning his wings" but I became increasingly disturbed at not seeing the third chick. I invested more time at the telescope, peering into the Throgs' recesses. I hadn't seen either of the fledgling's nest mates all day but I knew there had to be at least one in the eyrie because the adults were continuing to take kills there.

The second Sunday in June was a glorious peregrine day. At 6:00 A.M., I rushed out onto the terrace and observed two peregrines on the Bronx tower. The one that was perched on the topmost railing really got my attention because the adults almost never use that railing. I scoped that peregrine carefully and came to the conclusion that is was a fledgling. Later, the Queen was perched atop a tower while Rio hovered near her. Suddenly he mounted her, apparently in mock copulation to cement their pair bond.

I continued my observations from the beach area. At 8:30 A.M., the fledgling flew to the roof of Cryder House. His landing was excellent and he sat very serenely. While he was perched there, an adult took a kill into the eyrie. This indicated that there was a good likelihood that at least one other youngster was at the nest box, hopefully two. There were frequent hunting forays and some fancy flying. However, the best was yet to come. I had rushed down to the water's edge, joining the other watchers who had gathered there, to follow a hunt that carried the adversaries to the west. While we stood there expectantly awaiting the next hunt, we saw a pigeon flying toward us from the Throgs. It was being closely pursued by Rio. The pigeon headed on a downward trajectory and thereby gained substantial additional speed. Rio had the same advantage and did not appear to lose an inch on his quarry. They zipped by us at well over fifty miles an hour at a distance of no more than ten yards. We were able to clearly hear the air rushing across their wing surfaces. We felt as if we were a part of the action. The pigeon veered sharply left into a stand of trees and Rio broke off the chase by gracefully gliding to the right over the water.

The next hunt was a joint effort in which the adults isolated a pigeon over the water and took turns diving at it. The Queen grabbed the bird to end the chase. A short while later, they again were on the prowl for prey. They were in the hunting mode and a blue jay became their next victim when it made the mistake of flying across the water. They both went after the hapless creature and, after several spectacular dives and maneuvers, they hit it into the water. It paddled with flailing wings for less than a minute before it became exhausted. The peregrines circled it as if they were going to snatch it from the water; but they soon lost interest and abandoned their victim to a watery grave.

On the next hunt, again a joint attack, a fledgling tagged along. The quarry took refuge on the anchorage by cowering in a corner of its lower ledge. The peregrines seemed reluctant to go into that confined space and merely buzzed the pigeon, trying to get it to take wing. They failed to move it and alighted on the ledge nearby. The fledgling had followed the action very closely and alighted closer to the pigeon than had his parents. He advanced toward it with the same bearing we

172

had seen exhibited by the adults in similar situations. It was exceptional for a young peregrine to act so adultlike.

Eventually the pigeon became flustered and left the ledge; but it did not go far. It fluttered down to the thick layer of barnacles beneath the ledge and held on for dear life. The peregrines circled it a few times, trying to scare their intended victim into flight, but it did not budge. Again, the peregrines lost interest. After they left, the pigeon moved back up to the ledge and stayed there for several hours before making its final escape.

In the midst of such serious hunting activities, there were lighter moments. The fledgling was perched on the Cryder House roof very contentedly one day. A mockingbird took great exception to his presence and repeatedly dove at his head. The little aggressor then perched nearby, rested briefly, then resumed the attack. The young peregrine did not react to this display of bravado. Birds of prey seem to be programed to accept this type of harassment from smaller birds.

An adult black-crowned night heron, flying toward the Throgs, enraged the adults. They dove at it with exceptional ferocity. The heron could not fly away from danger and offered its only defense, a very loud guttural, croaking, and plaintive series of calls. It sounded like a combination call of distress and keep away. Several sharp passes at it culminated in a hard smash to its back. Feathers billowed out and I thought that it might be badly injured. The heron flew down toward the base of the anchorage and touched down on the very deep water; it then flew to a nearby barge for refuge. Although the peregrines took no further notice of the heron, it was so dazed that it could not even muster the effort to check itself or preen. After a long rest, it went on its way.

I found it interesting that black-crowned night herons are attacked by the peregrines when they have young that have fledged. They do not attack them when they have eggs or unfledged chicks. Evidently they consider the herons a danger to the young only when the young are out of the eyrie. Also, double-crested cormorants, which frequent the area in far greater numbers than night herons do, are never (normally) attacked by the adult. I can only surmise that somehow the peregrines understand that the cormorants do not present a danger at any time. Maybe it is the fact that, unless they are on water, cormo-

173

rants are never seen with food in their mouths, which cues the peregrines to recognize their exclusive status of fishermen.

Next we were treated to a classic type of hunt. A pigeon was flying over the water at a height of about fifteen feet. The peregrines sped toward their quarry with Rio quickly dropping down to just above the water. He streaked upward and grabbed the victim before it realized it was under attack. The peregrines have attacked prey from every angle and apparently enjoy varying their approach techniques. It makes our "job" of watching so much more interesting. We never know in advance what the scenario or the outcome will be.

Early one Sunday evening, with stiff winds providing good lift, the fledgling was using the force of the wind very skillfully. He rode the elevator, held position over the anchorage, went up the Cryder House wall of wind, and looked like he had been doing it for weeks instead of mere days. It was edifying to see the flying techniques that the fledgling had mastered in less than two months since he had hatched.

That day was marred by the increasing concern over the absence of the other two nestlings. The observation of a carcass being taken to the eyrie that morning held out some hope that there could still be more nestlings. The most troublesome aspect was the failure to see any nestlings on the Throgs all day.

Despair continued the following day because we could find only the adults and a single fledgling. It rained very hard for an hour and Rio took refuge in the rain spot. We could see the fledgling near him. Seeing Rio and his offspring together was a pleasant sight.

That Monday morning, the single fledgling perched on the roof of the nearest LeHavre building. He was facing us but we could not read his band because the sun was behind him, creating a silhouette. Later, the fledgling had "lunch" on the ledge above the 1983 eyrie. After lunch, he inspected some plastic sheathing tied to a railing post. The youngster pecked at it, footed it, and finally lay down flat on it. The plastic was in the sun and no doubt its radiated heat had attracted the bird.

I telephoned DEC to register my concern regarding the missing nestlings. It was decided that it would be safer to wait one more week before inspecting the Throgs because a disturbance could possibly cause a chick to leave the eyrie before it was ready.

At 5:00 P.M., I again observed the fledgling on the anchorage. The

174

Queen flew by our terrace and went around the south side of Cryder House on an upward cant. She seemed to be looking for her fledgling. I then checked the fledgling on the anchorage and found Rio no more than a foot away from him. Several minutes later, a peregrine flew from the top of Cryder House toward the Throgs, using the usual glide technique for a tail wind. I noticed that it looked dark and bulky, the configuration of a fledgling. I watched it closely as it made a perfect landing on a beam just below the roadway that was almost never used by the adult. I couldn't believe my eyes; it was a fledgling. I had two fledglings under observation at the same time. Dolores checked both fledglings and corroborated my observations. The release of tension was very much appreciated. This second fledgling had landed so expertly that it undoubtedly had had much practice. In seven prior seasons of observing peregrine fledglings, I had never seen any fly as well as these two within the first two or three days of their fledging. Evidently, these fledglings had frequented locations that were not under our surveillance. Another possibility was that we had been seeing the fledglings alternately and erroneously assumed it was one individual.

Then, one evening, we heard a youngster's food-begging call and spotted a fledgling on the bridge. It was on prey and eating heartily. Rio was perched, not ten yards away, on the catwalk railing. I absorbedly watched for twenty minutes as the fledgling tore off and very determinedly swallowed small bits of flesh. He then moved off a short distance from the now half-eaten carcass and feaked (wiped his beak clean). This signaled that he had finished his supper. Rio waiting for his share, immediately alighted on the remains. The youngster rushed over, displayed a mildly threatening posture, and pushed Rio away. Rio didn't contest the issue and flew off. Several minutes later, the youngster hopped away and Rio was back in a flash. He ate the carcass down to a nub in twenty-five minutes.

Two days later, when I commenced my evening observations, I spotted a male fledgling on the anchorage and Rio on the first side pier. The youngster was atop a headless pigeon, pulling meat from the opening where the head had once been. Rio watched the youngster from his lofty perch and, after the fledgling had dined very determinedly for ten minutes, he flew down to the ledge and alighted nearby. Although he did not challenge the fledgling, it charged him and drove him off the edge. Rio relocated several yards farther along the ledge and watched the fledgling as it moved away from the remains. His ten-minute repast was enough because he had eaten a meal three hours earlier. Rio quickly moved onto the leftovers and dug in. Within five minutes, the Queen alighted a foot away from Rio. She was interested in the remains but did not make a move. Suddenly the fledgling boldly charged the Queen and pushed her off the ledge. The Queen flew off out of sight but returned several minutes later. She again approached Rio and easily displaced him from the carcass. She fed on it without interference for about ten minutes. It was a beautiful family portrait, three peregrines in my scope sight at the same time.

This behavior was similar to that which we had observed in prior seasons. The fledgling is belligerent toward his parents and they give way. In this instance, the male fledgling was slightly larger than Rio but smaller than the Queen. Young females have longer wings and tails than either of the adults but are not heavier than the adult female. However, they frequently bully both their parents during this stage of their development.

Sunday morning was foggy with poor visibility at the Throgs. The intrepid peregrine watchers who had gathered stayed on undaunted, surviving on retold stories of previous peregrine exploits. The sun dispersed the fog slowly and the adults appeared, joined soon after by a fledgling. There was no wind and they did not hunt. But, when a willet flew into the arena, the peregrines were instantly rejuvenated and pursued the intended victim with great elan. The willet was forced down close to the water three times but was able to recover and avoid the grasping talons. The fourth escape took the little shorebird to safety and we marveled at its flying ability. It had shown tremendous speed and agility as it zigged and zagged at just the right times.

That June 17th was the last time that Dolores and I recorded seeing a fledgling. It had been out of the nest for only two weeks and a few days, and no one had yet reported observing it making a kill. As the days wore on, I despaired for the plight of the third fledgling because we had failed to confirm a sighting. Dolores and I had observed two chicks simultaneously on only one occasion, and we had confirmed the presence of two fledglings in one sighting, but the third chick failed to materialize.

Each breeding season produces a group of fledglings that disappear from their natal sites before they, apparently, have attained the skills to survive independently. The primary survival factor is the ability to capture prey. Conservatively, one may not count these fledglings as satisfactory dispersals, but, hopefully, some of them may acquire the ability to hunt successfully when stimulated by the pangs of hunger. Of course, the overriding loss factor, estimated at 50–70 percent for all peregrine fledglings for their first winter of life, is applied against those young that develop to independence. Only three New York City youngsters are known to have attained breeding status, though there may be other unknown breeders. It would be wonderful if some of the early dispersers, two- to three-week post-fledging, were to be identified as breeders.

Inside the Bridge. I conferred with Barbara Loucks concerning the lack of chick sightings at the Throgs and we agreed that the previously discussed inspection of the nest area was now needed. We had postponed performing a site inspection because of the possibility of frightening the unfledged third chick into a potentially dangerous premature first flight.

I was accompanied by Ted LeViness and Dave Gardner on this very important inspection. When we approached the first staging position, Rio and the Queen cacked loudly. As we scanned the area, they performed their usual defensive flight patterns between us and their nest. I changed my position to obtain a direct view into the nest box. To my great dismay I saw a large lump on the catwalk about thirty feet from it. Sadly, it appeared to be a peregrine chick. We moved toward the object, to the great consternation of the defending peregrines. They redoubled their loud vocalizations and made closer passes at us.

The object on the catwalk was indeed a dead chick; it was "M11M," one of the two males. The body had no flesh left on its frame. There were sheaths on some of its flight feathers, signifying that it had died prior to developing to the age of flight of about five weeks. We collected the body and forwarded it to the DEC laboratory for toxicologic analysis.

Because of the possibility that there might be another chick on the Throgs, be it dead or alive, we made a thorough inspection of areas that had not been inspected all season. We walked halfway to the Bronx tower and found only castings and prey remains. Returning to the eyrie, we then proceeded to the Queens anchorage. We entered

177

the anchorage structure and were engulfed by a dank dimness. The large room which we had entered was not the main section of the anchorage. We walked forward gingerly, unable to see the floor, went through an opening, and stepped out onto a catwalk. The interior of the anchorage was a sight to behold. After having looked at the anchorage from the outside for so many years, I had created a mental image of its essence. What a surprise to discover that, contrary to the solid image I had conjured up, it was mostly hollow. I had thought that it needed its massiveness to anchor the weight-bearing steel cables that support the thousands of tons of weight of the bridge itself and of the vehicles traversing it. A science-fiction movie could easily make use of the cavernous vertical space, confined yet so vaulting as it is. A catwalk runs from the north end to the south end and there are many ladders criss-crossing the interior, creating a surrealistic quality.

The heart of and the reason for the structure, the cables, take up a disproportionately small part of this extraordinary structure. The essence of the steel's strength is highlighted by the gleaming cleanness of the cables. They are completely uncovered. We could see the individual strands of steel that had been braided to make the smaller cables which were then interwoven to provide that fabled strength and flexibility that is the essence of a suspension bridge. The simplicity of the cable and anchorage system somehow does not seem so simple when one is physically inside the system.

We walked to the south end of the catwalk and I entered the first-year eyrie (1983). It felt strange to stand in the spot where it had all begun eight years ago. I looked over the water toward my apartment and savored the Queen's view from her first eyrie. It was very instructive to see the Throgs perspectives from so many different locations. But we found no sign of our missing chick.

It was important to determine why the Throgs' nesting effort had failed. Therefore, Chris, Ted, and I met at the Throgs on July 11 in to make a thorough inspection. Chris hoped, more than expected, that we might find a fledgling there, although it had been more than three weeks since one had been sighted.

I was anxious to discover whether the peregrines would defend their eyrie as strongly as they had during our last inspection now that there appeared to be no young at the site, dead or alive. The answer came as soon as we descended below the roadway, with the loud vocalizations of the Queen; she was soon joined by Rio. They screamed at us and put their bodies in our path. It was their territory and we were not welcome, whether they had young or not.

As expected, we found no evidence of any young. We also inspected the Bronx tower and anchorage. Chris took specimen castings from the nest box and catwalks. The nest box was very dirty because the hatchlings had excreted onto its sides before they had learned to use the open end. There were a few fresh prey carcasses on the catwalk and beams, as we said good-bye to our friends Queen and Rio. Our next visit to the eyrie would probably be just prior to the 1991 breeding season, to upgrade the nest box.

Dolores and I always considered our peregrine neighbors as friends and we continued watching them, although at a much reduced level now that there no young at the site. We saw them throughout the quiet period from August until the next breeding season. In August, we learned that the chick that had been taken in May from the Throgs had been hacked near Lake Jocassee in South Carolina. We wished her good luck and hoped that she would survive to raise progeny of her own. It would be wonderful if we could learn of her success. No matter, we would continue to monitor and enjoy our peregrines.

On August 26, an unbanded adult male peregrine briefly visited the Throgs. Peregrine visitors always started us wondering how many others went undetected when there was no one on watch to observe them. An extrapolation using the very low percentage of observation time invested in relation to total daylight time available would yield large numbers. Therefore, we did not dwell on those ethereal prospects and enjoyed the visitors that we were lucky enough to chance upon.

September produced some interesting observations. The Queen and Rio hit a pigeon into the water. The victim was unable to extricate itself from the water but had sufficient energy to propel itself. To no avail, it intermittently thrashed and flailed. The peregrines watched its efforts but made no attempt to claim it from the water. The bird flapped both wings unceasingly for about a hundred beats before it finally gave up. The peregrines still did not approach it. The pigeon's head was now very low in the water and evidently no longer presented an attractive target. The peregrines flew off without a backward glance. They apparently like to have their water-trapped prey exhausted but still with its head and neck out of the water. The pere-grines frequently display great tenacity in their pursuit of prey but seem to have well-defined parameters that determine their course of action in specific instances. Their prey base is so vast that they have the luxury of being very discriminating.

The Queen alighted in the 1983 eyrie and shuffled about in it. I wondered if she had any memory of it. It had been her first nest and it was nostalgic, for us, to see her where it all began for us more than eight years earlier.

12

Roundup

(1990 - continued)

News from the other peregrine nesting sites in the New York City metropolitan region varied in 1990 from wonderfully successful to disastrous. Success at the Verrazano-Narrows was a welcome turnabout from its five previous seasons of failing to produce even a single chick that survived to dispersal. This year, however, three chicks grew to independence at the Verrazano and a fourth one was taken and hacked in South Carolina. In early April, Chris Nadareski had observed four eggs in the nest box, located near the Brooklyn tower. On May 3, he recorded seeing only three of the four nestlings and the fact that his view had been restricted.

Chris scheduled an inspection of the Verrazano eyrie for May 19 to evaluate the nest conditions preparatory to Marty Gilroy's site visit. Marty's agenda included banding the chicks at the Verrazano, as well as those at the Throgs, and taking one chick from each for release elsewhere. Chris asked me to assist him in the inspection and I jumped at the chance. I had never taken part in an inspection of the Verrazano, although I had spent many hours observing the site. I had driven across it hundreds of times, to and from work, and even bicycled across its lower roadway several times as one of the more than 20,000 people who annually participate in New York City's Five Borough Bike Ride. Inspecting the eyrie would enhance my interpretations of future observations. I always feel the need to put my body where the peregrines make their home so that I can get their view of the environment.

Chris and I met at a location beneath the Verrazano to make some preliminary observations before going up on it. I arrived at the site early to gain more viewing time. My extra hour was well spent, as I watched the adults capture three birds. The first kill was a simple grab of a pigeon from among a small group that had emerged from beneath the roadway. The peregrines were in perfect attack position, above and behind them. The second kill, by the male, began with a spectacular stoop from the top of the tower to within several feet of the water. The quarry was gravely injured on the first strike and easily gathered in on the short second pass. The third capture was a collaborative effort but I missed much of it because my view was blocked.

Chris arrived and postponed the inspection because Marty was delayed. So, instead, we drove to the Outerbridge Crossing and were greeted by an adult soaring above the bridge. Shortly, another adult flew from the structure and they both alighted near the nest box on the New Jersey end of the bridge. However, there was no indication that there was any nesting activity there or at any other local site.

Chris and Marty went to the Verrazano the following day and found two male and two female nestlings. After banding the nestlings, they removed one female and shipped it to The Peregrine Fund facility in Boise.

On June 22, Dolores and I went to the Verrazano to observe the three recently fledged young. We spent a memorable two hours with them. They were cavorting on the main pier of the Brooklyn tower when we arrived and, from that moment to the moment we departed, they were in our full view. For most of the time, they were aloft enjoying the breezes and their own talents. They flew with good control and great verve. At times they zoomed to within inches of the swirling water and continued to wing their way as close to it as possible, as if to show their flagrant disregard for any fixed medium. I thought they were about to touch the water many times and remembered the instance in 1986 when a fledgling plunged into the water at the Verrazano never to be seen again. But they had infected me with their lack of fear and I felt sure that even if one were to go into the water, it would be able to extricate itself. They were the masters of all they surveyed and showed unbridled enthusiasm and confidence, the quintessential peregrine spirit. We had our lunch while we enjoyed the birds and the beautiful setting. The adults did not show themselves but that did not disturb us because the youngsters could not be in such an excellent state of health without attentive parents.

Great Peregrine Roundup

Two days later, I revisited the Verrazano with Dave, Ted, and Tony. It was Sunday morning, June 24, and we had convened at the Throgs for a "Peregrine Roundup Day." We planned to visit several of the productive peregrine nesting sites in the New York City metropolitan area, having our usual goal in mind: to observe wild peregrine behavior, especially the hunting. We had mused about trying to set a world's record for entry into the Guinness Book of Records by observing the highest number of peregrines in one day in one city. But we decided not to make an attempt to visit each and every site because that would require artificially shortened observation sessions, detracting from our enjoyment of the peregrines in our preferred manner. Instead, we opted to visit as many sites as possible.

Starting at the Throgs, we observed the adults by 8:00 A.M. Next, we kept an appointment with Ron Bourque of the New York City Audubon Society to observe the Marine Parkway Bridge site as a follow-up on observations that he had made in April and May. He had observed peregrines at the Marine Parkway/Gil Hodges Memorial Bridge. This small vehicular and pedestrian bridge connects Brooklyn and Rockaway. Ron had observed the birds hunting cooperatively and frequenting an area suitable for an eyrie. Now, on June 24, we observed two one-year-old peregrines at Marine Parkway. Each had a band on each leg. Could they be New York City youngsters? Potential new peregrine nesting sites generate great enthusiasm and are important to responsible governmental and private organizations. For me, they are a tonic and energize me to revisit a site until all pertinent facts are known.

Ted and I undertook a thorough inspection of the bridge on June 28. We rode an elevator ninety-five feet up to the machine room. The roadway is fifty feet above the water but, to accommodate taller vessels, its entire 595-foot-long center section can be lifted to provide additional headroom. The machine room houses the motors and other equipment needed for the raising and lowering of the roadway. The bridge once had the distinction of having the longest lift section of any bridge in the United States.

Once in the machine room, I went to the west window and immediately discovered a peregrine perched on the outside ledge. Unfortunately, I had approached too quickly and the bird saw me at the same instant that I had noticed it. We made eye contact. We were both startled by the encounter but, as much as I enjoyed the interaction, I despaired because I knew the bird was uncomfortable and would fly off. In fact, it quickly did so. It had brown subadult plumage but lacked the vertical streaking and white terminal tail band of a hatching-year bird. Ted found the prospective nest but I could see only the peregrine's head. We made eye contact and the bird flew off.

Early on the morning of July 20, Dolores and I traveled to the Marine Parkway Bridge. We made our observations from the pedestrian walkway and observed a subadult peregrine below the machine room. This was the same location where I had seen the birds on my two previous visits. We held a vigil for more than an hour, during which time the bird did not move. Although we clearly saw one of its bands, there was no chance of reading it from our poor viewing angle.

My next observation of a peregrine at the bridge occurred on September 8 as a consequence of my taking part in a hawk watch at Fort Tilden. Fort Tilden is located at the southern end of the bridge in Rockaway. Each fall, many migrating raptors travel along the barrier beaches on their trip south. As I was counting the migrating raptors on September 8, I observed a peregrine perched on the bridge.

On December 2, Steve Kazianas, a raptor enthusiast, observed a peregrine perched on a radio tower at neighboring Floyd Bennett Field. He had seen the bird there before and watched it use the tower as a vantage point from which to launch its hunts. On this date, he photographed it and was able to read the letter "K" on its band in the photo. It almost certainly was the same subadult whose "K25K" band had been read in July, one of Red-Red's offspring at the hospital site.

Verrazano-Narrows Leg Three. Now on the third leg of our Peregrine Roundup, we approached the Verrazano site. As we did so, we observed an adult peregrine on the wing. After it alighted near the nest box, we quickly found two fledglings. The youngsters took to the air and performed some aerial maneuvers with great exuberance. They flew with tremendous confidence, skimming the water by inches.

184

The adult "sat tight" while the youngsters played. We also observed a fourth peregrine on the wing but could not identify it. Seeing four peregrines at the site was a thrill for us. We had now seen eight peregrines at three sites and the day was still young.

On June 28, Ted and I visited the Verrazano site again and observed the adults and a fledgling on the catwalks near the Brooklyn tower. We saw nothing of the other two fledglings but they could have been perched in any one of many places not visible to us.

July 9 was a beautiful summer day at the Verrazano. Chris and I performed an in-depth inspection to fulfil a three-pronged mission. The adult female had been observed drooling copiously during a recent inspection. That symptom frequently indicates a disease process and an assessment of her physical condition was to be made, if possible. The fledglings were about eleven weeks old and it was important to establish whether or not they were still at the site and, if they were, to assess their condition. The third task for Chris was the gathering of castings to provide material for laboratory examination for a research project on which he was working. Chris and I carried a scope, tripod, and video camera equipment in addition to our regular complement of binoculars, cameras, etc.

Chris scheduled our inspection for a time when the lower roadways would be closed to traffic, in both directions. On previous occasions, the peregrines had flown across the lower roadways when disturbed at their eyrie. A fast-moving vehicle could easily crash into them in that situation.

The adult female alarm called as soon as our bodies were visible below the roadway. It was a welcome sign; she was on duty and sounded strong. But we were anxious to get a good look at her. We did not want to stress her any more than absolutely necessary, so we held our position while she perched where she could watch us. I humorously wondered who was in charge of today's operation and who was monitoring whom. Chris set up the tripod and scope and managed to scrutinize her well enough to ascertain that she was not drooling and appeared healthy. He could not read her band numbers due to the bridge's very high tremor level, which felt two to three times greater than that which I had experienced on the Throgs. But shaking that was barely perceptible to us was, of course, increased by the optical magnification of our binoculars, and by an even a stronger factor in the higher magnification power of the scope. Certainly the female's voice was in fine shape as she regaled us with almost continuous cacking at a decibel level that was unnerving. Of course, veteran peregriners like Chris and myself have built up an immunity to the ear-splitting alarm calls. In fact, while we had not talked about it, I presumed that he had developed a fondness for their vocalizations, just as I had.

During our search for the fledglings, I stepped onto a catwalk—and all three fledglings took flight. I clearly saw the white terminal bands on their tails. Luckily they did not go far; they alighted on nearby catwalk railings. They appeared to be in perfect condition. The failure of the adult male to make an appearance during our visit spoiled our chances of observing the entire family but, no matter; we were happy to have determined that the fledglings and their mother were healthy. As we walked about, Chris picked up castings for his research project. When we departed, the three youngsters were still perched on the catwalk eyeing us with displeasure. How could they have possibly begun to understand that the pleasure was all ours?

On July 20, Dolores and I went to the Verrazano for our last visit of the 1990 season. We saw only one peregrine, very briefly, as it flew about the Brooklyn tower.

Two items of good news concerning the Verrazano fledglings developed after they had dispersed. Tom Burke, an accomplished birder and hawk watcher, who operates the New York City Rare Bird Alert telephone hotline, observed a peregrine perched on a tree at the Marshlands Conservancy in Rye, New York, on August 5. He read its band number "L09L," which identified it as one of the two recently fledged males from the Verrazano. It had traveled thirty miles from its eyrie and appeared to be in excellent condition. Parenthetically, Tom had occasionally observed peregrines near his place of work in the 42nd Street area. The second news item concerned the female nestling that had been removed for release at another site. She had been successfully hacked at Lake Jocassee in South Carolina. The Verrazano had had its most successful breeding season ever.

Outerbridge and Goethal's Fourth and Fifth Legs. Pairs of peregrines had been observed at both the Outerbridge Crossing and the Goethal's Bridge, which connect Staten Island and New Jersey. On the fourth stop on our Peregrine Roundup Day, the Outerbridge Crossing, we were greeted by an adult peregrine. After it flew out of our view, we reluctantly decided to go on to Leg Five and the Goethal's Bridge. Our plan was to drive slowly along its approach road and to exit quickly if we spotted a peregrine. But we saw none and continued on our way. Evidently we had not invested enough time at the Outerbridge and Goethal's because, the very next day, Chris observed pairs at both bridges. Still, our roundup day was going well.

Riverside Sixth Leg. The Riverside Church site had successfully developed two fledglings to independence in its initial 1989 season. By March 28, 1990, Tony Holton had observed one egg at Riverside. He saw a second egg the following day. Eventually, a clutch of four was produced. Only two of the eggs were fertile but two chicks hatched during the first week of May and the chicks fledged during the second week in June.

On June 24 Dave, Ted, Tony, and I went to Riverside on the sixth leg of our peregrine tour. We were treated to several hours of heart-warming observations of a peregrine family. The session began on a high note when the adult female captured a pigeon near Grant's Tomb and was immediately pursued by the two fledglings. She dropped the prey item briefly in an attempt to encourage an in-flight prey transfer, but she quickly recovered it when they failed to do so. Alighting on a building adjacent to the church, she began to share the meal with one of the fledglings. The youngster then fed itself competently while the female sat very close to her.

The second fledgling was perched higher up on the same building gazing down on the dining session. It had no interest in food. Its crop was full to bursting. Then the adult male appeared and the family picture was complete. After the fledgling finished eating, there was a long flying session, in which the youngsters reveled in crabbing, soaring, diving at one another, and riding the air currents. A female American kestrel flew by and the peregrines immediately pursued it. She received a glancing blow from the adult male but escaped below the Riverside Park canopy. I was able to read the letter "K" on an adult's leg band, which identified her as the resident female that had been banded at the Riverside the previous year.

We had seen a total of thirteen peregrines at five different sites that day. The rising numbers of nesting sites and chick production in the New York City area presaged a bright future for the peregrines.

Hospital site

Although it was not part of our Great Peregrine Roundup, the New York Hospital/Cornell Medical Center was an important peregrine nesting site, and Dolores and I were keeping watch on it. It had two chicks develop to dispersal in its first year of existence, 1988, and that fine start was surpassed in 1989 with three successful fledglings. The first chick of the 1990 nesting season hatched on April 26. Dolores and I went to Roosevelt Island on April 29 and took up a position across from the nest ledge on a residential building's eighteenth-floor sundeck. There were two chicks sitting upright in the nest box; two days later, we spotted a third chick.

My next visit was during the last weekend in May. The male nestling was more advanced in plumage than were his two sisters; he had a richly streaked brown chest and very little down anywhere while the females' plumage contained more down than brown.

Red-Red, the adult female, was on her perch pole surveying the scene. As soon as her mate arrived with a kill, she hopped over to him and relieved him of it. After a moment, the male flew off with a small morsel and landed on the north face of the building. He ate it there while Red-Red fed the chicks.

The first fledging took place on June 3 and the second one occurred the following day. Dolores and I went to Roosevelt Island on June 6 and observed both adults and two young, but the action was unremarkable.

The middle part of June brought a dramatically downward turn of events at the site. Barbara Loucks of DEC advised me that the male fledgling had been found injured on the roof of a building adjacent to the hospital. He had been taken to a veterinarian for assessment and treatment. The news went from bad to worse; a female fledgling was discovered the following day, dead of a broken neck, on the same roof where her brother had been found. Apparently, the peregrines had trouble seeing the building's dark, clear glass and were flying into it. We could only hope that the third fledgling was still on the wing and that the injured male might respond to treatment and eventually be released.

Moving to another location, an important sighting was made at

188

Floyd Bennett Airfield during July by Craig LeShack, who, while working on an avian research project unrelated to peregrines, observed a pair of peregrines. They hunted successfully and alighted on the ground to consume their prey. He worked his way close enough to them to read one of the two bands each of them wore. It was "K25K." She was the same 1989 fledgling from the New York Hospital site that I discussed earlier. We were joyous. We had been waiting since 1983 for evidence that a New York City area fledgling had survived its first year of life. Her companion was a one-year-old male. The Floyd Bennett Airfield is twelve miles from the New York Hospital eyrie. We hoped that this was only the first of many such events and that the next one might involve a nesting situation. It was of paramount importance that the dispersed chicks carve out new nesting territories or replace lost adults at established sites.

My last visit to the hospital site was on the crisp, clear morning of November 26. I bicycled the eleven miles from my home to Roosevelt Island. I scanned the hospital building and the other structures in the vicinity; in vain. I gave up my search and had ridden less than fifty yards when, directly above me, I heard the loud call of a peregrine. I looked up and saw Red-Red, the resident female at the hospital. She dove through a dozen pigeons, which scattered in a frenzy in all directions. She hurtled downward so low to the ground that it took my breath away; then she zoomed upward on the power from the stoop. It was the peregrine's characteristic aerial hunt maneuver which I had witnessed many times but about which I could never be blase. As she broke off the chase and drifted away, she gained altitude almost effortlessly by merely adjusting her flight feathers to catch the air currents. As I watched her circling, it seemed evident that she treated the hospital as her personal property and Roosevelt Island as a colony to be plundered for prey. Red-Red continued to soar higher and higher over Manhattan, out of binocular range, as I departed.

I pondered this season's tumultuous events at the hospital site. Following two successful seasons, which had produced five healthy fledglings, the three chicks born in 1990 seemed to presage a third banner season. Unfortunately, one accident caused a chick's death and a second one caused another chick to be severely injured, rendering it unreleasable. Still, the discovery of one of the hospital's 1989 fledglings in good health, after it had been a year in the wild, was very encouraging. It seemed to me that reversals of fortune were a natural phenomenon and we had no choice but to accept and study them.

13

Oops!

(1990 - continued)

Ironically, it seemed that just as soon as we discerned an upward trend, the pendulum would swing in the opposite direction. Although the Tappan Zee site had started out auspiciously in 1988 with two youngsters reaching independence, its second season had ended in disaster when its lone fledgling met its death on the roadway. Now the 1990 season was proving a complete failure, with no known egg production at all.

On April 22, Dave, Dolores, and I went to the Tappan Zee and met James Vellozzi, a college student, who had devoted many hours to monitoring the site during the early portion of the 1990 season. It was a pleasure to meet him after having had so many telephone conversations with him. Together, we observed an adult peregrine perched on and near the west tower nest box.

On May 3, James observed the adults at the nest box. The female entered it and seemed to be arranging the substrate. This was the most encouraging behavior witnessed here to date. I visited the site the next day and found a peregrine perched on a beam near the box. On May 15, I observed the female going in and out of the box. Ten days later, James also observed the female in the box. There were no additional observations that indicated a nesting attempt was in progress. The bridge personnel also kept a watchful eye while engaged in the performance of their duties. Their observations corroborated our conclusion that the peregrines had not produced any eggs. My last visit to the Tappan Zee was on September 3. Dave and I had spent the morning at the nearby Hook Mountain Hawk Watch watching the migrating raptors. We had seen more than forty, among which one was a juvenile peregrine. On our trip home across the Tappan Zee, we spotted an adult peregrine flying about the east tower. That was my final observation at the site for the 1990 season.

Pan Am Building. The 42nd Street/Grand Central Station vicinity of midtown New York City, at first blush, would seem to be an unlikely location for a peregrine nesting territory. But the area is blessed with the city's usual abundant supply of pigeons and provides tall buildings for a peregrine eyrie. Although not directly over water, both the Hudson and East rivers are visible from the upper reaches of the buildings. Adult peregrines had been observed in the area for several years and, although there was no known nesting, their consistent activity pattern indicated that this area was their year-round territory.

The Lincoln Building and the Pan Am Building, across the street, provided their favored perches. Alison Okinaka, an attorney whose office was in the Lincoln Building, had shared her observations of the peregrines with me during the 1989 season. Her first 1990 sighting, on February 8, was of an adult flying over 42nd Street. Her next observation, on March 22, was much more significant: she saw two adults. My curiosity about whether this peregrine pair was nesting or not was so strong that I made arrangements to make an inspection of the site. On Sunday morning, April 4, Ted and I met Alison in the lobby of the Lincoln Building and went up to her office on the thirty-ninth floor. We stationed ourselves on a balcony facing north toward the Pan Am Building. The Pan Am rises vertically from its lowest level without exterior balconies, setbacks, or decorative protuberances on the upper portion which would provide prominent perches. The exceptions were the massive "PAN AM" signs.

Less than a quarter of a hour had elapsed when an adult female peregrine flew directly in front of us. She turned her head when she saw us and seemed startled at our unanticipated proximity to her. She flapped hard several times and alighted on a setback six stories above us. A few inches of her tail were visible as we craned our bodies to get a look at her. After several minutes, she flew to the southeastern face of the Pan Am and we distinctly heard the call of a second peregrine. Then the calling male moved to the front of a ledge on the fifty-seventh floor and into view. Both birds vocalized as the female alit close

192

to her mate. They sounded that special "chirruping" which peregrine pairs utilize during the breeding season.

The male flew off and the female settled down toward the rear of the ledge. We were ecstatic; we were very sure that we had just witnessed a nest exchange whereby the female replaced the male for incubation duty. I looked forward to apprising Chris Nadareski of our finding. He would surely conduct an intensive site inspection to determine if the peregrines had eggs. We left the site feeling wonderful; in a twenty-minute visit, we had almost assuredly established the fact that New York City had another pair of nesting peregrines. Chris inspected the Pan Am site on April 11 and observed at least one egg. Unfortunately, the substrate was very jagged and Chris felt that it very probably would create problems for the eggs. He was correct in his assessment. His revisit of May 11 yielded no peregrines at the nest nor any material which would provide any information concerning their failed nesting attempt.

On May 23, Alison observed the adults apparently inspecting various ledges on the Pan Am facade. The adults were possibly still in the breeding mode and engaged in nest site selection behavior. However, there were no signs of another nesting attempt.

On November 17, The British Broadcasting System arranged to have Dr. Heinz Meng fly two of his personally owned peregrines from atop the Pan Am as part of a journalistic project to produce a documentary. The ill-conceived endeavor ended in a heart-breaking loss for Dr. Meng when, in the course of this stunt, his ten-year-old female peregrine was attacked by a "wild" peregrine (most assuredly one of the Pan Am resident adults) and was last seen fleeing with the attacking peregrine in hot pursuit. An aggressive, territorial defense response by the resident peregrine directed against all interlopers, whether human or avian, was certainly predictable. Dr. Meng asked me to notify him if I were to hear of his lost bird. I certainly would cooperate but the likelihood of spotting and recapturing the creature was remote. The bird's jesses (leather leg straps) had been removed to create the normal look of a wild peregrine. Unfortunately, this reduced the chances that anyone observing the bird would recognizing that it was not a truly wild peregrine.

Hope Returns

In 1989, the Hell Gate Bridge had been the site of an unsuccessful nesting attempt. I began monitoring the site on February 11 and made an additional five visits through April 1, 1990. On four of the visits, I observed a single adult peregrine but there was no indication of the presence of a second peregrine at the site.

Those sites which are attractive to peregrines for nesting are frequently occupied by them during the fall or winter periods preceding the spring breeding season. We had had examples of this phenomenon at the New York Hospital, which hosted three peregrines beginning with the fall of 1987, and at least one of the Riverside Church peregrines had been observed at the site by Christmas of 1988.

This line of thinking encouraged me to start monitoring the Hell Gate site during the fall of 1990. On November 16, I bicycled to the site and was elated, but not quite surprised, to find an adult peregrine perched on the Queens tower of the Triborough Bridge. I hoped that it was staking out a territory rather than merely using the location as an off-season headquarters. Finding that its left leg was unbanded at least determined that it was not one of the local peregrines; they were double banded.

Ten days later, I again visited the site, after having had a wonderful interlude with Red-Red at New York Hospital. When I was still a third of a mile away from the Hell Gate, I observed a peregrine perched on top of it. On December 2, I returned and again found an unbanded peregrine on the Triborough. A peregrine had been there on each of my three post-season site visits; hopefully, that bode well for the ensuing 1991 season.

The Wall Street area had hosted a pair of peregrine high flyers in 1989. Four eggs had been laid in a failed nesting effort. Steve Walter, an intrepid hawk watcher, opened the 1990 season on March 14 when he observed two peregrines while lunching in Battery Park. Enzo Volpe, a devoted peregrine watcher, observed a single peregrine from his office in the World Trade Center's Twin Towers on April 12, May 2, and May 3. There was no known nesting but it was possible that an eyrie might have been established somewhere in the financial district and had gone undetected.

Barrett Station. Long Island observer Tony Tierno had observed an adult peregrine over several years at the Long Island Lighting Company's Barrett Station, located in southern Nassau County, in the town of Island Park. On March 17, Tony, Ted, and I drove to Barrett and gained entry through the courtesy of cooperative LILCO personnel. We found a peregrine with an extremely broad, black helmet perched on a window sill. It did not move and we planned to return to observe it again; no peregrine was safe from our adoring eyes. The Barrett Station was eminently suitable for a peregrine nesting site because it possessed high nesting cavities, hordes of pigeons and other birds, and creeks were nearby.

On June 3, Ted and Tony returned to Barrett and went on a guided tour through the plant's interior. No peregrines were observed but they did find fresh prey remains. On July 16, I biked the eighteen miles to Barrett and checked every structure that a peregrine might perch on, but saw none.

Brian Milano, a worker at Barrett, called me on October 2 to report that he had observed a peregrine at the plant. Two days later, Brian guided me through the plant and, although we did not find a bird, there were fresh prey remains. When we were about to give up our search, and as darkness was setting in, we spotted an adult peregrine on a railing atop one of the two smokestacks. It had prey and fed heartily. Tony Tierno observed a peregrine at Barrett on October 22, and I did also on November 2. But the best news was yet to come the very next day. Brian observed two adult peregrines sitting together. The newcomer was obviously a larger bird, seemingly a female. The "pair" was observed together on November 3 and 4. Brian touchingly related, "The male lets her sit in all his favorite places."

Brian's next report was extremely distressful. On December 3, a dead peregrine had been found. Its body had not been retrieved and his inspection of the area involved was fruitless. The workers thought that the dead bird was the resident male because of its appearance and small size. Because no one had seen a peregrine recently, the likely scenario was that the male who had been frequenting the site had been joined by a female. The male by then was bonded to the site and probably would have remained there had the newcomer died or disappeared. On the other hand, the newcomer had no such attachment and could be expected to leave upon the loss of the original resident. It seemed ironic that just when the situation at Barrett had improved, it suddenly turned sour.

14

Limited Success

(1991 at the Throgs Neck Bridge)

We started the year 1991 early, and well. On the seventh of January, I saw Rio flying toward the Throgs in a suspiciously purposeful attitude. Moreover, as he passed above the cables near the tower, he dipped down and buzzed a bird perched there. Peering at the bird through the terrace door, I could see that it had brown plumage. I called out to Dolores, "We've got an immature peregrine on the bridge."

But the bird did not quite have the look of a peregrine; it had no facial markings. I rushed onto the terrace so fast that I did not feel the sting of the icy air in my hurry to focus my binoculars on the stranger. It was definitely an immature falcon but not a peregrine. Could it possibly be a gyrfalcon? Through my scope at 60X magnification, the visitor appeared to be slightly larger than our Queen. Its tail was considerably longer than its wingtips. We were sure that it was an immature dark-morph male gyrfalcon. We watched it for a half an hour before it flew off.

We observed the Queen and Rio irregularly during the winter, but their increased activity became evident in March at the onset of the breeding season. Rio began frequenting the nest box area, indicating that the Queen was either sitting on eggs or preparing to do so.

Chris Nadareski observed a scrape in the nest box on March 18; he also saw the adults copulate, an even more encouraging sign. When he returned on March 27, he saw two eggs in the box. In the ensuing week, Dave Gardner observed the adults conduct a prey transfer near the nest box and attempt to copulate. Ted LeViness witnessed Rio capture two passerines in a brief hunting spree and present his second catch to the Queen. On April 6, Chris was able to count at least three eggs being incubated. The 1991 breeding season was off to an excellent start, with the eggs safely in the box and the attentive parents in prime breeding condition.

Dolores and I returned to New York on April 23, from our winter vacation in Florida, starved for the sight of a peregrine. The next morning, Rio flew into view and we felt that we were really home. We observed Rio regularly without the Queen, a strong indication that she was sitting on eggs. One evening, I discovered a peregrine perched on the rail on top of the Queens tower. Since this vantage point is rarely used by the resident peregrines, I carefully scrutinized it and found that it was a one-year-old male, banded on each leg. The youngster flew to the 1983 eyrie and then to the first pier. It perched there serenely for thirty minutes, until 8:00 P.M., when it dove down at a black-crowned night heron that was contentedly feeding. I did not see the visitor again that evening. Undoubtedly, it had not been challenged by the resident adults because they had not seen it.

The following morning, Rio stooped at a blue jay and hit it into the water. He did not retrieve his victim. Two minutes later, he struck another blue jay into the water, again failing to claim it. Then he narrowly missed snaring a passerine. After two quiet hours, the peregrine visitor of the previous day boldly flew onto the scene. He had the temerity to chase the resident adults. The Queen took up the gauntlet and flew at the interloper. But it seemed clear that she and Rio recognized his immaturity. They displayed a mild territorial defense and avoided injuring the youngster. Apparently, because the residents did not act overly threatening, the young male again made himself at home on the Throgs. He enjoyed a meal on top of the Queens tower and pursued some birds. After several hours, the intermittent protestations of the residents finally encouraged the visitor to leave.

On May 1, Chris and I inspected the Throgs eyrie. Rio gave the alarm cry and sat on a railing where he could guard the path leading to the nest. The Queen was ensconced in the box on her eggs and joined in his vocal demonstration of horror at our transgression into their sanctuary. We tried to accomplish our mission with the least possible disturbance to them and moved to a spot that provided us with a view of the box's interior. To keep a low profile, we crawled forward like soldiers beneath barbed wire. The accumulated filth and jagged debris, across which we were scraping, was the fallout from the millions of vehicles that had traversed the Throgs plus pigeon droppings and other unpleasant items.

Chris raised his body just enough to focus his binoculars on the Queen. She saw Chris, increased her alarm vocalizations, and moved a bit, allowing him to see one chick under her and possibly two. We hastily retreated; all seemed well for this ninth consecutive breeding season.

In the morning of May 11, Rio captured two pigeons and two blue jays. The Queen was aloft but did not seem to display her usual dynamism, and failed to snare any prey. On May 14, when Chris and I again inspected the Throgs nest, there were three chicks there. We were ecstatic. We hoped that the only task before us at this site would be to band the nestlings.

The next afternoon, the Queen behaved very strangely. While on a Bronx tower shroud, she "spread-eagled" herself by pressing her body, wings, and tail downward. Both wings were in a fully extended position and the tail was moderately fanned. We had never before observed her in this position. She seemed to be peering about in a curious manner. The Queen then stooped at an osprey, which distress called, did a quick wingover, and wisely beat a hasty retreat. The Queen returned to the cable shroud and again prostrated herself for five minutes before resuming her normal activity pattern.

Several days later, Rio harassed some gulls before moving on to his major responsibility: providing food for his mate and offspring. He pursued a pigeon and gathered it in his talons on his third diving attack. No sooner had he snipped his victim's neck than the Queen streaked toward him and demanded that he give up his prize. Rio could not bear to part with the bird immediately and continued flying toward the eyrie, with his mate close behind. He disappeared from sight for a few seconds, within the Throgs structure, and flew out empty-taloned. The next morning, after Rio had snared a blue jay, the second successful hunt was the Queen's when she caught a pigeon on her third dive after she had forced it down very low to the water. She flew up to the Throgs and deplumed it. As a shower of feathers ensued, we hoped she would not be cited for littering the less-than-pristine water of the East River.

On May 21, Chris and I banded the three Throgs hatchlings. We were accompanied by Dave Gardner and three press photographers. The three newcomers were mesmerized by the continuing drama of the peregrines' near-extirpation and reintroduction as well as the tales of our personal experiences. We make a continuing effort to harness the power of the media by educating them and enlisting their aid to benefit all wild creatures.

When we drove onto the Throgs, Rio was perched high up on the tower. The Queen challenged us from the instant we began descending toward the eyrie by perching close to us and cacking as loudly as she could with hardly a lapse. We positioned the photographers on a safe ledge which provided them with an excellent vantage point. The Queen was roused to flight and made a few passes at us but, due to Rio's absence, she seemed unable to muster her usual level of aggressiveness. Having experienced the full fury of their combined attacks on many occasions, I hoped that he would not appear. I think that the three photographers on the ledge, Chris and me on the catwalk, plus Dave and the absence of Rio to help her was more than she could deal with. In one way, this may have been beneficial because it discouraged her from taking any potentially dangerous actions and actually calmed her by coercing her into inaction.

We made our way toward the nest box, fully expecting Rio to zoom onto the scene at any moment and precipitate a full-scale attack. However, Rio did not appear. The three nestlings vocalized when they saw us, adding to the cacophony already being heaped upon us by the Queen. The Queen perched on a pipe above us and screamed at us intermittently. Then she alighted several feet from Chris's foot, stared intently at us, and cacked loudly. She sat unmoving in that spot during the entire banding session. Not once did she avert her stare from us nor did she pay any attention to the photographers. The banding of the two females and one male nestling proceeded like clockwork. Chris took advantage of the Queen's unusual proximity and read her band numbers, which corroborated her identity. When Chris and I moved away from the box, the Queen jumped onto it and redirected her aggressive cacking toward the photographers. We took our leave with everyone having a feeling of elation because of the special happening that we had had the good fortune of witnessing. The photographers obtained some wonderful shots, which appeared in several newspapers. Later on the afternoon of the banding, Dave observed the Queen capture a pigeon and deliver it to the eyrie. All was well at the Throgs "Peregrine Palace."

The Queen increasingly spent more time away from the nestlings and began initiating more of the hunts. The peregrine pigeon-killing team was back in full force; there were three hungry chicks to feed.

On weekends when the Throgs site was being monitored continuously from approximately 7:00 A.M. to noon, the average of three prey deliveries seemed to be much lower than the observed morning-delivery rate in previous seasons. It seemed likely that several kills were being made before our morning sessions began, so I began my next observation day at first light, 5:00 A.M.; sunrise was 5:27 A.M. At 5:50 A.M., Rio flew to the eyrie with a small bird, or the remains of a larger victim. Rio was very active during the ensuing forty-five minute period but he did not go on the hunt until 6:35 A.M. when he snared a bird and took it directly to the eyrie.

Ten minutes later, both adults were alternately soaring and gliding above the Throgs. Then three bridge workers ascended the main cable to replace burned-out light bulbs. The peregrines zoomed toward them, but their attack was muted because the workers were very far from their nest. They merely voiced their displeasure and circled above them. At 7:15 A.M., they captured the third prey item of the morning, indicating that about half of each morning's feedings took place within the first two hours of sunrise. At 8:20 A.M., another catch was taken to the young, with a fifth meal being delivered in the next hour. Five feedings were accomplished during a five-hour period; sufficient food for three chicks.

On a Sunday morning, by 6:30 A.M., half a dozen peregrine watchers had assembled at the beach. The Queen flew to the Throgs burdened with a pigeon. She alighted about thirty yards from the nest box and deplumed the bird steadily, seemingly preparing it for her hungry chicks. Instead, she fed on it herself for several minutes and then took the still sizable remains to her chicks.

A few moments later, Rio was in hot pursuit of a mockingbird, which wisely sought refuge within a myriad of beams. Rio followed it in and displayed his most menacing attitude in an attempt to scare the bird from its sanctuary. After several unsuccessful attempts at flushing his quarry, Rio lost interest and flew off. The mockingbird was observed half an hour later, speeding on a beeline to land. Later, Rio chased a robin over Little Bay, but this victim had no place to hide within 500 yards. Rio drove it down close to the water and gathered it in. Then an immature red-tailed hawk flew directly above us and, to its good fortune, escaped the notice of the resident peregrines.

The following afternoon, Rio was on a catwalk near the nest, with a look of concerned interest. This was a signal that a chick had moved out of the nest box and made its way onto the catwalk. Rio would now need to stand guard over the chicks, who would increasingly leave the safety of their nest, without reducing his food-gathering activities. Rio deftly struck a pigeon, disabling it and causing it to go into the water. He circled it several times but made no attempt to retrieve it. Unfortunately, Rio does not have the strength to extract a pigeon from the water and it is lost unless the Queen lends a talon.

The next milestone for this season was the first sighting of a chick from a viewing position off the Throgs. From our apartment, I observed a chick on the catwalk where I had seen Rio two days earlier. The chicks were then about five weeks old and were expected to be clambering about the catwalks at that stage of their development. The next day, two chicks were together on the catwalk. They engaged in bouts of wingflapping and shared a meal. The only improvement in that scenario would have been that of seeing all three chicks.

There were six observers at the beach the next morning and the adults were visible from 6:00 A.M. on. They captured a blue jay and a pigeon by 7:00 A.M., when three bridge workers ascended a cable to replace burned-out light bulbs. Rio was aloft but did not attack them at first because he was busy pursuing a crow that had strayed too close to the Throgs. After Rio had escorted the crow out of the danger zone, he turned his attention to the workers. He flew close to them but did not display a high level of ferocity because the interlopers were far from the chicks.

At 7:15 the next morning, Ted and I spotted a chick on the main pier below the eyrie. This was the first sighting of a fledgling at the Throgs for the 1991 season. It moved actively about the pier and we identified this left-banded bird as a male by his small size. Twenty minutes later, the Queen carried a pigeon to the pier and fed the youngster for more than twenty minutes. She took the prey remains up to the eyrie. Rio alighted on a platform about thirty feet above the fledgling, no doubt to guard him. The Queen soon joined her mate; it was a proud pair of peregrines that sat inches apart gazing down at their brown chick. We felt both excited and privileged to have been able to witness a fledged chick's first day and his parents' efforts to feed and protect him.

The Queen raced after a pigeon. At the instant when she was about to dig her talons into its body, it dove down to the level of the water and actually touched it. This action seemed to slow the Queen for a second, providing the wily quarry with the opportunity to streak away to safety. We were also entertained by the antics of the fledgling as he hopped, ran, and walked on the pier. He jumped up to higher perches with ease by pushing off with his legs and exerting a well-timed wingbeat. He did everything except fly, which was the one activity that he most needed to master in order to survive. During the many hours that we observed him that day, not once did he even attempt to fly. In fact, he did not even engage in wingflapping, the hallmark of both newly fledged birds and nestlings that are almost ready to take the great leap forward. We hated to even think about it but, though the main pier was very spacious, if the chick were to stumble off and fall into the water in the space between the pier and its protective fender, it would almost assuredly not have been able to extricate itself.

As the morning wore on, odd behavior was exhibited by both adults. Rio alighted on the south ledge of the anchorage and lay on the jagged pieces of concrete and other items of debris that were strewn there. He spread his wings out so that at certain points they were actually touching the rough debris. The sun was strong on that warm day, making that particular spot much hotter than the surrounding area because the sun's rays were being absorbed into the concrete causing radiant heat to be reflected outward. We wondered why he would choose to subject himself to the additional heat of that location and why he would allow his precious feathers to touch such irregular debris. To add to our perplexity, while Rio was on the anchorage, the Queen flew to a shroud on the Bronx tower and flattened herself upon it, significantly increasing the ambient heat applied to her body. We could think of no plausible reasons for this behavior but, because they both appeared to be in robust health, we did not worry. Rio lay prone on the ledge intermittently for an hour.

In the afternoon, the Queen snared a pigeon and fed on it for a short time. Then, instead of flying to the nest, she flew off with the remains on a circuitous route, obviously calculated to lure either the fledgling on the pier or the chicks that were still at the eyrie. On the second go-around, Rio flew after his mate and, finally, both went to the eyrie.

The fledgling on the pier was observed regularly until 4:30 P.M. The adults attacked all gulls near the Throgs because the youngster was in a very vulnerable location. I kept a vigil until dark but did not again observe him. I feared the worst. My experience of observing fledglings for nine seasons at the Throgs and at other sites dictated that if a newly fledged chick does not have the confidence to fly, it may remain on its first landing platform for many hours, or even a day or two. The parents will minister to it there or at any location it may move to. I saw no evidence of any activity related to the fledgling and despaired that it was lost.

I could not find the fledgling the next morning, either. My worst fears were corroborated when Chris advised me that the body of a male fledgling had been recovered from the water at the Throgs. This was the first known loss of a fledgling from the group of fifteen young hatched in New York City this breeding season. Losses are to be expected each season, and life must go on, so we turned our attention to the other two chicks and their parents.

I had not seen a chick for several days, but the adults continued to deliver prey to the eyrie. Occasionally we could hear the chicks' vocalizations. I learned later from Chris that he had seen a fledgling on the Throgs when he had made an inspection two days after the male fledgling had been found dead.

June 13 provided splendid opportunities to observe the adult peregrines in their full flying glory. The wind was out of the northwest and exceeded fifteen miles an hour. The action commenced before 7:00 A.M. when a pigeon flew past Cryder House "going with the wind" and the Queen tried for it even though it was close to cover. She missed her one chance and glided into Cryder House's wall of wind, where she took time to soar over the top of the building.

In the early evening, both adults were aloft. A male adult mallard flew past the Throgs and noticed the peregrines. His instincts cried out, "They weren't called duck hawks for nothing." What he could not possibly have known was that the Throgs peregrines had never been

204

observed attacking a duck. Due to the available cornucopia of pigeons, doves, and other prey, there was no need to pursue prey that could not be carried whole. The panic-stricken duck changed its flight course and flew upward on the wind. There was no attempt to move away from the peregrines, only a desperate upward movement to obtain a height advantage which would prevent the predators from stooping downward to conquer. When the mallard had risen to a height of several hundred feet, it streaked out over Little Bay toward the nearest land. The peregrines ignored the entire event but I enjoyed watching the duck play out its genetically programed response and wondered if it felt anything approaching satisfaction at its successful escape.

Two days after Chris had spotted the second fledgling, I at last saw it, at 6:30 A.M. near the eyrie. At 1:15 P.M., it was on a cable near the Queens tower. The Queen arrived with a prey item and fed the fledgling right on the cable. A half-hour later, the Queen unsuccessfully attacked a dozen pigeons near the Bronx tower while at the same time the fledgling was walking up the cable toward the tower. Walking on the cable was typical fledgling activity each season at the Throgs. It was reassuring to witness the same behavior exhibited by the young each succeeding year. There is a sense of continuity and consistency that is appreciated by those who have had the experience of observing peregrines raise young over many seasons. However, there was a pall being cast upon the scene. In addition to the loss of the first fledgling, the third chick had not been seen since my inspection of the eyrie six days earlier.

The fledgling made a short flight and alighted on a shroud, where she lay almost flat for half an hour taking a much-needed rest. Two hours later, the Queen fed the youngster there while Rio was perched on the other shroud proudly watching. The Queen then flew off with the remains, which prompted Rio to chase after her, no doubt to beseech her for a tidbit. The fledgling, still flat on the shroud, dozed off. I clearly saw her nictitating membrane come across her eye. It was wonderful to be able to observe these intimate activities without intruding. Rio returned to the other shroud and stood guard over her for over an hour. He left at 8:00 P.M., well before nightfall, obviously satisfied that the youngster intended to sleep all night on the shroud.

I checked the shroud several times after dark and found the fledgling in the same position.

At 6:00 A.M. the following day, the fledgling was perched on one shroud and Rio on the other. The fledgling then flew to the top of the tower and the adults shifted into the hunting mode. Rio twice stooped unsuccessfully on a passerine but within half an hour flew in with prey. At 5:00 P.M., the fledgling fed, while on the shroud, and Rio remained until she went to sleep there at 8:30 P.M.

At 5:30 the next morning, the fledgling had already left the shroud and was perched on the cable. Later, an adult carried prey to the top of the Bronx tower, where the youngster enjoyed her first meal of the day. The fledgling was still on the Bronx tower in the afternoon when the Queen circled her with prey. It was an attempt to entice her to take flight. The fledgling was asleep on the shroud by 8:30 P.M. Rio terminated his guard duty session much earlier than he had done previously, no doubt due to the consistency of the fledgling's behavior at nightfall. Sadly, no other fledgling was observed, which meant that it was very likely that there was only one.

More of her later.

15

Bikes and Films

(1991 - continued)

June 17 was a peregrine bicycle touring day. At 7:15 A.M., I pedaled off to the Riverside Church site where there were three young on the wing. I had visited the site only once that season and I missed the special ambience of the location; the beauty of the church itself, the seemingly unending stretch of trees in Riverside Park along the expansive Hudson River, and the imposing Grant's Tomb. I planned also to visit the New York Hospital and the Pan Am sites.

I crossed the Queensboro Bridge, worked my way west to Central Park, and plunged into it with whirring legs. I enjoyed the change of pace afforded by the park's dearth of vehicular traffic and people. Most of the people in the park were walking to work on that particular Monday morning at eight o'clock. I zipped northward to the park's 110th Street exit, turned left, and continued going west until I reached Riverside Drive. Turning northward, I had half a mile to go to Riverside and I was becoming anxious; but when I stopped a few blocks south of Riverside, I immediately found a fledgling perched on a Riverside gargoyle. What a thrill to find a fledgling so quickly and to observe its apparent health and serenity while it meticulously preened its tail feathers.

My mind raced through the first hour and a half of my already successful excursion. An important aspect of my pleasure related to my mode of transportation. Travel by bicycle generates a special feeling for the areas traversed because the visual elements are close and personal. I had traveled from my own neighborhood of residential dwellings, apartment buildings, and one-family homes through increasingly more commercial sections until I was moving through a heavily trafficked business and factory area. The Queensboro Bridge provided wonderful views of the East River, Roosevelt Island, and the crowded island of Manhattan. Then I was immersed in the congested streets of Manhattan, where the buildings seemed to be piled one on top of another. Every square foot of space that was not occupied by a structure was covered by a vehicle or a person. Central Park appeared like an oasis in a mirage except that it was vibrantly real: walkers, runners, bikers, loungers, lakes, birds, and cars. Then onto hot, crowded streets for the last segment to get to Riverside where spirits are uplifted for many in many different ways.

From Riverside Drive, directly across from the church, I observed an adult peregrine perched high up on the edifice. I continued on for one more block to Grant's Tomb, where I heard a fledgling plaintively calling. Then I spotted it as it craned its head in every direction looking for either its siblings or parents. A youngster flew around the church and alighted on it but, due to the timing of my observations, I was unsure as to whether I was observing one individual or two. At any rate, I had seen an adult and two of the three young at the site.

My energy level was high and I headed downtown to the Pan Am site. I raced down Riverside Drive and along West End Avenue to get to 42nd Street, where I headed crosstown to Grand Central Station. Scanning the upper reaches of the Pan Am and Lincoln buildings was unsuccessful. However, I did find an adult peregrine perched on a Chrysler Building antenna. Since it showed no inclination to leave its perch, I moved on to the third site on my itinerary, the New York Hospital.

I pedaled eastward to York Avenue, then north to the hospital. Several blocks from the site, I spied a fledgling perched on the west side of the building. Riding two more blocks gave me a view of the building's north side, where I observed an adult. I checked the hospital's smokestack and found another fledgling. Try as I might, I could not find any of the other peregrines. I had already seen seven and possibly eight birds at three sites and still had the Throgs to survey. As before, I asked myself, "Where else but in New York City could one bicycle to three peregrine nesting sites within three hours and see seven or eight birds?" I anticipated that, in the years to come, the number of nesting sites would increase in this urban peregrine stronghold, allowing even a greater number of birds to be seen on such a trip.

When I returned home, I could not find any of the Throgs peregrines. But in the afternoon, I saw an adult and the fledgling. The last observation for the day was that of the youngster asleep on a shroud at the Bronx tower. The third chick still had not been seen and we were sure that it was lost. The toll of two lost chicks was very heavy. Yet we rejoiced in the good fortune of the surviving fledgling and gradually the living bird erased the thoughts of the absent ones.

On June 20, the American Broadcasting System sent a crew to New York City to televise the peregrine story for their "Good Morning America" program. They had already taped an interview with Chris at the Riverside site and now were going to cover the Throgs site. Dolores and I rendezvoused with Chris, Barbara Loucks, and the ABC crew at the Throgs. A traffic lane was blocked off to vehicles and the videotaping started right on the roadway with a shot of the Queen perched above us on a handcable. Interestingly, when we drove onto the Throgs, Rio had been perched on a drainpipe near the top of the tower and there he remained throughout the taping period.

We entered the eyrie area, to the great consternation of the Queen. She yelled vigorously but did not fly at us. Three factors reduced the impact of our intrusion and took the edge off her aggressiveness: first, her fledgling was not in the area; second, we did not approach the nest box but remained behind a group of beams; third, Rio did not appear at the eyrie to help defend it. I was filmed making an inspection of the eyrie. When we departed from the site, Rio was still perched on the tower and the Queen was soaring above it.

The ABC crew returned to Cryder House with Dolores and me. They filmed the Throgs from our terrace and the birds whenever they flew. We were interviewed in an effort to chronicle a day in the lives the peregrines and to educate the public. A five-minute segment of film was aired two weeks later.

The ensuing days were filled with interesting observations, such as the fledgling chasing a white pigeon; it was to no avail. Trying to hunt, at this stage of her development, is almost as important as actually making a kill. Shortly after, Rio also attacked a pigeon. Hunting provides the utmost drama because the peregrines' consummate flying skills are exhibited and the outcome is never sure.

One morning, the fledgling alertly eyed everything that moved. She made passes at many different creatures but the well-executed dive at a rat scurrying along the beach was unprecedented. The rat gained sanctuary under an abandoned pier. Twenty minutes later, the fledgling returned. She obviously remembered the furry stranger and wanted to check the area for it.

The youngster also streaked after the Queen whenever she was aloft. When that game was unavailable, she attacked crows. Her entire world was encompassed by an area of only a few thousand square yards adjacent to the Throgs; but that contained a vibrant melange of many wild creatures that truly characterized the area as wild despite the encroachments of humans.

On another morning, the Queen had hunted unsuccessfully several times by 8:00 A.M., prompting the fledgling's food-begging vocalizations. The Queen pursued five pigeons over Long Island Sound and her perfect approach yielded a kill. She alit on pier 5 with her prize and fed her youngster. Later, the fledgling attacked a great egret and a double-crested cormorant. The Queen assisted her youngster on these sorties. No doubt the size of the adversaries must have prompted the Queen to become involved because she would not otherwise have participated in such foolishness.

The last hunt of the day occurred after 7:00 P.M., when the Queen flew directly at a pigeon, rattling it to the extent that it could not muster an adequate escape attempt. She gathered it in and flew with Rio in hot pursuit; often he did not receive his meal until late in the day and only after the youngster had been fed.

Steady rain the next morning did not deter the fledgling from harassing a gull. Rio flew with prey, inspiring the fledgling to give chase, whereupon Rio dropped the carcass into the water; neither of them tried to retrieve it. Rio landed above the 1983 eyrie and the fledgling followed suit. The very wet youngster, finding that the ledge had some dry areas, promptly placed her body down flat.

Two hours later, the fledgling was again chasing after her parents with great vitality. She flew after Rio, calling loudly. This was clearly a request for food, which Rio did not choose to heed. The youngster ascended and dove down toward Rio as if he were the prey. Then she pursued Queen and tail-chased her for thirteen minutes without a rest period. She was robustly developed and she seemed to have inherited her mother's tenacity in the pursuit of flying objects. The Queen was a master of the tail-chase technique, frequently doggedly pursuing birds until they fatigued or failed to maneuver out of the clutch of her talons. She had captured many birds that would have eluded a less determined predator.

Later, the fledgling was aloft clutching a small bird. The Queen stooped at her, causing her to drop it. In the afternoon, Rio flew to the anchorage with prey and indulged in a quiet repast. While Rio was dining, the fledgling harassed crows and gulls at the Cryder House and Cryder Point boat piers. The fledgling perched on a pier railing but the Queen evidently did not approve of the fledgling's companions. She went to Rio, appropriated his meal, and flew close to the youngster, trying to lure the wayward fledgling back to the Throgs. Rio joined his mate in this attempt but the ploy did not work and they returned to the Throgs with only the food for solace.

The fledgling finally flew back to the Throgs and chased her mother. Rio was perched on the tower, a tempting target that she could not resist. She approached his perch as if she were going to alight on him. At the very last second, he jumped off his perch and the youngster kept on flying. Rio then made himself scarce, prompting the fledgling to again pursue the Queen, who stooped down and into the eyrie area.

The next evening, the fledgling sat on pier 1 quite contentedly with a full crop, having fed during the five-o'clock hour and again after six o'clock. The Queen arrived and commenced feeding on the remains of the fledgling's dinner. The youngster seemed unconcerned with her mother's appropriation of the leftovers. A mild breeze swirled the feathers off the pier as soon as the Queen separated them from the pigeon's body. Then the fledgling seized the carcass from her mother's grasp. The Queen fled the pier with an anguished vocalization and flew to the second pier. The fledgling resumed dining on the remains, followed by a complete beak wiping to indicate that her feeding session had been completed.

Both the Queen and I had been watching. Like myself, the Queen evidently took the youngster's signal at face value, for she flew back to pier 1 and landed directly on the remains. Regardless of whether she was hungry or not, though, the fledgling refused to give up the remains. She charged her mother, but instead of shouldering her off the edge, her usual tactic, she protestingly stood facing her, beak to beak. The Queen flew off rather than contest the irascible glutton; but she quickly returned to claim the remains. An identical scene was enacted. Then Rio tried his luck. But the fledgling had tired of the game and chose rather to dive at a great egret fishing from a moored barge below. There also were two black-crowned night herons feeding there but they did not receive any direct assaults. The heron croaked its distress call when the youngster made a pass at it but did not think enough of the attack to give up its fishing position.

During the last week of June, the youngster flew more often and started showing increased interest in chasing pigeons. One morning, she chased pigeons at the fender for over an hour, and when the pigeons were not flying, she tried to flush them off their perches. In one instance, Rio dove at a pigeon that the fledgling had flushed into flight. The outstanding event of that day was an in-flight prey transfer in which the Queen passed a prey item to the fledgling. The Queen flew toward the anchorage carrying prey, the fledgling flew to her, and, in the next instant, the fledgling had the carcass. A short while later, a male American kestrel flew through the area. Although the Queen undoubtedly had spotted him, he failed to provoke her wrath and went on his way unmolested.

Later, the fledgling had footed a pair of wings from a prey item. She held fast to them and flew along the ledge just as the adults do. While the youngster was playing, Rio was engaged in more important work. He spotted a monk parakeet and snared it before the wayward victim could gain sanctuary in a tree or building.

The fledgling continued harassing gulls and the pigeons at the fender. Her attack tactics had improved to the point where some gulls were choosing to dive into the water rather than risk being slashed by the talons of this young pest. In one extended sequence, the fledgling pursued a gull for several minutes over the East River. When the gull was able to break off the farce by diving down to the water, the pursuer instantly changed direction and chased after a pair of black-crowned night herons. One changed its course while the other continued on and the fledgling honed in on the second individual. The heron soon divined that this was no ordinary adversary. It began to take evasive action, which served it well enough to allow it to reach the shelter of the fender. The fledgling alighted above the heron but the heron

212

wisely did not stir for a quarter of an hour. When it did try to leave the safety of the fender, the fledgling attacked it again. The heron retreated into the fender and eventually the youngster lost interest in it; there were so many other interesting things to do.

The fledgling had been on the wing for more than two weeks and her flying skills had improved markedly. She seemed to enjoy landings which required pinpoint accuracy, such as on the thin handcable. Often she alighted with extra verve, evidenced by an increase in speed on the approach and the flare of the wings and tail which enabled her to decelerate and to land as lightly as a feather. The amazing transformation from unsure, sloppy landings to elegantly fluid ones was almost complete.

The aftermath of one peregrine hunt resulted in a disabled pigeon grasping onto barnacles on the anchorage. While the peregrines displayed no interest in this vulnerable creature, we had learned that, despite their apparent indifference toward a pigeon in this situation, peregrines often bide their time until it is ripe for capture. Of course, there are instances when they simply abandon a downed bird.

In this instance, the tide rose, immersed the barnacles, and the pigeon had to struggle to retain its precarious foothold. The Queen alighted on pier 1 and eyed her victim below. The wounded pigeon went into the water and floated away, prompting the Queen to change her surveillance position to a set of three pilings. The fledgling had been chasing gulls and stooping on a double-crested cormorant but when she saw the Queen on this rarely used perch, her interest was piqued and she alighted nearby. She immediately noticed the pigeon in the water and riveted her eyes on it. The pigeon finally expired and, as it sank deeper into the water, the Queen started flying short circles around it. After a few tentative attempts at snatching the bird from the water, the Queen deftly footed the bird and flew to the anchorage. This was a good lesson for the youngster, who had been mesmerized by the scene. The youngster followed her mother and was rewarded with a meal.

By July 1, the fledgling was two months old and had been on the wing for almost three weeks. Her flying ability had improved to the point where, at times, we mistook her for one of her parents. But she had not yet begun hunting for herself. On this day, the Queen again retrieved a pigeon from the water and delivered it to the fledgling on the anchorage. On July 3, the youngster was observed carrying a large insect in her talons. She released it and quickly recaptured it. It was a sure sign that her hunting instinct was beginning to stir. Later, she chased a gull just above the water, which, in and of itself, was not a remarkable feat; but she had had to put on a very determined burst of speed to overtake the gull. This was important. The practical application of her flying prowess to the accomplishment of a goal, albeit still in the play stage, was very important for the development of her hunting prowess.

Independence Day morning at the beach viewing site opened with another predator at work. A great black-backed gull was on a nearby barge and had come into possession of an immature starling. The gull struck the dead bird several times as if trying to penetrate it. Then, changing its strategy, it picked up the bird in its beak and proceeded to swallow it whole. We could see the bulge in the gull's neck as the creature slid down to the digestive juices below.

The first peregrine hunting safari of the day was a classic attack directed against a huge flock of pigeons. The Queen flew directly at the flock and the first bird that broke ranks was thereafter the only one in her sights. She snared it on her second dive and took it to the Bronx anchorage to prepare it for her youngster. In the meantime, the fledgling was chasing pigeons at the fender but still had no good chance to capture one because it still lacked sufficient adroitness to overcome their wily tactics. The Queen arrived with her prey and the fledgling immediately gave chase and called for her meal. Rio also flew by, completing the family picture. They flew out of sight; end of scene. One hour later, the youngster was very doggedly tail-chasing a pigeon. Her determination was so akin to the Queen's frequently demonstrated tenacity in chasing prey that at first we mistook her for the Queen. We observers love to be fooled by youngsters. There is no greater accomplishment for a fledgling than to be able to emulate adult behavior.

The next morning there were some interesting behavioral observations in addition to the two pigeon kills that we, the watchers' claque, witnessed. A belted kingfisher had been frequently observed fishing near the barge moored adjacent to our beach vantage point. When the fledgling spotted the kingfisher, she tenaciously chased it, giving it no respite. The continuous swooping attacks of the youngster caused it to dive into the water, which befuddled the young peregrine for a few seconds. That was long enough to allow the kingfisher to take to its wings and escape. Until the peregrine again overtook it. This scenario was repeated six times before the quarry was finally able to make its escape.

A third pigeon capture later in the day employed an interesting tactic. The Queen was on the first pier across from the 1983 eyrie and observed a pigeon in it. The essence of her successful attack was in the approach. She dropped off the pier, flew toward the opening at a level just below it, which prevented the prey from seeing her, swooped up, and alighted directly onto the pigeon.

Ted recounted observations that he had made on the mornings of July 10 and July 11. The fledgling started by chasing her parents and a great blue heron that chanced to fly by. She dove at it repeatedly for eleven minutes. Despite these extremely energetic efforts, the youngster showed no sign of flagging. This display of tremendous stamina augured well for her future in the wild.

Next, she harassed a double-crested cormorant but soon lost interest and captured a monarch butterfly. The fledgling flew toward the Queen just as she had alighted with a fresh pigeon kill. But the youngster was more interested in chasing than eating and when the Queen flew, she pursued her all the way to the Bronx tower, leaving the pigeon remains behind. Then the Queen flattened her body against a Bronx tower shroud as if she were embracing the shroud.

The next morning produced the most meaningful observation of the post-fledging period. The fledgling was observed flying just above the water carrying a live pigeon. The location of the parent birds precluded the possibility that they had caught the prey and transferred it to the fledgling. This was her first known successful hunt. She alighted on the barge with her booty but waited a few minutes before starting to feed on it. The piteous pigeon was very much alive, a fact which seemed to be of no interest to the fledgling. She continued to pull at the bird, mostly about the neck area, until she inadvertently killed it. It had taken a full nine minutes for the pigeon to expire. After a few minutes, the youngster flew off toward the Bronx tower with the remains firmly clasped in her talons. She made no attempt to land. Rio then pursued her in a manner suggesting that he wanted some of the prey. How the tables had turned; the fledgling had made the kill and, having possession of the food, she would for the moment be the leader.

Shortly after this incident, the fledgling was again on the hunt. She pursued a pigeon close to the water. Rio was perched high above on the tower and the Queen was not in view. After the youngster had launched two unsuccessful dives, the Queen stooped at the pigeon with great speed and snared it. This lone fledgling was receiving invaluable experience and training that would hone its skills and turn her into a masterful predator. Enough so that the topic deserves some treatment of its own; hence the following chapter.

16

Training and Instincts

(1991 - continued)

The next series of activities relate to the way parent birds nurture their young; and how the peregrines' instincts are revealed in their actions. The subject of training is interesting to behaviorists because it is enmeshed in the essence of a creature's innate abilities versus learned techniques. For example, there are particular acts involving prey which the parent birds engage in only when they have fledglings on the wing for several weeks.

On this particular morning at the Throgs in mid-July, 1991, the Queen was carrying a live pigeon and flew an inordinately long distance with it. The fledgling approached the Queen, which prompted her to release her captive. The pigeon wisely flew into the Throgs to seek sanctuary. The Queen and the fledgling followed but neither pigeon nor peregrine came out of the area. It was an example of the adult's attempt to train the youngster to attack a pigeon. I believe that the adults are genetically programed to perform this type of behavior. Another example of this behavior occurred a short while later. The Queen was pursuing a pigeon with the youngster following close behind. She hit the pigeon lightly and the fledgling dove at it before it escaped, unscathed. The Queen could have just as easily dealt the quarry a crippling blow but she obviously wanted the fledgling to have a go at it.

By the third week of July, the fledgling had sharpened her skills and increased her hunting frequency, often with the adults' assistance. As an example, when the fledgling initiated a hunt of a white pigeon, the Queen joined the fray, seized it, and released it after two wingbeats. The pigeon flew for its life, with the youngster in pursuit. The pigeon won. Later, the fledgling chased after Rio, quite determinedly, although she must have realized that she did not have a chance of overtaking him. The speedster easily kept her at a distance and could maneuver in ways that she could not hope to match. Again, there was a pigeon in the water and the Queen made some feeble attempts to pull it from the water while the fledgling looked on. The pigeon went to a watery grave rather than into a peregrine's maw. The lesson might have been that a determined effort is often required to obtain a meal even when the prey has been disabled.

On July 20, while the Queen was perched on the tower, the fledgling flew to Cryder House and went after a parrot that was assuredly an escaped pet. It took haven on a terrace railing until the youngster flew off. The highlight of the day occurred later, however, when Dave Gardner observed the fledgling capture a pigeon. From its perch on a handcable, it stooped downward at a pigeon and captured it on the first pass. This was the fledgling's first kill that had been observed and recorded in its entirety.

The air was heavy with heat, moisture, and ozone the next morning. The Queen, Rio, and their fledgling were on the fifth and sixth piers south of the anchorage. The fledgling was dining on a prey item that had been reduced to a small tidbit. When the youngster flew off to an adjacent pier, Rio alighted upon the remains and started to strip what little meat still remained. After a few minutes, he flew from the pier down to the anchorage ledge with the miniscule leftovers. The fledgling followed him to the ledge and also alighted but did not try to reclaim the prey. Rio started feeding and the youngster hopped along the ledge until she turned a corner and went out of sight. Rio continued to feed but abruptly flew from the ledge and, oddly, dropped the remains into the water. A short while later, the fledgling returned and circled the remains. She lowered her legs as if to grasp it but never really made a serious attempt to pick it from the water. Again, this appeared to be an attempt to encourage the fledgling to practice hunting techniques.

At 8:00 P.M., the fledgling was alone on the very top of the tower. Darkness had started setting in early because the sky was heavy with clouds. This was the time that the peregrines usually settle in for the night. But the fledgling kept looking around very alertly. While I waited to see what she would do, I could not help thinking that her remaining time at the Throgs, her only home for all of the twelve weeks or so of her life, would soon be up. It was sad to contemplate that even if she were to survive to adulthood, very likely we might not learn of her success.

For this evening, however, encouraging signs of her successful future came quickly when she leaped from her perch and chased a pigeon as it traveled from the Throgs toward land. The youngster pursued its quarry past Cryder House and followed it when it turned inland and flew between the many buildings. The pigeon's only escape tactic was to fly faster than its pursuer. The fledgling alighted on a cable; alert and agitated, she was still in the hunting mode. In two minutes, she flew west, out of my view, with a purposeful, methodical flapping motion that indicated she was on the prowl again. She returned flying several feet above the water and gained altitude within the last fifty yards of the second pier so that she could land on it. Her behavior was normal for her tender age but demonstrated her need to further hone her hunting skills. While she had twice captured prey, and possibly more than twice, she was still too slow on the wing and was not capable of performing the adroit aerial maneuvers required to attain a higher kill rate. She may have gone to bed hungry that night but that condition might serve to motivate her the following morning and help sharpen her attack tactics.

Ted witnessed a kill by the Queen in which she raked the pigeon on her first pass and bound into it on her second. Later, while the Queen and her fledgling were aloft, Ted observed another (large brown) peregrine. The fledgling joined her mother in pursuing the visitor. The Queen was very aggressive toward the interloper while the resident fledgling merely trailed close behind. The interaction continued for several minutes with the three females wheeling about over the Little Bay area. The Queen twice intertwined her talons with those of the intruding youngster and shook her vigorously; she inflicted no injury. At this time, there could be as many as five fledged females at large in the New York City area but we could not tell whether this youngster was one of them.

At 5:00 P.M. the following evening (July 22), seven cormorants were winging their way westward below the Throgs several feet above the water. Suddenly there was a brown streak flapping furiously over them as it headed toward a target well beyond them. It was the fledgling on one of her attempts to capture prey over the East River. A few minutes later, the fledgling returned, flying just inches above the water. The wind was rising steadily as a weather front rapidly moved in to the area.

The sky darkened as the rain clouds increased and flashes of lightning flickered across the eastern sky. Peals of thunder boomed through the heavy, moisture-laden air but, strangely, there were many more bolts of lightning than thunderclaps. I wondered where the fledgling was now that some of the wind gusts were exceeding thirty miles an hour and the light level was more appropriate for 8:30 P.M. rather than the present time of 5:30 P.M. I looked upward and saw the youngster soaring with perfect aplomb several hundred feet above me. She would turn in one direction and then another with no particular goal except to use the wind. She moved with the wind for a short distance and then against it. The wind was the power and she was the art form; she could move in any direction, upward or downward, performing almost all her aerial choreography without the need to utilize her own motive power. At about twelve weeks of age, she was a marvelous creature that epitomized the future and yet, at the same time, probably stood a less an than even chance of surviving her first winter. Finally, heavy rain cascaded down and I could no longer see my special young neighbor.

July 25 was a mostly rainy day and at 8:00 A.M. I found the fledgling perched on the fourth pier. My primary goal each day was to find the youngster because the longer she remained at the Throgs the better would be her chances of surviving. She was very wet and was emitting that plaintive call that we had heard so many times before. After a few minutes, she repositioned herself onto the lip of a beam that placed her out of the rain. It was her "rain spot" and was similar to the location which her parents used in inclement weather.

On July 28, at 8:20 P.M., the Queen alighted on the Throgs. She appeared agitated, looked all around the area without moving, and then clomped inward out of my view. I tried not to read anything into her actions but it seemed that she might have been searching for her fledgling. This was the first day, since the chick had fledged, that she had not been seen at all. Dave and I had observed a total of seven hours during the day, but did not see or hear her. We could expect the youngster, at almost thirteen weeks, to emancipate herself at any time. The ensuing days would disclose whether or not she had taken her leave of the Throgs. Whatever the case, she was in our thoughts.

July 29 was rainy but visibility was good when Rio flew from pier 1 to pier 5. The Queen landed near him and Rio moved to the thirteenth pier and again the Queen followed. Rio took to the air and, surprisingly, flew right at his mate as if he were performing some post-season courtship etiquette. He moved to pier 15 with no slackening in the Queen's interest in accompanying him. This was the second consecutive day that the fledgling had not been observed; it appeared that she had finally moved on to investigate the rest of the world. The Queen and Rio had been steadfast mates for six seasons. Their behavior of the past two days of staying close to each other was a marked change. Were they searching for their fledgling or did they just want to be together because suddenly they had no responsibilities? Of course, one cannot surely know what leads to certain behavior in a truly wild animal but it is fascinating to try to comprehend the factors that might have precipitated a particular pattern of behavior.

On the first day of August, as I stepped out onto our terrace at 7:30 P.M., the sound of a peregrine in trouble intruded into the serenity of the balmy summer evening. I saw two peregrines moving toward one another at the tower. Even without the aid of my binocular, it was clear that the bird that was diving downward was the smaller of the two. It was Rio and his target was a recently fledged female peregrine. Could this be our own Throgs fledgling returning to her natal territory? If it were she, would Rio be able to recognize her? After only a four-day absence, one would expect that he could. And, if he did, would that alter his attitude toward her? He stooped at her and passed very closely but there was no attempt to strike her. The youngster turned to present talons but neither seemed to want to make contact. They vocalized intermittently while they played out their aerial acrobatics. When the interloper finally headed west, both the Queen and Rio flew past Cryder House. It was quiet and they were so close to me that I was able to hear one of them call. It was a strange kind of chirping that I had not heard before.

Rio returned to the Throgs in less than a minute and alighted on a handcable. Within seconds, the Queen landed fifteen yards from him. They sat facing west with the setting sun illuminating them. They were clearly disturbed by the intrusion into their territory. Ten minutes passed before either one of them mustered up the effort to leave its perch. They were immobile except for the Queen, who, for half a minute, stretched her wings fully into a rarely seen pose. Finally, the Queen flew to midspan and then out of sight to the west. Rio sat for an additional seven minutes before leaving.

When the episode was over, I reviewed it to try to make sense of it. Resident peregrines must repulse all transgressors because without a territory they cannot procreate. Once the breeding season is completed, as marked by the dispersal of the fledglings, any peregrine, be it a dispersed young or not, is treated as an outsider by the residents and is escorted out of the territory. Whether or not the adults were able to recognize their own progeny is still questionable.

I compared this event to a similar occurrence at the Tappan Zee Bridge in 1989, when a fledgling was taken from the site for a period of several days. When I placed the fledgling back up on the bridge, the adult male checked it out very carefully before feeding it. Of course, that situation was very different in that the adult was still in the feeding phase of the breeding season whereas Rio was through with his procreative chores. We will never learn the truth about this happening but for me it was a moving experience nevertheless.

After the fledgling had been gone for about a week, the adults more and more exhibited a decided interest in each other. They perched close to one another, followed each other, and shared meals. It seemed as though they had a need to recement their pair bond because their progeny was no longer there to provide the common thread of their lives together. Interestingly, I found the Queen in the 1983 eyrie on three consecutive days. On the third occasion, Rio was with her; they sat side by side, only inches apart. This space has no meaning for Rio because he was not at the Throgs in 1983 when it had been the eyrie. The question of whether the Queen remembered it as a special space where she had fledged her first young was unanswerable. More likely, it was just another area that impinged on her memory with no specific association.

The Raptor Research Foundation's (RRF) 1991 annual meeting was held in early November in Tulsa, Oklahoma. Dr. Dean Amadon, and I traveled there together. Dolores and I had first met Dr. Amadon several years earlier at a Hawk Migration Association of North America conference in Cape May, New Jersey. His interest in our peregrine work prompted his subscription to my *NYCAERIES* newsletter and then to meetings and communications which developed into a lasting friendship.

RRF oral papers included that of Ambrose & Swem (U.S. Fish and Wildlife Service), which stated that the arctic peregrine falcon *(Falco peregrinus tundrius)* and the American peregrine falcon *(F. p. anatum)* in northern North America, currently listed as threatened and endangered, respectively, will be reviewed for delisting because of the support for such change deriving from increased population statistics. Craig and Enderson of the Colorado Division of Wildlife reported that the improved rate of reoccupancy and productivity, coupled with reduced eggshell thinning at peregrine nesting sites in Colorado, lead to the opinion that the Colorado population is secure. Moen & Tordoff (Bell Museum of Natural History) and Redig (The Raptor Center, University of Minnesota) stated: "The reintroduced peregrines differ both genetically and demographically from those which occupied the Midwest prior to extirpation in the 1950's," and "genetically . . . show a high level of inbreeding. . . . The population is partially migratory . . . roughly 65% urban. Historical eyries along the Mississippi River remain unoccupied."

Back on the home front, early on the morning of November 30, I found Rio perched on the south side of pier 1. I scanned the Throgs searching for the Queen. Instead, I discovered an almost totally white pigeon sitting on the sill of the large, louvered opening on the south side of the anchorage. I surmised that the pigeon had taken refuge there in response to an attack by Rio. The pigeon did not seem to be injured but also showed no inclination to leave the relative safety afforded by this awkward perch. I stepped away for several minutes and returned to find the pigeon deeply immersed in the water. Undoubtedly, it had taken wing and had been intercepted by Rio, who either drove it or hit it into the water. It was still alive but did not make any effort to use its wings, probably being exhausted beyond recovery. As the victim floated away from the anchorage, Rio appeared increasingly anxious, but he made no effort to extricate it from the water. He had never been observed to retrieve a pigeon from the water but I did expect the Queen to arrive to pick up an easy meal. Suddenly a gray shadow passed across the anchorage; the Queen indeed had arrived to claim the prize.

She circled the pigeon slowly at a distance of several yards. Her next two passes were much closer but there was no attempt to touch the waterlogged bird. She alighted nearby on the top of a set of piles. The pigeon still held its head erect but did not move. The Queen then circled the pigeon, moving closer and closer to it, and on her third pass extended her talons down toward the sinking body and touched it. Her next approach was even more determined and she hit its head hard and the bird flipped onto its back. It was then floating upside down, which prompted the Queen to turn sharply and fly directly back to it. She thrust her talons at the now inert body, striking it but missing her attempt to bind to it. On her next attempt, she was obviously very determined to claim the prize before it disappeared beneath the enveloping waters. She approached with fanned wings and tail as if to land on the pigeon. She was going to claim the bird even if she had to get wet. Skillfully, without immersing herself, she snatched it and flew to the anchorage.

Rio had witnessed the entire episode and joined his mate. He waited patiently while she checked her surroundings in that matter-of-fact way that many wild creatures do when they are about to eat or rest. Finally, she tore into her meal. The head came off first. Depluming was interspersed with the swallowing of chunks of meat. When the intestines were stripped out, she gulped down only a portion of them, allowing the remainder to fall to the side. She purposefully downed some of the smaller feathers while discarding the larger ones.

Rio twice called to his mate, plaintively. No doubt he was asking for his share, reminding her that he had downed the bird that she was now enjoying. She ignored him and continued feeding very determinedly. An immature herring gull flew very close to them, which elicited their warning vocalizations. The gull's second pass drew a stronger protest and it left the area. Rio's patience ran out after twenty minutes. He moved very close to the Queen but did not immediately try to take any of the prey. Then he deftly reached through her legs and snared a chunk of meat. She moved off several inches with a disturbed look on her face. She gazed outward, obviously planning her next move, which would be escaping to another site with her meal intact. The Queen flew from the ledge and disappeared from view. Rio dug into the tidbits that were strewn about the ledge: head, intestines, and legs. After finishing these items, he flew off in the same direction as had the Queen. He surely knew her every haunt and would find her. Just as surely, she would eventually share her meal with him.

Peregrines share their kills despite the abundance of prey in their hunting territory. It is their way. It is their way of continuing to strengthen their bond. It is efficient; there is no waste and fewer hunting attempts are required. Each hunting episode generates some danger to the predator. From an observer's viewpoint, this sharing propensity also provides added opportunities to witness interactions.

17

Marine Parkway

(1991- continued)

The first observation for the 1991 season was on March 9 when a male peregrine took prey to its female partner at the south tower of the Marine Parkway Bridge. This courtship behavior indicated great potential for an initial breeding attempt. The peregrines were frequenting a gusset (a steel plate that connects beams) that was inaccessible to interlopers and provided protection from adverse weather; however, it seemed too small to accommodate developing chicks. The slightest mishap could result in a chick being pushed off its ledge and a perilous fall to either the roadway or swirling water below.

This galvanized DEC. To provide whatever assistance this new breeding pair might need, Chris Nadareski inspected the site and determined that any attempt to install a nest box would be extremely disturbing to the nesters. Instead, he planned to monitor the site frequently and to enlist the aid of the Triborough Bridge and Tunnel Authority workers and administration at the bridge and that of the Rangers and National Park Service staff headquartered at the adjacent Floyd Bennett Field. I notified all of the peregrine watchers I knew of the need for site monitoring. Hopefully, this approach would provide us with an early-warning system if a problem were to arise. As the season unfolded, this network of watchers would prove to be invaluable.

During spring, the bridge underwent repair work that included the resurfacing of the pedestrian walkway. Its closing made the volunteer watchers' task more difficult because they were not able to view the eyrie from the walkway, the best location to do so. One watcher, Paul

Keim, president of the Brooklyn Bird Club, made his observations from Riis Park in Rockaway, one-third of a mile away. One reward for his efforts occurred on April 26 when an adult alighted on the top of a light standard near his viewing position. The peregrine seemed to be scrutinizing him and they actually made eye contact. What a thrill for a new watcher who had already been fascinated by the peregrine mystique. Paul's observations continued to disclose very encouraging behavior patterns. On May 4, the female captured a pigeon and carried it up to the south tower. Shortly, the male snared a mockingbird that had made the fatal mistake of flying into the confines of the tower.

The people who informally report their observations form an important foundation of the monitoring process. I was gratified to be able to be part of the network. The peregrines were the primary beneficiaries of these efforts but their importance to those who were directly involved and to the scientific community were additional factors.

On May 14, Chris and I spent several hours at the bridge's south tower and observed the adults frequenting the gusset that appeared to be their nest. The female was perched on one side of the gusset and five blue jays were perched on the other side of it. The jays were rooted to their perches, obviously aware that the peregrine was their mortal enemy and that any move out into the open would most likely be their last. While our attention was temporarily elsewhere, the jays slipped away. We thought that they had escaped but a few moments later the female arrived with a blue jay and fed it to her chicks. While we could not see the nestlings, the adult's bending, tearing, and other movements clearly indicated that she was feeding young.

Chris was able to read the letter "K" on the female's band, identifying her as being the 1989 New York Hospital fledgling whose band had been read the previous year at Floyd Bennett Field. She and her mate were constantly at the gusset, strengthening our belief that they were tending to nestlings. We wanted to corroborate this conclusion but there was no easy access to a position affording a view of the nest. Our problem was solved when Vince Zambetti, a consulting bridge engineer, whom I first had met at the bridge a year ago, described a route that we could climb which would afford us a clear view. When we declined the use of this route, because we felt that it was perilous for inexperienced climbers, Vince offered to go up himself. He insisted that he had climbed the route many times and, furthermore, that he needed to inspect some work in that area.

We were concerned for his safety and advised him of the two main dangers related to making an inspection of the nest. First, we fully expected that the adults would attack him when he approached their eyrie. He had not yet faced two angry, attacking peregrines who were determined to defend their nestlings. It could be very unnerving, especially for a newcomer to the peregrine scene, to be caught in an exposed position. The second danger related to the potential disturbance to the nestlings and the possibility that they might be flushed from their nest prematurely. While we were discussing the uncertainties of the situation, the adults practically made the decision for us. They launched an archetypical hunt against five pigeons that took them far from the bridge. The male initiated the hunt and was quickly joined by his mate. She strategically took a nearly parallel route that allowed them to converge on the hapless birds from two directions about five hundred yards from the bridge.

The three of us watched the spectacle with rapt concentration. The pigeons were close together as the male dove toward them. I alerted Vince to follow any pigeon that might break away on its own. Indeed, the very first pass caused one pigeon to flee by carving out its own path. This spelled its doom as the peregrines alternately stooped at the lone bird, driving it down to within a few feet of the water. On the eighth attempt, it was snared by the female and the peregrines flew off toward Brooklyn with their prize. It was apparent that they were not going to return to the bridge directly, prompting us to seize this opportunity to have Vince climb up to the nest area without the danger of the adults attacking him.

Obligingly, Vince climbed the ladders and beams until he was positioned across from the nest. He peered into the dim space while Chris and I kept a sharp lookout for the peregrines' return. The combination of good timing and a little luck held, allowing Vince to complete his entire inspection and then to descend without interference. He observed two white objects that were very close to one another. He was very sure that they were chicks because, in addition to the movement of feathers caused by the brisk wind, he detected movements that could only be those of a live body. We had not provided him with binoculars but now we wished we had done so because

228

his observations would have been more definitive. Nevertheless, we were now almost positive that the Marine Parkway/Gil Hodges Memorial Bridge held our newest peregrine eyrie. This site had succeeded in producing the first known brood of chicks to issue from a peregrine that had been born in the New York City metropolitan area since the peregrine reintroduction program that started in the 1970s.

Our euphoria was short-lived because the adult female was killed two days later at Floyd Bennett Field, apparently as a result of colliding with a vehicle. She died two years after her birth at the New York Hospital site. The questions that leaped to mind were whether the surviving male would abandon the chicks and, if he were to stay with them, would he be able to provide sufficient food and protection to carry them through their developmental phases to independence? Because both male and female peregrines have a strong drive to nurture their young, we expected that the male would not abandon his chicks. Whenever he had to go afield to hunt for prey, the chicks would, of necessity, and of course, have to be left unprotected. We hoped that there were only two nestlings because having fewer mouths to feed would lighten his burden.

Single Parent

In the ensuing days, the male continued to deliver prey to the nest and apparently feed the young. Chris and I arrived at the site at noon on May 20, after having spent the morning banding the chicks at the Verrazano-Narrows Bridge and making observations at the Outerbridge Crossing. We saw the adult male capture a blue jay and consume it. We had hoped to observe the male feed the nestlings, because if it should be determined that the chicks were not being fed adequately, it would have become necessary to remove them lest they starve. Chris had to go to another site and I continued the monitoring. I set up my scope on the walkway and was prepared for as long a vigil as might be needed. The male perched near the nest and did not move appreciably for an hour and a half. Undoubtedly, this particular perch was selected because it afforded him an almost 180-degree view southward toward Rockaway.

When two mourning doves flew close by the bridge toward Rockaway, he eagerly pursued them. This sort of scenario especially interested him now because, since his mate had been lost, the dual responsibilities of feeding his nestlings and protecting them apparently had changed one fundamental element of his hunting logistics. He was loath to leave the chicks alone for any appreciable length of time. Therefore, instead of employing the more usual attack tactic of pursuing prey over the open expanses of the surrounding water, he now chose to make shorter pursuits of birds closer to the bridge.

On one such attack, he failed to capture a dove, but within ten minutes, he returned with a pigeon. I first discovered his return when I noticed a shadow moving along the walkway directly toward me. The sun had formed a sharply defined silhouette that clearly depicted the peregrine as it carried a pigeon. And to further raise my level of excitement, the shadow stopped directly over my head. I looked up but could not see the bird, although it was on a beam only thirty-five feet above me, because my viewing angle was too acute. A shower of feathers wafted down as he speedily deplumed the pigeon. I took my scope and quickly moved along the walkway in hopes of obtaining a better viewing angle and possibly read its bands. Unfortunately, the bird's position did not afford me a view of it from any location on the walkway. My disappointment was assuaged when it flew up to the nest carrying the prey and for ten minutes engaged in what was an obvious feeding session. I could not actually see the nestlings, but the adult's position and body movements indicated that he was feeding chicks. I left the site with a joyful feeling because I was sure that the youngsters were being fed.

I drove to the bridge five days later with Dolores, Dave Gardner, and Tony Tierno. We saw the adult male deliver prey to the young at the nest, although we were unable to see them directly. It was edifying to contemplate that one peregrine was doing the work of two and succeeding at it.

I traveled the twenty-four miles to the bridge by bicycle for my next visit. Vince Zambetti was there and I brought him up to date on the nesting status. We watched an exciting drama unfold when the male avidly pursued two pigeons and skillfully slashed one, causing it to go into the water. The peregrine did not even try to retrieve it from the water. This represented a parallel with the peregrines at the

Throgs, where the female is strong enough to pull a pigeon from the water but the male is not.

The male returned to the eyrie but was soon aloft again. I could not see the object of his attention but I knew that he had to have had a target in mind because his flight was very purposeful. The unwavering, vigorous wingbeats were surely speeding him on a collision course with a creature that most probably was not yet aware that it had transgressed into a peregrine's territory. Pity the bird that did so during the breeding season when defensive drives and food requirements are at their highest levels. As I followed the peregrine's flight, he turned sharply and I saw a large, black bird. It was a turkey vulture. No injury was inflicted, the vulture continued on its journey, and the peregrine returned to his guard duty at the eyrie.

We still did not know this male's origin. I had always suspected that he might be his mate's sibling because he very probably was the same male that had been observed with her at the bridge a year earlier. They had probably dispersed from the New York Hospital site in 1989 and traveled together until they had found this excellent territory only twelve miles away. Jean Bourque observed the male standing in a rain puddle on a Floyd Bennett Field runway early one morning. His use of the runway was worrisome because his mate was killed at a similar site. Peregrines are not equipped to deal with a fast-moving vehicle because there was nothing like it in its previous history. It takes multitudes of generations for a factor to be meaningfully introduced into a creature's ken. The peregrines will continue to suffer the dangers inherent in their new urban environments. The following day, Chris read the "J28J" on the male's alphanumeric leg band. That identified him as having been banded at the New York Hospital site in 1989. He was indeed the brother of his mate, the now dead female.

The male seemed to be feeding his young adequately but, in case there was insufficient food, Chris tried to assist him by providing day-old, frozen (thawed) bird chicks, raised and contributed by a falconer. The male declined these gifts and was able to provide enough food through his own efforts. Possibly the fact that the offering was already dead rendered it unattractive.

Chris observed the male being chased by a crow during one of his trips to Floyd Bennett Field. The crow was extremely dogged in his harassment and flew as close to the peregrine as it could without

231

actually touching it. The crow was very probably defending its territory against the peregrine's intrusion, just as the peregrine would have defended its territory.

Several days later, a nestling was recovered from the bridge walkway by National Park Service personnel stationed at Floyd Bennett Field. Chris took the bird, intending to place it back up on the bridge as soon as possible. It was a male less than four weeks of age and definitely not ready for flight. It needed to be placed on a spacious ledge within the adult male's view while he watched the other chick, still in the nest. The installation of a nest box would provide a secure spot for the nestling. The best location was a few yards below the nest, on the counterweight, which is six traffic lanes long and ten yards wide. Regrettably, it is lowered whenever the bridge roadway is lifted to accommodate a passing vessel. As luck would have it, however, the bridge was scheduled to be raised the very next day. Chris postponed the placement of the chick until the following day.

I met Chris that morning at Floyd Bennett Field, where he had secured the assignment of three National Park Service staff to assist us with the chick placement. We went to the bridge prepared with wood and nails for the nest box, crushed stone for the substrate, and tools. We arrived at the eyrie to find the male perched in his usual position adjacent to the nest. We unloaded our materials and, although we were quite close to him, there was no discernable reaction on his part. Despite the noise of the hammering as we put the box together, and our presence so close to the nest, he did not show any interest in us. Peregrines are very tolerant of noise, and other types of disturbances, if they are unable to see their origins. In this case, while we could at least see his tail, he could not see us at all. Because there is always the danger that a chick will bolt when put in a new location, Chris had managed the chick's diet during the two days that it had been in his custody so that the chick was hungry at this time. He placed fresh food in the nest box, a few minutes prior to putting the chick into it, hoping it would feed rather than flee. Also, we moistened the chick's wings with water to discourage him from flying immediately after being released. Normally, a bird tends to preen its wet, disturbed feathers rather than take to the air. The food ploy worked like a charm; the chick took no notice of its new surroundings and eagerly fed. Three of us quickly withdrew but Chris remained hidden on the counterweight to monitor the site. He wanted to be sure that the chick would stay at its new location and that the adult male would accept the chick in its new spot away from the natal ledge.

One of the National Park Service staff had mentioned that she had twice observed a peregrine perched on the main pier of the Cross Bay Veterans Memorial Bridge, three and one-half miles to the east of the Marine Parkway Bridge. As chance would have it, she would pass beneath the Cross Bay Bridge that very afternoon on her regular weekly trip to check on the progress of an ongoing water quality experiment. I took the opportunity to go along in order to check for peregrines. It would have been revealing if we were to find one because with Chris monitoring at the bridge we would have been sure that any peregrine that we found elsewhere would have been a different individual. We did not see a peregrine but we were rewarded with a remarkable raptor nesting discovery. A pair of ospreys were on a platform in the center of a small bay. The platform was set on pilings that provided a permanently posted sign warning mariners of shoals. The female was sitting as if she were on eggs and the male was right alongside her. There were sticks covering the entire platform and, although not numerous, they were in proper nesting position. The birds were either in the nesting mode or they were youngsters that were going through the motions.

I returned to the Marine Parkway Bridge, where everything was going as planned. The chick roamed around the top of the counterweight with obvious abandon but showed no inclination to go over its edge. The adult had accepted the new conditions and had fed the chick. We left the site with a wonderful feeling of accomplishment. Now we hoped that the youngster would stay on the ledge for the two additional weeks that were needed for his flight feathers to grow in and his flight muscles to develop sufficient strength to sustain flight.

Chris checked the site the next day and observed the male feed the chicks. He used a new perch that enabled him to watch both nestlings at the same time.

The following day brought more unwanted excitement. The second nestling had fallen to a beam about twenty-five feet above the roadway. This was dangerous because the next stop downward would be the roadway, or, if the chick were to miss the roadway level, the water fifty feet below would come next. Chris and I met at the bridge and obtained the help of the TBTA workers, who provided a motorized lift platform. The equipment lifted us to the chick and Chris retrieved it.

This female chick showed a great deal of spunk, unlike her placid brother. She yelled and tried to escape our clutches using her beak and talons. We appreciated her aggressiveness because it boded well for her survival potential but, for the moment, we had to deal with her feisty behavior. I held it while Chris affixed an identification band to its leg. He examined her and found her to be in excellent condition. Chris was concerned that because of this female's aggressiveness, there was a good possibility that, on placing her on the nest box ledge, she might flush off the edge. The same problem pertained to the male chick. He very well might flush from the ledge during the disturbance that was bound to be caused by both our presence on the ledge and the introduction of another chick into his area. In view of these potential perils, Chris arranged for the bridge to be closed to traffic for a few minutes during the release procedure. The Coast Guard patrolled below to rescue any chick that might have the misfortune of falling from the bridge. It was heartening to see the enthusiastic spirit of cooperation among such diverse organizations as the TBTA, the staff at the bridge, the United States Coast Guard, DEC, and the National Park Service.

Chris and I placed our equipment and the caged peregrine chick into the elevator for the trip up to the counterweight. The elevator did not function despite our ministrations and those of engineer Zambetti. Finally, we climbed ladders one hundred feet to the counterweight level.

The male chick was sitting in the nest box displaying a quizzical mien. We thought it very fortunate that he was safely in the box but he did not remain there and started clambering about in an agitated manner. The transport cage was too large to fit through the small opening from the elevator area to the counterweight. So we removed the chick from the cage and passed it through the opening by hand. She squirmed, yelled, and tried to bite our hands. To secure her and avoid damaging her flight feathers, we wrapped her in a foam pad forming a cylindrical shape. When Chris was ready to release the chick onto the ledge, I gave the signal to stop traffic. Chris released the chick and she merely stared at him as he withdrew. Evidently, she needed only a modest distance to feel secure.

Throughout the placement operation, the adult male remained nearby. He did not approach us but he did fly nervously. We climbed down the many sets of ladders delighted that our mission was accomplished without a hitch. We hoped that the remainder of the chicks' tenure on the ledge would be uneventful. It was gratifying to observe both chicks safely cavorting on the commodious platform. The nagging worry that still plagued us derived from the occasional need to lower the counterweight; its movement downward could be as much as ninety-five feet, lowering the chicks most of the distance down to the roadway. The bridge staff usually scheduled lifting operations in advance and promised to alert us whenever one was planned.

The chicks remained on the counterweight until they fledged during the third week of June at the optimum age of about six weeks. They did, however, obtain at least one free ride prior to their fledging. Five days after we had placed the female nestling on the counterweight, an unscheduled ship passage required the lift section of the bridge to be raised. The event caused no problem for the chicks.

On a quiet Tuesday morning, when the fledglings had been on the wing for a week, I rolled out my bike and pedaled the twenty-four miles from home to the bridge. As I approached the north tower, I observed the adult male perched about halfway up its north face; there was no sign of a youngster. I continued on to the south tower and heard the plaintive calling of a fledgling. It flew directly over me and I knew from its large size that it was the female. After flying back and forth between the towers, she alighted on a beam only thirty-five feet above me. I had a clear view of most of her body and her right leg band corroborated my reading that she was the female.

She vocalized, from time to time, with a fretful call that experience told me indicated her unhappiness. I wondered whether it was a plea to be fed or if it was merely caused by the need for company. At any rate, my presence did nothing to assuage her despondency. I looked up at her and she peered down at me. We made eye contact, which seemed to be of absolutely no significance to her as she turned away and resumed her discontented calling. I studied her every move and enjoyed ogling her at such close quarters. She never again even glanced in my direction during the remainder of the one hour that I spent with her. I searched for the male fledgling on the south tower without success.

I returned to the bridge several days later with Dolores and a few friends and observed the robust female fledgling flying from tower to tower, occasionally vocalizing. Suddenly the adult winged his way toward the youngster, carrying a small prey item, which prompted her to speed toward him, then fall in behind him. When she had followed him for a short distance, he let the prey fall. The fledgling made no attempt to retrieve it and the male gathered in the item before it had fallen two yards.

The peregrines entertained us with some exciting flying routines. The young female alighted with prey and the male fledgling zoomed down toward his sister, causing her to take off. He trailed very closely behind her and when she performed some graceful turns, he duplicated them. Their size differential was so markedly obvious that an observer ignorant of the size difference between the sexes in peregrines would have surely thought the male needed to do some more growing. The birds vocalized during their aerial display. The program finished with both fledglings pursuing their parent with great zeal that obviously was born of a combination of dependency and fascination.

One week later, Ron Bourque of the New York City Audubon Society observed both fledglings on the radio tower at Floyd Bennett Field. It was good to learn that the youngsters were venturing away from the bridge and using the same structure that their parents used regularly.

On July 15, Chris observed both fledglings and an in-flight prey transfer between the female fledgling and her parent. The fledgling had taken another step on the road to independence. Shortly thereafter, only one fledgling was observed at the site; the second youngster dispersed early in August.

During September and October, on eleven days, I observed one or two peregrines at the bridge while counting migrating raptors at the Fort Tilden Hawk Watch in Rockaway. On September 28, I observed two peregrines on the bridge and a successful hunt. It appeared that the resident male had attracted a replacement female. Two weeks later, Ron Bourque definitively corroborated that the newcomer was a double-banded adult female.

After the Marine Parkway bridge nesting territory was established this spring, we peregrine/hawk watchers wondered if the resident bridge peregrines would challenge the migratory peregrines traveling along Rockaway. Many of the migrators would be visible from the bridge. Would the bridge birds treat the flyway track as part of their territory? If they did, the interactions could be numerous with the scores of peregrines moving through each fall.

On October 19, the resident male intercepted a migrating immature peregrine at Fort Tilden, in view of the hawk watchers. The attacker overwhelmed the traveler with aggressive passes but allowed it to continue on its way unscathed. Undoubtedly, there were more skirmishes that were not observed but the lack of observations indicated that it was not a frequent event.

At any rate, the Marine Parkway site was providing hope for the reintroduction program.

18

A Record Season

(1991 - continued)

Eggshell fragments were observed in the vicinity of the New York Hospital site by April 12, 1991, signaling the hatching of at least one chick. On April 23, two chicks were observed, and by the twenty-sixth, three chicks had hatched.

Dolores and I went to the site on May 2 and found the resident mother, Red-Red, and P.J., her male partner, on guard at their eyrie. P.J., named after Peter Jenny, the man who donated him to the release program, set off on a hunt and his mate joined him. Red-Red returned with a pigeon in her grasp and both adults sat on the nest ledge for a few minutes. Then Red-Red took to the air, flew for a minute holding the prey, and glided past the nest ledge calling to the chicks before she finally alighted and fed them.

Two days later Dolores, Dave Gardner, and I observed a red-tailed hawk traveling high over the area. It obviously was no threat to the peregrines but Red-Red and P.J. gave it the usual nesting-season transgressor treatment. P.J.'s repeated stooping on the hawk elicited no response from it; apparently undaunted, it continued on its route. After the excitement of the territorial defense was over, P.J. fed on the ledge above the nest, then transferred the remains to his mate while aloft. She took the meal to the nearby smokestack and consumed it. Three nestlings were observed in the box.

The chicks were banded on May 8, the first ones to be banded in the New York City area for the season. Despite Red-Red's frantic defense, Chris Nadareski of New York City's parks and recreation department carefully gathered in each chick. Unexpectedly, there were four nestlings, all females. They were in excellent condition, except for the minor problem of feather lice. It is a very common affliction among many birds, especially raptors. Generally, feather lice do not endanger healthy chicks but Chris sprayed their wings with a lice-killing chemical as a precaution.

Several days later, I spent three hours at the site observing the adults and the four young. In one instance, P.J. was perched on his favorite spot above the nest ledge when Red-Red flew in and displaced him. He then flew to the smokestack, where he fed. Shortly, he delivered the remains to Red-Red, who fed the nestlings. During the ensuing two hours, there were two more feeding sessions. One chick was much less developed than its siblings, showing only white except for dark wingtips, whereas the others were a mix of both dark and white.

On May 16, Dolores and I arrived at the site and found all four nestmates on the nest ledge. Red-Red, perched on the nest box perch pole, appeared very relaxed as she proudly eyed her chicks. The serenity of the scene was in sharp contrast to the bustling activities that continuously paraded through our field of view. Commercial airplanes were flying by constantly and on that day we were also visited by three military helicopters. The East River Drive traffic was in its usual slow crawl routine for as far as the eye could see. The window washers and other building workers were engaged in their seemingly never-ending maintenance work.

One chick still had so much down that we saw her clearly from Roosevelt Island without the aid of our binoculars. The disparity between the white chick and its sisters was striking. They were mostly dark-feathered with tufts of down in several spots while the less-advanced one showed dark coloration only at its wingtips. The darker chicks' chests had the characteristic vertical brown barring. The tremendous difference in development caused us to wonder how many days of life separated these siblings.

We kept an eye on this family, though our viewings were, admittedly, spotty.

P.J. appeared and he and Red-Red went aloft. They circled over the hospital building several times before winging toward Central Park, probably on a hunting foray. We hoped that they would be successful because we wanted to see a feeding session. The three advanced chicks stretched their wings and engaged in wingflapping, sometimes quite vigorously. They sat bolt upright, very close to one another, for fifteen minutes while the other chick had lain down. Later, when Red-Red returned, two chicks assumed the food-begging position and repeatedly charged their mother, who responded by merely dropping off the ledge. The less-developed chick did not engage in any of these activities. I began to refer to that chick as "Whitey" to differentiate her from her nestmates. The appellation would, of necessity, be short-lived because Whitey would soon develop the darker plumage similar to that of her sisters.

Two days later, Ted and I arrived at Roosevelt Island at noon and observed both adults and two chicks. The most noteworthy event was some wingflapping by Whitey, the first such observation recorded by anyone for her. A herring gull flew past the nest ledge, drawing Red-Red's wrath. She stooped at it several times in quick succession, missing it by mere inches. Finally, she hit it lightly, eliciting an anguished wail and the gull's invigorated departure.

This episode stimulated the adults and they geared up into the hunting mode. First, they flew past the nest ledge several times. Red-Red called to the chicks in a manner apparently designed to prepare them for a feeding session. All the chicks became enlivened and were visibly more alert. Together, the adults circled higher and higher until they were in a position to attack prey in any direction. After a few aborted approaches toward prey, the full spectacle of the hunt unfolded before our eager eyes. P.J. began his precise, rapid wingbeats toward the quarry. Any witness, whether knowledgeable or otherwise, would be bound to recognize the purposefulness of his flying. Ted LeViness and I had observed this behavior hundreds of times and had learned to recognize the telltale clues. We kept our binoculars trained on him and soon found that his mate had joined him in the chase. Sometimes the prey comes into one's field of vision prior to the peregrine's strike, and sometimes one is able to scan ahead of the attacker to pick up the intended victim. But in this instance, the birds were moving so quickly and had flown so far that staying on them was our only possible course of action. Suddenly, P.J. dove downward at a mourning dove, missing his intended victim by mere feet. The two hunters alternately stooped at the dove and P.J. captured it on his third try.

They returned to the eyrie where Red-Red took possession of

their prize. Whitey rushed to Red-Red and was fed for four minutes without any interference from her siblings. Then one of her sisters clambered over to Whitey's side, though she did not beg or interpose herself. Whitey continued to feed for another minute, until a second chick displaced her. This prompted the other two chicks to gather about Red-Red, who stripped off pieces of the prey and fed all three of them. Whitey was preening. When her three sisters moved away from Red-Red, Whitey returned to her mother, who resumed feeding her. It seemed as though the entire family cooperated in catering to the one who was the weakest and needed special attention. This was the second instance in which I had observed Whitey being given this type of consideration.

Our last observation of the day was P.J.'s six-stoop attack of an immature red-tailed hawk. The hawk's route, over Queens County and well away from the eyrie, was decidedly not a threat but P.J. felt compelled to intercept the interloper and escort it out of his territory. The young hawk made some mildly evasive, if ineffective responses, but the peregrine did it no harm.

Several days later, Dolores and I found that the chicks were developing satisfactorily. Whitey had grown so many new feathers that she now appeared to be half white and half brown. One chick wingflapped while perched on the nest box pole. It looked ready to fledge at any time. It also sat on the outer edge of the ledge, dangling one leg over the side. It peered down and displayed that wistful look that we had seen many times when a chick is girding itself for its first flight.

We observed a youngster on the ledge adjacent to the nest ledge and conjectured whether or not this small move should be interpreted as a fledging. Later, we learned that two chicks had fledged two days earlier. P.J. hunted above Roosevelt Island and snared a pigeon, which he cached whole on the hospital facade. A short time later, Red-Red carried a blue jay to the nest ledge.

Two days later, Dave and I observed the site for two hours. Three chicks were on the nest ledge and one was on a nineteenth-floor terrace. A great black-backed gull incensed the adults and they collaborated on a concerted stooping attack. The gull maintained its course along the East River and, when it moved out of their territory, they lost interest in it. Red-Red took prey to the nest ledge and fed Whitey first. Soon, another chick muscled her out of the way and fed. Whitey's dark feathering now covered more than half of her body. She was healthy and there was no reason to fear that she would not fledge in her own time.

Two days after that, I could spot only three chicks. P.J. was alone, relaxing on the smokestack with a prey item. Red-Red barged right in, grabbed the carcass, and delivered it to the chicks on the nest ledge. Next, as I watched, one of the chicks jumped off the ledge and flew off to the south side of the building. This was the first youngster that I had seen fly during this 1991 season. It is always a special treat for me to observe newly fledged peregrines fly and the first experience of each season is the most thrilling. Half an hour after this first solo, Red-Red gave Whitey a private feeding.

On June 1, Ted and I arrived at Roosevelt Island at 12:15 P.M. and, after diligently scanning each nearby building with the aid of the scope, we located P.J. perched on an apartment tower. He apparently had positioned himself there to monitor the fledglings. Shortly thereafter, we found two fledglings on the lower ledge of the hospital's smokestack. Then Red-Red and P.J. commenced soaring above the hospital and zeroed in on a hapless pigeon. On her second pass, Red-Red delivered a blow that allowed her to bind into it on her third approach. After administering the spine-severing neck bite, she flew toward the smokestack, now occupied by three youngsters. Red-Red deliberately flew past them, prompting two of them to pursue her. There is no stronger lure for a recently fledged peregrine than to chase a parent carrying prey. Finally, Red-Red flew out of sight, leaving the three fledglings to fly in an aimless fashion but obviously enjoying their recently acquired gift of flight. It was wonderful to see this robust peregrine family flying about the tall buildings of New York City.

The following day, Dave and I arrived at Roosevelt Island in the early afternoon. I was eager to find all four fledglings because I had observed only three of them during my previous two visits. On my arrival, two fledglings were on a ledge and the adults were flying aimlessly above the hospital. One youngster moved out of sight and then two house finches shared the ledge with the remaining young peregrine. The diminutive ones looked at the larger bird inquisitively but the fledgling did not deign to take notice of their presence. The finches flew away and returned several times. In one instance, the finches flanked the peregrine and I feared that they might be a special breed of "attack finch."

Later, three fledglings were on the nineteenth-floor terrace taking short flights, hopping, shuffling, and wingflapping. Then, happily, I saw a fourth head on the terrace. One week later, the body of one of the fledglings was retrieved from the water adjacent to LaGuardia Airport. The reason for its demise was not determined but it was not Whitey, the youngest chick of the brood.

The three surviving youngsters dispersed satisfactorily, a wonderful achievement at any "wild" peregrine site. I visited the site at least ten more times from June 30 to the end of 1991. Most of the trips were made by bicycle and were less than an hour. P.J. or Red-Red, or both of them, were there but there was nothing remarkable to report.

Grand Central

Peregrines nesting at 42nd Street overlooking New York City's railroad passenger hub, Grand Central Station! Incredible as it might seem, it was true. The quintessential urban peregrines had produced eggs during the two previous years in their failed nesting attempts at the Pan American Building. The substrate on the nest ledges was too jagged to safely nestle the eggs and there was not much hope that these birds could find a satisfactory ledge at the Pan Am.

This year, 1991, to assist the peregrines in their nesting attempt, Chris installed a nest box on the fifty-seventh floor of the south side of the Pan Am. On April 1, Chris observed at least one egg on a ledge at the northeast corner of the Pan Am but again the substrate was unsatisfactory. As anticipated, the egg or eggs were gone by April 12. On April 23, another egg was observed at the southeastern corner of the Pan Am, providing some hope that they might nest successfully. Why they chose not to use the box that had been installed for them was an enigma not dwelled upon. We had learned that humans can only try to help but cannot delve into the mind of a wild creature. Of course, there are many interactive relationships between humans and animals that depend entirely on a "meeting of the minds;" falconry is a sterling example. But when it relates to a wild animal not responding to something a human has proffered, whether it be food or a nest box, who can truly fathom the creature's decision-making process? It seems that whenever one begins to feel that some understanding has been gained, events will quickly conspire to dispel that notion.

The British Broadcasting Corporation had obtained the approval of DEC to photograph the peregrines in New York City for use in their forthcoming documentary on the relationship between wild animals and humans in an urban setting. On April 29, BBC's crew was ensconced on the sixty-seventh floor of the Chrysler Building with its camera trained on the Pan Am, diagonally across the street. Chris and I went to the Chrysler Building to observe the conditions at the nest site and to assist the BBC crew.

For us, the important event of that particular day was the discovery of a third egg. Moreover, there was an extraordinary singularity related to that egg in that it had been laid in a different spot from that of the two previous locations. The egg lay on a ledge at the most easterly section of the Pan Am's south side, just around the southeast corner from the second egg. (The first lost egg, you will recall, had been laid on a northeast ledge.) To add to the uniqueness of the already unusual situation, the male was sitting on the second laid egg while, at the same time, his mate was on the third egg. This strange behavior was very disturbing to both the peregrines and their human monitors. We knew that the birds were being stressed by the continuing disturbance emanating above their nest ledge. Workers were frequenting the area above the eyrie, although entry had supposedly been restricted. It was interesting to note that the third egg was laid in the identical spot in which the eggs had been placed the previous year in a failed nesting effort.

It was a most extraordinary scene. The male was hunkered down on an egg in an apparently serious incubation attempt; his mate was very close by on another egg; they could not see each other. She did not warm her egg consistently but stood up frequently. Even when she had seemingly put her body onto the egg, she did not appear to take care to position her brood patches properly. The male, at this point, seemed not to be unduly concerned with the activity in the area, including birds flying by and people creating noise on the utility roofs above. She, on the other hand, was alert to every sound and sight and repeatedly turned her head to one side and peered upward, obviously

244

agitated by the activity above. However, they both stayed on their respective eggs for one hour.

The pair engaged in courtship behavior and I had the good fortune of witnessing some of their flying routines and their most intimate moments. The male pursued a blue jay, which tried to escape by darting into a recessed exterior terrace. The peregrine perched on the outer edge of the terrace and waited patiently for his intended victim to reappear. That failing, he jumped onto the terrace and promptly snatched the bird from its hiding place, then flew upward above the Pan Am with his prize. He flew large, circular patterns, interspersed with moderate stoops—beautiful courtship choreography. His mate soared above and watched his every move. Whether she was enamored of his flight prowess or was more interested in the bird he was holding was open to question. The male finally presented his catch to her and she took it in midair.

Later, the pair was at the south ledge near the last laid egg. Their courtship manner was thrilling. They touchingly moved their beaks across one another's and allopreened. The posturing was very dramatic; she bent down and forward in a begging position while he stretched himself to his full height to appear as upright as possible. All this while, we clearly heard them "talk" to each other. The bowing and vocalizing mesmerized me because I had never before had the opportunity of observing it. The display seemed almost ritualistic. I envisioned peregrines the world over going through these mutual displays during their breeding time. A thread of atavistic continuity traveling through the ages suffused the scene.

The peregrines often perched on the antennas of the nearby Chrysler Building, the only structure in the vicinity that is taller than the Pan Am. This allowed them to monitor both of their egg sites simultaneously. The BBC cinemaphotographers spent many days at the site and came to know the peregrines' habits very well. Their appreciation of their flying mastery and uniqueness was a pleasure to share. They recorded many hours of peregrine exploits and I looked forward to enjoying their work on television.

One week later, the second egg was abandoned and the adults concentrated their efforts on the third egg. Eventually, that one was also deserted, thereby ending their breeding attempt for 1991 in total failure. The adults remained on their territory in the ensuing months.

Verrazano-Narrows

Brooklyn Bird Club members Paul Keim and Joe Bertuna observed a pair of adult peregrines at the Verrazano-Narrows Bridge in early March. By March 18, Chris observed at least two eggs in the same nest box that had been utilized during the previous breeding season. On April 12, Chris again observed two eggs and was reasonably sure, from the female's position on them, that she had three and possibly four.

The breakthrough came on May 1 when Chris saw the female guarding three chicks. The next three weeks were uneventful and the chicks were banded on May 20. To minimize the danger to the adults, Chris scheduled the banding operation for a time when both lower roadways were closed to vehicular traffic, 5:00 A.M. to 6:00 A.M. During previous nest intrusions, the adults had flown between the upper and lower roadways in defense of their eyrie area, thereby exposing themselves to the danger of colliding with a moving vehicle.

Chris and I were at the site by 4:30 A.M. and, with the Verrazano supervisor and his personnel, drove to the eyrie. TBTA workers set up lights, unfastened the grille above the eyrie, and positioned a ladder. Chris donned a climbing belt and attached a safety line from it to a beam. The adults vocalized their alarm and flew circular patterns. They flew very close to Chris as he gathered in the three chicks, but did not make contact. He placed the chicks into boxes and we hoisted them to the roadway. Chris banded the two females and one male chick which, were about three weeks old and in perfect condition.

The chicks were developing satisfactorily but the bad news arrived on June 11; the body of a female fledgling had been found on the roadway. She had lost her short life in a collision with a vehicle. The parallels between the Throgs Neck and Verrazano bridges in 1991 were unfortunately all too close. Both sites had two female and one male young. Each had lost an early fledgling, one to the water below, the other to the traffic above. We hoped that their seasons would now switch to a successful track. The questions at the conclusion of each breeding season as to how the fledglings would fare after their successful dispersals represented an unknown that we accepted. But we did hate to lose young even before they had had a chance to become independent.

On June 30, Ted, Dave, and I observed the site for several hours. Joe Bertuna happened by and informed us that he had seen three birds there one week earlier. As we spoke, the adult male flew into view; he was on the hunt. A pigeon was his victim and several short stoops put it into his clutches. The prey was entirely consumed on the Brooklyn tower. A female fledgling chased several different pigeons but to no avail. Finally, she pursued one that was not as swift as are most of its kind and was able to hit it lightly. The youngster was about nine weeks old, and chasing pigeons represented for her the proper developmental stage. Chris observed both surviving fledglings during the first ten days of July. On July 11, Chris, Ted, and I made an inspection of the Verrazano, primarily to try to ascertain the presence of the two fledglings and to monitor the physical condition of the young and adult peregrines alike. If a bird were to exhibit a disease process or other malady, an intervention could be attempted. Even the retrieval of a dead body could provide valuable information.

The adult birds were on guard and the female tracked our every move. She did not attack us at first because we were far from her young. But as soon as we moved closer, she and her mate stridently vocalized and flew at us. Their attack was somewhat muted because the fledgling was fully capable of flying away. We left without finding the second fledgling but were not overly concerned because the Verrazano is so gigantic that there are too many excellent perching spots to check. At this stage of a youngsters' development, it separates from its family members for progressively longer periods of time.

Several days later, Chris again observed only one fledgling; it was a male with a left leg band. The fledgling that we had observed on our prior visit was a female that had a right leg band. Therefore, there were still two fledglings at the Verrazano on July 21, and they apparently dispersed satisfactorily. This was the second consecutive successful breeding season at the Verrazano.

Riverside Church

The first noteworthy event at the Riverside Church site was an exciting territorial defense battle waged by the resident adults against a female peregrine interloper. On January 4, Barry Freed, the peregrine watcher at the hospital site, observed the resident male leave his favorite perch on the antenna atop the church tower, fly along the Hudson River, and then turn inland. He then stooped on the unwelcome visitor and zoomed upward to gain altitude for another dive at it. A second female peregrine flew onto the scene, prompting the male to break off his pursuit. Although Barry was unable to determine the ages of the females, the second one was almost assuredly the Riverside resident. She dove at the visitor and followed with an upward surge. As the antagonists came together, both lashed out with their talons and actually intertwined them. They spiraled downward, making no attempt to use their wings to arrest their fall. They disappeared from view behind a building and neither one was seen again in the ensuing half hour. Later, a red-tailed hawk soared above the site. All else was quiet.

The following morning, Barry observed a female peregrine aloft at Riverside. She was carrying prey. Having consumed the prey, she joined the male at his perch. The resident adults were on their territory; yesterday's intruder had been successfully repulsed.

Territorial defenses probably occur more frequently than is realized. Sites are monitored for only a small fraction of the total daylight hours. Therefore, if one were to extrapolate a figure for total intrusions based upon those actually witnessed, the number would be sizable. There are many peregrines in the New York City region that have no home territory, making it inevitable that they journey through occupied territories. Fortunately, interactions resulting from intrusions rarely lead to injury. This statement relates to the New York City area; in truly wild locations, the outcomes have not always been so benign.

Early in February, Chris observed the adults copulate at Riverside. He also saw two scrapes in the nest substrate. By April 1, there were five eggs being incubated. On April 29, Chris observed several pieces of eggshell on the nest ledge. Two days later, there were at least two chicks in the nest and on May 8 there were three.

The chicks were banded on May 23 with Barbara Loucks in attendance and in the presence of a very special observer, Dr. Dean Amadon. Chris unlocked the special gate that he had installed to prevent access to the window nest ledge. He carefully removed each chick and handed it to Barbara. The adult female had become aware of our presence from the moment Chris first touched the protective gate. She began her alarm vocalizations: anguished cries, which continued intermittently throughout the banding session. All three nestlings were healthy females. Interestingly, eleven of the thirteen nestlings that we had already banded this breeding season were females. The chicks had some feather lice, and, therefore, their wings were sprayed with a lice-killing chemical. Chris examined the nest substrate and found both of the unhatched eggs hidden deep in the substrate. They were forwarded to the state laboratory for analysis.

By June 6, one chick had fledged; two days later, a second one left the nest ledge. On June 12, a fledgling was on the sidewalk adjacent to Riverside. It was taken into custody and taken to the Animal Medical Center, where it was found to be in good condition. Chris placed the youngster back up on the nest ledge. There were no further incidents at the site and the three fledglings developed normally.

On June 17, I visited Riverside during one of my three-pronged bicycle trips which also covered the New York Hospital and Pan Am sites. I observed at least two fledglings and an adult during my short visit. Chris monitored the site regularly and continued to observe the three fledglings. Ted, Dave, and I conducted a four-site peregrine roundup tour on June 30 (Throgs, Verrazano, Riverside, New York Hospital). At Riverside, we observed both adults and two of the three fledglings. There were no further untoward events at the site and all three youngsters dispersed successfully.

Tappan Zee

In early May, Chris monitored the Tappan Zee Bridge site regularly and observed a pair frequenting the east nest box. During one observation session, he observed two kills, but the prey were not taken to the nest box area. Although several eggs were laid in the east box in early June, they were abandoned. On July 10, when the time had elapsed for any possible renesting attempt, Chris recovered three unhatched eggs from the nest box.

While attending the Hook Mountain Hawk Watch, a site which is within view of the Tappan Zee, Paddy French, the hawk watch leader, advised me that the body of an adult peregrine had been recovered on

August 8 from the Hudson River at Piermont, New York. This location's proximity to the Tappan Zee indicated the distinct possibility that the bird was one of the resident peregrines at the Tappan Zee. However, because the Tappan Zee residents' bands had not been read, this fact could not be established.

World Trade Center

Steve Walter sighted a pair of peregrines soaring amid the upper reaches of the World Trade Center's twin towers on March 8. Ten days later, Chris observed a scrape in the nest box substrate at the 48 Wall Street building. The pair regularly engaged in courtship behavior but no eggs were laid during the months of March and April.

On May 8, Chris and I found that the nest box contained the remains of a pigeon. At least the peregrines were using the box, albeit not for nesting. This was the fourth consecutive season in which a pair of adult peregrines were in the area but failed to nest successfully.

19

Queen's Reign Ends

(1992)

Dolores and I sojourned in Florida for three and a half months until March of 1992. I returned to New York City for a one-week period in both January and February and was greeted upon my January arrival by the sight of the Queen and Rio perched on the Throgs tower; Rio was enjoying a meal. The following morning, they were soaring in tandem above the anchorage and I was engulfed with that special feeling one experiences when confronted with the beauty of peregrines aloft in their element. It was the dead of winter but their togetherness assured me that the spring breeding season was not a very long way off.

That same day, Ted LeViness related to me some interesting observations, which he had made a week earlier at the Jones Beach water tower on Long Island. Parenthetically, this tower first gained raptorial distinction on November 24, 1987, when Ted discovered an immature male gyrfalcon perched upon it. The gyr used this structure as a night roost for the entire winter. Hundreds of bird enthusiasts were able to view this, the largest of the four species of North American falcons, of which only a few travel as far south as Long Island. Interestingly, Ted also observed an immature female peregrine perched on that water tower at the same time.

Returning to the January, 1992, observations, Ted observed two peregrines on the Jones Beach tower on January 4. One was an immature, the other an adult, probably a female. He clearly heard them chirruping and saw the female going into the nest box that had been installed prior to the 1991 breeding season. This was the second consecutive winter that a pair of peregrines had used the tower for their headquarters and we hoped that they might find its conditions satisfactory for nesting. Peregrines were not known to have nested on Long Island. However, just as bridges and buildings had become a new source of nesting sites, it seemed possible that a tall edifice such as the tower, which overlooks water and has an abundant prey base, could become a viable nesting site. Peregrines sometimes use odd, tall structures such as smokestacks and the superstructure of vessels as nesting sites.

On February 4, Lester Short, curator of birds at the American Museum of Natural History, New York City, observed an adult peregrine perched on a telephone pole as he drove across the Henry Hudson Bridge, which connects the Bronx and New York (Manhattan) counties. Then a second peregrine alighted on an adjacent pole. Since the peregrine eyrie closest to that bridge is at the Riverside Church, a distance of less than five miles, these peregrine could have been the Riverside pair. However, the possibility that this was an unpaired duo just traveling together could not be ruled out.

During my February stay in New York, I observed the Throgs adults on a fairly regular basis. On the twentieth of February, Ted witnessed two kills and a possible copulation. By March 25, Chris had observed at least one egg in the nest box. When I returned to New York at the end of March, I made sporadic observations of a single bird.

The news from the other nesting sites in the New York City area was very encouraging. Peregrine pairs were observed incubating eggs at the Verrazano and Marine Parkway bridges, New York Hospital, Riverside Church, and the Pan Am Building. Additionally, a pair was seen on its territory in the Wall Street area, and pairs were also seen at the Outerbridge Crossing and the Goethal's bridges. At the Tappan Zee Bridge, considerable courtship had been observed, including copulation. However, no eggs had yet been laid. I looked forward to another record breeding season, possibly eclipsing the 1991 total of fifteen chicks. I anticipated at least one new producing site coming on stream and a new high total of eighteen to twenty young. The established sites, namely the Throgs and Verrazano bridges, New York Hospital and Riverside Church, each could reasonably be expected to average three young, and the Marine Parkway Bridge should contribute an additional three, thereby equaling the previous year's total.

On April 10, I monitored the Tappan Zee site for an hour and observed an adult pair. The female guarded the west nest box and the male perched on a ledge above her. They flew together briefly and then returned to the box. The female went into it several times but I did not see a behavioral pattern that denotes incubation, though the temperature was a cool fifty-two degrees Fahrenheit.

Returning home, my observations took a startling turn. For one entire hour, an unidentified one-year-old female peregrine sat on the west edge of the Throgs, about fifty yards north of the nest box. This visitor wore a band on each leg, had a very dark head and facial markings, and no white bib at all on her chest. She lazily preened for the better portion of the hour, and was not challenged by the resident adults. I did not see the adults and I doubt that they saw the interloper. The visitor's nonstop departure flight to the Bronx was my last observation of the day.

During the next two weeks, only Rio was observed. On April 26 at 3:00 P.M., I found an adult female peregrine consuming prey in the 1983 eyrie. I was astonished to see that she was not the Queen. The bird was of a darker coloring and wore two leg bands. The right band was a silver U.S. Fish and Wildlife type and the left was black. Having eaten for fifteen minutes, the visitor flew into the bridge structure about thirty yards north of the nest box. One hour later, she flew off, out of sight. It is interesting to note that this visitor was not challenged, just as had been the case with the peregrine interloper of April 10. It was possible that this bird had also gone unnoticed by the resident pair. The affair seemed strange, indeed. Neither of the resident peregrines was observed while the visitor was visible. Rio was seen often during the next three days while the Queen was observed briefly near the nest box on only one occasion.

One afternoon, I bicycled to Roosevelt Island and observed Red-Red sitting on the ledge above the nest ledge while P.J. remained perched on the north side of the building. I was advised by Dr. Aronian, that there were at least three chicks in the nest box and that they had hatched on or about April 13. The hospital site has been a wonderful producer for five consecutive seasons. Two chicks were hatched in 1988, three in both 1989 and 1990, four in the 1991 (of which three fledged), and now, as it turned out in the end, four in the 1992 season for a total of sixteen chicks.

Another interesting peregrine report came to me from Tony Tierno, who, for years, has been spending many hours observing all kinds of wildlife on Long Island. On April 26, he observed two peregrines perched on the Robert Moses Causeway Bridge. One was an unbanded adult female but he could not identify the other as to sex or age. As he drove southward to Fire Island, he spotted a third peregrine, on the smaller Captree Bridge. The large female on the Moses Bridge seemed to be the same bird that Tony had been observing in the area throughout the winter. In fact, his most recent observation had been on April 5 when he saw a pair of peregrines in the same area. We speculated as to whether the Moses Bridge could support a peregrine nesting effort. Since the underside of the bridge did not appear to contain suitable ledges or cavities, we came to the conclusion that a closer inspection was needed to determine the exact conditions. Historically, as I have noted, peregrines are not known to have nested on Long Island. But the world has changed drastically for the peregrine and maybe this site would prove to be usable.

May 1 began quite uneventfully at the Throgs. In the morning, Rio captured a bird, ate a portion of it, and delivered the remainder to the nest. However, at 5:30 P.M., I spotted an unidentified peregrine perched on the tower. The bird appeared similar to the visitor that I had observed on April 26, but it could not have been the same one because it was wearing two black leg bands. After an hour, it flew off to the west. This was the third female visitor within three weeks that did not meet with any hostility from the resident adults. This was very remarkable, since this was the nesting season, a time when territorial defense drives are at the highest level.

On Sunday, May 3, I monitored the Throgs site almost continuously for six hours beginning at 7:20 A.M. The session began with Rio capturing a pigeon and feeding upon it for seven minutes. When he flew past the eyrie carrying its remains, the Queen intercepted him and forced him into the eyrie. Half an hour later, the Queen and Rio were seen aloft, buoyed by the northwest winds, waiting on above the anchorage. Later, the pair sat close to one another on the top of the tower. Presently a herring gull lazily flying by became the recipient of a languid dive; several passerines were approached with somewhat more purposeful dives. A change of pace occurred when an osprey appeared. Rio stooped at the large transgressor, flaunting his superior maneuverability in a manner obviously designed to induce the interloper to withdraw. The result was quickly achieved and the osprey was escorted away from the Throgs.

In midafternoon, I bicycled to Roosevelt Island to check the New York Hospital site. Both adults, as expected, were at their eyrie, but the nestlings were not visible. Rio was soaring above the anchorage at the Throgs in a waiting on attitude upon my return home. He hunted, unsuccessfully, from this position and also from perches on the handcable.

Good News

Good news flowed from many of the other nest sites during the first week of May. At New York Hospital, Chris had banded four healthy chicks. This site is perennially several weeks ahead of the others in the region. There was a lone chick in the nest box at the Pan Am Building. After several years of failed nesting, a chick was developing in a nest high above Grand Central Station. The use of a nest box greatly improves the peregrines' chances of producing live hatchlings and their ability to nurture them successfully. The peregrines at the Tappan Zee were incubating eggs in the west nest box. Although they were well behind schedule compared to all the other nest sites, there was sufficient time to progress through their developmental stages and have a successful breeding outcome.

On May 7, Chris and I inspected the Throgs Neck and Marine Parkway bridge sites. At the Throgs, we observed three chicks but could not spot the fourth egg. The three chicks appeared to be about a week old. Our visit was brief because we did not want to unduly stress the adults and prevent them from brooding the hatchlings.

At the Marine Parkway Bridge eyrie, we found four nestlings that appeared to be several days younger than those at the Throgs. We read the female's band number, which identified her as being a two-year-old, wild-raised bird from Virginia. This was the only the second known instance of a mated peregrine, in the New York City area, that had traveled in a northerly direction from its natal territory.

Ron Bourque, a few days earlier, had observed the adults facing into the nest box and bending down and inward in a position which strongly suggested that they were stripping meat from prey and feeding young. The dates of his observations correlated with the estimated hatching dates. He also witnessed the female, whom the observers had named "Marina," escort a visiting peregrine out of its territory. The incident started when her mate discovered a female peregrine and had begun his defense maneuvers. Marina joined in and the male withdrew. This is the usual course of action in territorial defense situations. A female intruder will be repulsed by the resident female and the male will repulse the male transgressors. The size matchup would seem to be the operative principle but intrasex competition is more likely nature's way.

One beautiful, sunny afternoon, during the second week of May, Dolores and I visited the New York Hospital site. We saw both adults, two of the four chicks and a feeding session. It is always a special thrill to see our first chicks of each breeding season.

The Verrazano and Riverside Church sites' three-chick broods were banded during the week. I attended the banding session at Riverside. It never fails to invigorate me to see chicks at such close range; the magic endures.

Bad News

On May 13, I observed an adult female peregrine on the Throgs. She was preening. I clearly saw her two black leg bands. She definitely was not the Queen. She appeared to be the same female which I had observed on May 1; her coloring was much darker than the Queen's and she had noticeably different facial markings. My consternation was immediate. This was the fourth unchallenged female "visitor" I had found at the site since April 10. But more telling was the likelihood that this bird was the same one which I had seen two weeks earlier. This led me to surmise that she was now the resident female and that the Queen was gone. I kept my eyes riveted on her as my mind reeled. The Queen had produced this season's eggs and the current female replaced her after the eggs were laid. I knew that this was the case because the Queen had disappeared from all watches after May

3, just about the time the chicks hatched. On May 3, Ted had observed Rio and the Queen for several hours. He had watched the Queen for many hundreds of hours during ten seasons and could not possibly have observed the replacement female for hours and not noticed that she had brown plumage as opposed to the slate gray of the Queen.

After preening for almost an hour, the female flew past the eyrie area out of my field of vision. Less than one minute later, Rio dove down from the eyrie in pursuit of a pigeon. A female followed close behind, undoubtedly the new female that I had just observed, and together they snared the pigeon. This cooperative hunt further buttressed my conclusion that the Queen had been replaced.

Three days later, I observed the new female for a third time. She flew from the main pier carrying prey and alighted on pilings, where she fed. The following morning, Ted and I started monitoring at the Throgs before 7:00 A.M. Within an hour, we were able to corroborate that Rio was paired with the new female: she hunted with him and went to the eyrie; we heard them call to one another as pairs do, especially during the breeding season. The Queen was gone. We could not even speculate intelligently regarding the specific cause of her disappearance after having reigned for ten consecutive breeding seasons at the Throgs. Ten years was a reasonable number of procreative years in the wild, although there have been reliably recorded cases of pairs attaining sixteen and seventeen nesting seasons. We would miss the Queen.

A decade of peregrine nesting data in the New York City metropolitan region (see Appendix for tables) has demonstrated that once a breeding territory has been established, it is not abandoned despite repeated failures. An established territory is here defined as one that has produced at least one chick. Furthermore, there are several territories, which, to our knowledge, have not produced young but continue to attract and hold pairs of peregrines year after year. Apparently, the peregrine's historical tendency for mating-age birds to seek to replace lost breeders in existing territories, rather than to try to create new ones, is being again lived out. In the period prior to the extirpation of the peregrine in the eastern United States and elsewhere, there were many well-documented cases of sites which continued to be used despite consistent failures caused by the systematic depredations by egg collectors, falconers, pigeon fanciers, and hunters.

It is also interesting to note that all of the New York City breeders that have been identified as to age were one or two years old when they commenced their breeding careers. No doubt there is a group of nonbreeders (floaters) perennially in the region waiting in "their" wings to fill any vacancy that develops at a nesting site. The fact that resident adults in the region have been promptly replaced after their disappearance amply corroborates this premise.

In the past, when there was a dearth of breeding territories or openings in them, floaters frequently did not commence breeding until they were three or four years old. This phenomenon has not yet been evidenced locally. Whether this signifies that there are no older birds as floaters in the region is questionable. But if that is the case, does it mean that local fledglings have not survived beyond their second year of life, or that they have gone farther afield in search of a nesting territory? Hopefully, as the years progress and the peregrine continues to prosper, some of today's enigmas will be clarified.

20

Most Productive Season

(1992 - continued)

On May 19, 1992, Chris and I went to the Throgs eyrie to check the condition of the chicks and to try to read the new female's band. The adults loudly called in alarm as soon as we approached the eyrie. Rio alighted close to us, which was unusual behavior for him. He would usually fly at us and then perch at a distance, whereas the Queen more often stood her ground close to us. Now that he was the senior and more experienced component of the duo, he had become the more aggressive defender of the eyrie. Our mission was very successful. We observed all four nestlings in the nest box. During our previous inspection, we had spotted only three chicks. In the past, eggs and chicks have been recorded as unobserved in early inspections because they simply had not been visible to the observer.

Chris read "M27M" on the female's leg band, which identified her as a 1990 Boston hatchling. Both adults currently at the Throgs originated in Boston. The female was readily distinguishable from Rio because, in addition to her larger size, she still had a preponderance of brown plumage and her facial markings contained much less white.

Later, I set out by bicycle to Roosevelt Island to observe the New York Hospital site. I was very fortunate to witness Red-Red feeding two chicks on the nest ledge during my short fifteen-minute observation session. I also saw the site's other two chicks and P.J. I had seen a dozen peregrines at two sites within two hours. Days like this are ample compensation for the many hours of work and anxiety that are part and parcel of ministering to an "endangered species." I looked forward to many more rewarding events in the continuing peregrine recovery.

At the Throgs the following day, the female called loudly as she circled some workers walking on the roadway. Rio half-heartedly assisted her but he knew the Throgs ambience. The men were not a threat to their young because they were on the roadway. In her time, the Queen, too, had learned to ignore the activities that did not intrude into the eyrie area.

On the afternoon of May 21, Dolores and I spent two hours observing the New York Hospital site. Three chicks were active on the nest ledge but we were unable to find the fourth one. We learned later that one youngster had taken its first flight earlier that day. Red-Red flew directly over us on a foray into Queens County. While she was away from the eyrie, P.J. carried prey to the nest ledge and fed three chicks. He had fed them for less than ten minutes when Red-Red alighted next to him. She unceremoniously took the prey remains and fed the chicks. One of the chicks still had much more down than its nestmates.

The next day, I assisted Chris and Barbara in banding the chicks at the Throgs. Dolores and Dave observed the banding session and marveled at Rio's flying ability in defending his young. I was too busy recording band numbers and defensively dodging Rio to fully enjoy his technique. Chris and Barbara examined each chick prior to placing a band on each of their legs. I recorded the numbers and alerted them whenever Rio approached. He came often and with great skill. Many times he struck Chris's helmet first and then Barbara's shoulder on the same pass. This double hit was an indication of the damage he was capable of inflicting if he chose to slash us. Rio's very forceful and tireless defense posture was in sharp contrast to the behavior he had exhibited during previous banding operations. In fact, I recalled, Rio did not even appear at the eyrie during the entire banding period in 1991. In earlier years, he had made passes at us but without displaying the ferocity shown this time. The loss of the Queen must have girded him to a higher level of defense.

The four male nestlings were in fine condition. Each was banded with both the usual Federal Fish and Wildlife band and a two-colored alphanumeric band. The color pattern indicates the geographic region in which the bird is banded. The letters and numerals on the colored band are large enough to be read in the field. All the chicks born this season in New York were double banded.

The Marine Parkway Bridge chicks were also banded that same afternoon. Dolores and I attended as observers. The male was a reticent defender and merely voiced his disapproval. The female was more aggressive and flew close to the banders several times. Once, she alighted on a nest box perch pole but made no effort to approach any closer. The four chicks were healthy and the banding operation proceeded in routine fashion.

The following day, a two-hour observation session at the New York Hospital site proved rewarding. We arrived and found two chicks of dark coloration at opposite ends of the nest ledge while the adults were soaring above. Suddenly, Red-Red alighted on the ledge and grasped a carcass. Jumping off the ledge, she circled just above it and then landed close to one of the two chicks. She presented the prey to one chick, which carried it the length of the ledge. We then observed a third chick, the youngest of the brood. Shortly, Red-Red delivered a prey item to this youngest chick and it fed itself. One of the two more advanced chicks flew to an adjacent building and adroitly alighted on a narrow window sill. In less than a minute, it returned to the nest ledge. This fledgling's competent flying and landing ability indicated that it had been on the wing for at least several days. The other chick hopped onto the nest box perch pole and perched there contentedly for over an hour.

By May 29, all four young were known to have fledged and, when I arrived there on that date, they were easily visible on the building. Three took to wing and flew with great abandon through the canyons between the highrise buildings. They chased one another and showed that crabbing was their favorite game. When the young had had their fill of flying, P.J. arrived with prey and began to feed one of the youngsters on a smokestack ledge. The feeding session did not last very long because the youngster edged P.J. off the ledge. P.J. still held the prey in his talons, prompting the three young to pursue him. He dropped the prey in an attempt to entice a fledgling to catch it in midair. When none of the young rose to the occasion, P.J. quickly retrieved the prey himself.

May 30 was a very special observation day at the Throgs. It started at first light, 5:00 A.M. I was at the beach area. The setting was calm and peaceful. The sunrise would not come until 5:27 A.M. The first birds to appear were herring gulls traveling east from their night roost to a feeding area. They came singly, two at a time, three together; there was no pattern. Two black-crowned night herons were fishing at the water's edge. Three great egrets flew to the west while a double-crested cormorant passed by them going in the opposite direction.

The sweet sounds of the singing land birds was occasionally muffled by the crash of a boat's wake hitting the shore. At 5:45 A.M., the female peregrine flew from the eyrie to the anchorage. I clearly heard her calling as she flew, but I could not fathom her purpose. At 6:15 A.M., the female flew to the west in pursuit of two pigeons. She returned empty-taloned but with Rio alongside. They hunted intermittently without success until 8:45 A.M. when, after many dives at it, they forced a starling into the water. They circled their victim but, before they could retrieve it from the water, a small boat chugged by, allowing a herring gull to drop into the water alongside the downed bird. The herring gull was immediately forced from its position by a great black-backed gull. This large predator quickly dispatched the little bird by snapping its neck and then swallowed it whole. Predation is the watchword in the wild and the prize is not gained until digestion takes place.

The first capture of the day was registered at 9:07 A.M. when Rio seized a starling after a joint attack. The starling's feathers burst outward as Rio bound strongly into its body. The female pursued Rio as he carried the prey and called in a manner suggesting that she was begging for the prey. Rio carried it directly to the nest.

Hunting continued and the next catch was taken into the nest by the female. Within a few minutes, however, she left the eyrie, still carrying the prey. Her behavior with regard to food, the chasing of Rio, the begging attitude, and the removing of prey from the eyrie seemed to indicate that she was still too young and inexperienced to consistently subordinate her own needs to those of the chicks.

At noon, the female snared a white pigeon and alighted on pilings to feed as Rio watched from the anchorage. After feeding for eight minutes, the female flew off with her meal but did not, as expected, go to the nest. Three-quarters of an hour later, the adults captured another starling, their fourth kill of the day.

The following morning, fellow peregrine watcher Tom Renner and I rendezvoused at Roosevelt Island and observed the four fledglings at the New York Hospital site. Upon our arrival, we found two fledg-lings perched on the hospital; then a third youngster flew into view. I very much wanted to see all of the fledglings at the same time as an indication that they were well. Two of the young birds took to the sky and cavorted with one another. This prompted the third one to join in the frivolities. Each took turns diving at the other and several times two of them almost locked talons as they playfully extended their legs. When P.J. alighted on the north side of the hospital, we had four peregrines in view and our adrenaline began to surge. When P.J. flew, two youngsters pursued him. They did not vocalize nor was there any apparent urgency in their attitude. Apparently, they were not moti-vated by hunger but by the need for exercise and play. After they had alighted on the tallest residential building in the vicinity, we observed a youngster on the hospital and another on the smokestack; we had all four fledglings in view. Red-Red then flew over the hospital and we had indeed seen all six members of the family.

Later that afternoon at the Throgs, I found Rio having a midafter-noon snack. Five minutes later, he zoomed past the first three piers south of the anchorage in his pursuit of a pigeon. As I followed his hurtling symmetry, the female flew parallel to him in the opposite direction. I kept my binoculars trained on Rio as he missed his in-tended victim and went out of view. The female alighted on the hand-cable. Her stance was the essence of alertness as she craned her neck in all directions, on the lookout for another victim. Peregrines contin-uously monitor their surroundings to detect any potential danger to themselves. This particular high perch is so inaccessible to other pred-ators that it appears to offer them a sense of security. Its location is a most favored one when they are in the hunting mode. It is interesting to witness how the adults sometimes get so comfortable on the hand-cable that they defer hunting and remain almost stationary for pro-longed periods of time.

Within two minutes, Rio started hunting; the female quickly join-ed him. They flew out of sight. Two hours later, the female was on the first pier energetically feeding on a mostly white pigeon. Occasionally, her beak would have so many feathers stuck to it that she would try to shake them off and, when this failed, she would employ her talons to rid herself of the encumbrance. She had been feeding for fifteen minutes when Rio alighted close to her. There was an expectant air about him as he calmly watched her feed. No doubt he wanted the prey for the chicks. This was an example of Rio trying to discharge an innate adult responsibility of feeding the young before feeding themselves. Rio remained on the pier for five minutes before returning to the eyrie. The female continued eating with gusto for another ten minutes (a total of thirty minutes) before carrying the remains to the eyrie. Rio flew out to intercept her when she approached the eyrie and they flew in together. Rio was at the eyrie more often than was his new partner. He seemed to have taken over the role usually filled by the female of a peregrine pair.

On June 3, I received word that a Riverside female nestling had been taken into custody the previous day by the New York City Police after it had alighted on top of an ambulance parked on the street below the eyrie. The bird had been taken to Vivienne Sokol, a licensed rehabilitator in Manhattan, who found it to be in perfect health. Chris Nadareski transported Vivienne and the bird to Riverside, where I met them. Arriving early, I observed the eyrie and was rewarded with the sight of the two other chicks exercising their wings and jumping onto the perch poles with obvious confidence. They appeared ready to leave their eyrie, if they had not in fact already done so. They were about six weeks old, the optimum age for peregrine chicks to make their first flights.

As soon as Chris approached the eyrie, the female began her usual loud clamor. Chris opened the window slowly, with great care, but before the window had moved but several inches, first one and then the second chick hopped off the nest ledge. Chris commented that the youngsters most likely had flown before, or had at least moved from the nest ledge to other nearby perches, since they exhibited no reluctance to leave the ledge on such short notice. His experience in these matters was very reassuring to me. Chris placed the chick on the nest ledge and we quickly left.

Chris then raced off to a pet shop in Brooklyn, where a chick from the Verrazano-Narrows site was being held. It had been taken as it lay on the ground beneath the Verrazano's Brooklyn tower. Chris would place it back up on the Verrazano if it were uninjured. Vivienne and I looked up from the street at the nest site we had just left to ascertain if the youngsters were satisfactorily situated. Two young were on the north side of the building. The adult female deposited prey on a ledge near one of the young and flew off. The adult male then alighted close to the two young. After a short wait, the chick which we had returned to the eyrie showed itself and an adult joined it. We left the site assured that the chicks were in good positions.

The next day, Tom Monaghan, another friend and fellow watcher, and I bicycled to Roosevelt Island to observe the six peregrines at the New York Hospital site. We were unable to find any of the peregrines for twenty minutes. Then Red-Red flew past the hospital carrying the better part of a pigeon. Tom wondered why she was flying such seemingly pointless circular patterns. I ventured the opinion that she might be trying to lure her fledglings into flight to provide them with both a meal and a lesson. Two youngsters suddenly appeared and vocalized as they chased Red-Red. I had heard that call many times before; it was the special begging call of hungry fledglings. Red-Red dove precipitously, as if to avoid them, but it was a ploy. One fledgling followed her closely and when Red-Red stopped in midair and extended her prey-filled talons, it deftly snatched the offering and flew off. Tom was enthralled by the spectacle.

Now that three young were aloft, they reveled in their newfound flying abilities and rode the wind with increasing skill, though still with noticeably less proficiency than their parents. Crabbing and diving at one another were their favorite pastimes. At this point, Tom Renner arrived at our viewing location and the peregrines unknowingly had three admiring observers. One fledgling alighted on a large metal duct on the roof of a building. Evidently, Red-Red did not approve of this particular location and tried to lure the youngster to an acceptable location by flying low over it, carrying prey and calling loudly. Later, the bird left the duct of its own accord and alighted on a wide roof parapet of another edifice. It was joined there by a starling, which seemed to be quizzically perusing its strange new neighbor. The peregrine took no notice of the other bird. We left the site with fond visions of the peregrines flying about the area.

The Throgs

A rainy weather system was fast approaching the New York City area on the morning of June 6. The sky was overcast and the winds were gusting to twenty-five miles an hour. Rio and his new mate soared together above the Throgs. They enjoyed the buoyancy of the moisture-laden air, flying in a manner that I could only describe as a kind of aerial ballet. A starling-sized bird flew into their view and the fun-flying immediately turned into a determined hunt. The quarry flew into the steelwork of the Throgs while Rio, in hot pursuit, attempted to force it back into flight. This little bird, however, had excellent survival instincts. When it exited the Throgs, it beat its wings as fast as possible and gained altitude as it made its way toward the nearest shore. The peregrines lost interest and returned to enjoying the wind currents. Often, peregrines will abort a hunt when the intended victim obtains an altitude advantage.

The early morning of June 6 had been enveloped in a dense fog, but by 11:00 A.M. the clouds had dissipated and the sun suffused the Throgs. The sight of a chick peering out from the Throgs was most welcome. This was the season's first sighting of a chick from a land-based vantage point. The adult female now frequently perched in this area to monitor the chicks as they tramped about the catwalks and beams. At 2:00 P.M., I observed two chicks. They were now brown-plumaged but still had many small areas of down. The chicks seemed to enjoy the view and having the sun in their faces. One chick scampered along the catwalk, flapped its wings strongly, and flew out of my view. I was sure that, although this flight was only a few feet long, the time for it to take its first full-fledged flight off the Throgs was near.

The following morning, I started observing from the apartment terrace at 5:30 A.M. The tower was again enveloped in fog and so visibility was low. I decided to continue my observations from the beach area and as I walked through the parking lot, Rio flew directly over me at height of about twenty yards. He flew to the tower and within five minutes had attacked a pigeon near the fender. Failing in this attempt, he alighted on a handcable to await his next opportunity. A dozen pigeons began winging their way, from land to the Throgs, several feet above the water. Rio was again on the attack and he was among them before they had realized their peril. They scattered and headed back toward land because its distance was shorter than that of continuing on to the Throgs. One pigeon made an evasive maneuver but continued toward the bridge. Rio dove at this individual three times in quick succession, making no contact. The pigeon was between the fender and the anchorage when Rio bound into it from behind. The victim was almost as large as Rio, making it exceedingly difficult to carry, prompting him to fly only several yards farther on and alight on the nearby anchorage rather than struggling to carry the heavy prey up to the eyrie. Seventeen minutes later, Rio flew from the anchorage with the much-diminished prey remains tucked in close to his body. He made one circuit around the anchorage and three around the tower, gaining altitude with each circuit, until he reached the eyrie, when I heard the chicks' cries.

On June 8, I finally observed all four chicks from the terrace. At one point, three chicks huddled together and touched their beaks, as in the act of kissing. They alternately engaged in bouts of wingflapping. One chick lay down flat and dozed for an hour. Sometimes two or three of them would draw side by side and make body contact.

At 1:00 P.M., I watched in wonderment as four chicks huddled together only several inches from the end of a beam. A sight such as this makes all of the months of waiting worthwhile. The chicks' feather development did not vary to a great extent. While the most advanced chick showed almost no down at all, the least developed one had only small spots of down. Two chicks appeared imminently ready to leave the security of the eyrie.

The June 9 observations at the Throgs began at 5:45 A.M. I was restless because, by my calculations, the chicks were just about ready to fledge. The prevailing northwest wind was providing ample updrafts at the anchorage and Rio and his new mate were soaring above it. The chicks were not in view but the adults delivered prey to the eyrie several times. Later, at 6:30 P.M., I observed two chicks near the eyrie. They had been in view for half an hour when a third chick joined them. By 7:30 P.M., all three had retired to the nest box area.

During the day, wingflapping is common, as is running along the catwalk and flying short distances along it. The young love to lay prone and to huddle close to each other. They touch each other with the utmost tenderness. One may place its head on its brother's back or put its talons on the reclining bird but always with care to avoid injury. On this day, one bird deliberately moved so close to the edge that its talons were over the side. Another perched on the edge with its back to the world. Their time to fly would come. The simultaneous flight of four male fledglings would be a fantastic sight to behold.

At 9:30 A.M. the next day, the alarm vocalizations of the adult female pervaded the apartment. I rushed out onto the terrace with binoculars in hand. The first fledgling of the 1992 season was sitting on the center of the main pier. The adult female was circling the pier raising the alarm because four men in a boat were tied up to the fender only twenty-five feet from the fledgling. The fledgling did not see them because the boat was well below the top of the fender and, conversely, neither could the men see the fledgling. After this initial aggressive display, the adults guardedly accepted the presence of the boat.

The fledgling had a black and red identification band on its left leg. The red coloring on the band glinted in the morning sun, inducing me to name the youngster "Red" for lack of any other more pertinent characteristic. One of the men in the boat was donning diving apparatus. I immediately advised DEC of the possible disturbance which the proximity of the boat presented. The diver entered the water to inspect the fender. The female continued to watch her youngster.

The female left the pier area but regularly returned to check on Red. At 11:30 A.M., I observed two fledglings, side by side, on the pier. I decided to call the second fledgling "Blackie" because the only identifying characteristic that I could discern was the black coloring of his bands. Ten minutes later, the female alighted on the pier with a pigeon and placed it next to the young. They quickly fed on it with great vigor, without any sign of competition between them. One perched on the prey and both carefully stripped meat from it. The female sat nearby observing them for five minutes before leaving the scene.

As the day wore on, I became increasingly concerned that I had made no sightings of the other two chicks. Wondering if they might be concealed in the catwalk area north of the eyrie, I went to the end of the Cryder House pier to obtain a better viewing point but half an hour of intense scrutiny yielded no sign of any young.

At 7:00 P.M., the female jumped off the tower, made a steep dive almost straight down the tower column, and snared a pigeon. Twenty minutes later, I observed one of the fledglings exercising on the pier; it alternately ran and flew short distances on the pier as only a newly fledged chick is apt to do. My observation day came to a close just before nightfall, with a lone fledgling on the pier being guarded by the female.

This day had been one of very mixed emotions. Having seen two healthy chicks together on the day they had fledged had certainly been a joyful experience, but this was also the first day that we discerned the dreaded trend that we face each breeding season at the bridge nesting sites and, to a lesser extent, at the building locations. Each year we anticipate the disappearance of chicks, both those who were not known to have fledged and those who had. In this instance, it appeared that two of the four fledglings might well have disappeared. While it was possible that they had merely escaped our notice, they should have been visible at some point during the day's observations. We could only hope.

On June 11, I started observing at 5:45 A.M. and, within a half hour, I found a fledgling on the Bronx pier. Then both adults alighted on the platforms above the fledgling. Later, a fledgling was on a weight-bearing cable. This perch on high certainly demonstrated the young bird's ability to fly competently, although it was very probably only its second day out of the eyrie. I observed a single fledgling first on the Bronx pier and then on the Queens pier. Was it one and the same bird or were there two different birds, one at each pier? I could not be certain.

The afternoon produced a spate of interesting observations. The fledgling Red was on the Queens pier when Rio flew at him in a manner suggesting that he wanted the youngster to take wing. Failing to move Red, Rio alighted on the west platform. A crow flew into the fender, causing consternation among the many pigeons in the area but eliciting no reaction from Rio. It is possible that the crow had escaped notice because Rio's view was blocked, since, when the crow finally lifted off the fender, Rio attacked it with great vigor. The crow wisely retreated into the fender and Rio alighted on the east platform, which provided him with a view of both Red and the fender. Shortly thereafter, the second fledgling landed on the pier and lay flat. The female then displaced Rio from the platform. The crow decided to make for land and incurred the wrath of the adult female. She pursued it and made serious attack dives at the crow until they reached landfall.

Later in the afternoon, I observed four peregrines aloft, though briefly. It seemed evident that two of the fledglings, at least, were alive and well.

It was Saturday, June 13. My observations began before 6:00 A.M. The female first hunted at 7:00 A.M., unsuccessfully pursuing a pigeon.

Fifteen minutes later, when Rio attacked a small flock of pigeons, she joined in the attack and Rio captured one. He then deposited his catch on the anchorage and flew away. Ten minutes later, Rio flew into view with different prey and consumed it himself. At 8:00 A.M., both fledglings came in viewing range as they flew between the tower and the anchorage. It was a most welcome sight to view two healthy young aloft and being watched over by two adults. The pain of the almost certain loss of the other two chicks was eased by the joyful scene unfolding before us.

Uninterrupted monitoring is essential in ferreting out the many behavioral nuances and the odd events that occur regularly at peregrine eyries. During the next hour, we observed a fledgling short stoop a pigeon and thus displaying a visible hint of things to come. Having completed this bold maneuver, he alighted very proficiently on a handcable. A short while later, we spotted a peregrine diving toward the water at midspan. Expecting to witness a hunt, all binoculars turned to the battle arena. Instead of a peregrine diving at its victim, we saw a great black-backed gull diving at a peregrine fledgling. The gull repeatedly went at the youngster, no doubt fully intending to force him into the water where he could quickly dispatch it. While the fledgling had no trouble in avoiding the relatively labored approaches of the large gull, we feared that any miscalculation on the part of the peregrine would result in disaster. Following a few more determined dives by the gull, which drove the fledgling close to the water, the fledgling finally realized that this was no game and fled the scene. We wondered why no adult came to the youngster's rescue. It might have been merely that neither adult was in a position to observe the danger to its young.

In the afternoon, the female alighted directly upon the prey that Rio had earlier deposited on the anchorage ledge, deplumed it, and flew off with it. Rio arrived at the ledge several minutes later and appeared to be perplexed because his cache was missing. It seemed strange that a meal that had been ignored for so many hours had became the focal point of both adults.

In the evening, the adults hunted together above the Bronx. They flew patterns that were very much like those courtship flights usually observed at the beginning of the breeding season. At a quarter to eight, Rio was perched on the Queens tower in a most relaxed stance.

The activities of the day are usually over by this late hour. However, a light brown pigeon winging its way along the fender toward shore proved to be such an attractive lure that Rio could not resist and instinctively zoomed straight down at it. The female entered the fray after Rio had already missed making contact with the bird several times. Their synergistic attack was fine-tuned to a degree that I had not often seen duplicated in ten seasons of watching peregrines. They alternated passes at the quarry breathtakingly fast, not allowing it time to plan any evasive maneuvers. The female snatched the bird from the air and flew to pier 1 with it. She sat on the pigeon as she regained her composure. Suddenly there was an unexplainable flutter of wings and the pigeon was free and several feet from the female. There was a look of consternation on the female's face and a look of disbelief on the face of a very puzzled pigeon. A few seconds elapsed before the pigeon realized it was "free" to leave. As soon as it had taken to wing, Rio bound into it. As he carried it past the anchorage, flying prey feathers gave testimony to the fact that he had delivered the fatal neck bite. It is very unusual for an adult bird to lose a victim in that manner, except when it intentionally does so to give a fledgling an opportunity to develop its hunting skills.

Shortly after 6:00 A.M. on Sunday, a white pigeon became the female's quarry. She managed to strike it once but the pigeon withstood the attack and took refuge within the fender. At ten minutes to seven, Rio captured a passerine. But the most interesting event of the day was yet to take place. Dolores and I spotted a brown peregrine winging its way eastward toward the Throgs. Because we had not yet observed a fledgling this morning, we presumed that this was one of the young from the Throgs. Although it seemed strange for it to have been away from the Throgs so early in the morning, we were not entirely prepared for what was about occur. Rio flew out to intercept the fledgling, and did so with a vengeance. The first few dives at it appeared to be a parent's way of chastising a wayward youngster. But Rio's approaches became increasingly more threatening and his new mate joined in the effort to turn the young bird back into the direction from which it had come. There was no question that this individual was not Rio's young. More than twenty passes were made at the transgressor before it was persuaded to reverse its direction. Rio hit it once, but ever so lightly. The two experienced Throgs birds could have easily

271

dispatched this juvenile but their intention was merely to remove it from their territory. They seemed to realize that it was just a youngster and that it presented no real danger to them. Although it had been thrilling to watch the aerial pyrotechnics, we nonetheless worried about this young bird, alone and probably not yet able to adequately fend for itself. The origin of this interloper almost assuredly had to be the New York Hospital. It was the only nesting site which, at that point, was hosting fledglings capable of staying on the wing long enough to have strayed into the Throgs territory.

The first of the two Throgs fledglings showed itself and the female attacked a pigeon, unsuccessfully. On her next hunt, Rio assisted, but this try was also of no avail. Fifteen minutes later, Rio captured a small bird, the second catch of the morning. Since the quantity of food provided by the flesh of the two small birds was insufficient to meet the needs of the fledglings, the female was compelled to continue her hunting. By nine o'clock, she carried the third prey item into the eyrie area. This was a very good sign because prey delivered to the eyrie area is usually intended for the young. Hunting continued irregularly and, by 10:30, the fourth catch had been taken in. One particular chase impressed us because an elusive dove flew several feet above our heads with the female in close pursuit. It was wonderful being so close to a peregrine without disturbing it as usually is the case when humans interact in close proximity with wild creatures.

In the evening, an adult harassed a great black-backed gull and, a short while later, we saw a fledgling circling over the anchorage. A second fledgling appeared but our observations for the remainder of the evening revealed no additional young. It was very disturbing to see only two young. It was now the fourth day since the first two chicks had fledged and the evidence was mounting that two chicks were lost.

On June 15, the adults were observed regularly but only one fledgling had shown itself. This was a depressing situation because now we were seeing only one of the two chicks that were known to have fledged on June 10. In addition, we were also lamenting the loss of the other two chicks that were unaccounted for.

The next day's observations did not bring any brighter news. Although the lone fledgling flew well, it was the second day in which we had failed to spot the second fledgling. It seemed almost certain that there was only one chick still alive at the Throgs.

Other News: the good and the bad

The news from other nest sites was considerably more heartening. Chris had banded two chicks at the Tappan Zee. This was especially welcome news because the peregrines at the site had failed to produce young for the past three consecutive seasons due to a combination of nesting failures. At the newest breeding site in the NYC area, the Pan Am Building, the single chick had fledged and seemed to be doing well.

The Marine Parkway Bridge's lift cables were scheduled to be inspected on June 17, necessitating the lowering of the counterweight. Although the nest box was not attached to the counterweight and the chicks were expected to have fledged by that date, it was nevertheless desirable to monitor the test in the event that the day's operations might adversely affect the peregrines. Arrangements were made and Tom Monaghan and I went to the bridge, equipped with a 60-power spotting scope and tripod, two video recorders, a 135 mm lens camera, and 10-power binoculars. We would be available to help the peregrines in the event of a problem; we also wanted to enjoy viewing the spectacle of a peregrine family, that might number as many as six members, on the wing. Photographing them successfully would provide a wonderful bonus.

As we trod up the bridge's gradual incline toward its north tower, the cool sea breeze chilled us as it washed across our bare skin and through our lightweight clothing. We were fifty yards from the tower when the adult male streaked past us, straight up the center of the roadway. To us, at first, it seemed dangerous for the peregrine to be flying only about ten yards above vehicular traffic, but the bird knew his territory and traveling this route was probably old hat to him. Suddenly there were adult and fledgling peregrines flying all around, just above us. Unfortunately, we could not photograph them because we had not yet readied our equipment.

At the south tower, we watched as the bridge inspectors took the elevator up to the eyrie area; the bridge's maintenance supervisor came over to tell us that the inspectors were very wary of the peregrines' behavior. The birds were diving at them menacingly and yelling very loudly. He asked us to consider going up to the eyrie to assuage the inspectors and at the same time monitor the birds. We agreed to help and shared the elevator trip with an inspector who told us that, at the Throgs Neck, one of his workers on a previous occasion had been cut so badly by the peregrines that stitches were required to close the wound. After we had entered onto the platform above the counterweight, I found that there were no fledglings in the vicinity. Of course, some inspectors had arrived earlier and any chicks in the vicinity would have flown at their appearance.

The adult male peered at the men from behind a steel mesh and remained there for more than two hours without uttering a sound, seemingly more curious than disturbed by the presence of so many interlopers. The adult female held quite a different opinion about the intrusion. She flew many circular sorties in front of the eyrie and vocalized very stridently. There was no mistaking her adamant opposition to our being in her eyrie area, nor did the passing of time mollify her. Again and again she dove in toward the eyrie, though she did not try to make contact or alight.

We scoped the area while there and three fledglings came into our view as they perched on the top of beams thirty-five feet above the roadway. They seemed very relaxed and lay down most of the time. The sun was directly on them, warming them and the beam beneath them. We scanned every inch of the bridge within our view but could not find the fourth fledgling during the two and one-half hours of our stay. The youngsters did go aloft for a while in a spirited flying session. They flew well and appeared to be in good condition. We enjoyed the unexpected pleasure of being able to see and photograph the adults at the eyrie. Above all, the most positive element of the day was witnessing the fine physical condition of the three young that we did see.

The Throgs. At 3:00 P.M. when I returned home, the Throgs fledgling Red was perched very adultlike on the edge of pier 1. His immaturity quickly manifested itself, however, when he lay on the edge of the pier with one wing hanging over the side. Later, he flew off and eventually alighted on a top-floor terrace of Cryder House. Rio flew by Red's perch, no doubt to check his safety, and Red returned to the Throgs. At 4:00 P.M., I heard peregrine calls and rushed out onto the terrace. Red was on the ledge above the 1983 eyrie feeding. This was the third day in which there had been no sign of the second fledgling. Not seeing the two young together was a bad sign. However, since there previously had been a similar two-day absence of one of these two fledged chicks, there was still a chance that wayward chick would reappear.

A fourth day passed with only Red being observed and then, on June 19, Chris phoned to give me the bad news; the body of one of the Throgs fledglings had been recovered from the roadway on June 17. That would have been Blackie. This corroborated our fears that there was only one surviving fledgling. It was sad to lose three of the four young but after ten seasons of following the peregrines' fortunes at the Throgs and other sites, one almost becomes inured to the attrition of fledglings.

The next morning, Red was on pier 3 dissecting a pigeon while Rio watched from his perch on pier 1. Five minutes later, the female alighted on pier 3, prompting Red to hop away, prey in foot, to the other end of the pier. No doubt this was Red's way of protecting his meal. Rio joined them on pier 3, completing the family portrait. Rio moved close to his new mate and both stood almost facing each other for seven minutes.

Ten minutes later, the adults were aloft flying tight circles around the base of pier 1. The quarry, a dove, attempted to seek sanctuary at the anchorage but was snared by Rio. As Rio alighted on the anchorage ledge, I transferred from my binoculars to the telescope. The dove escaped Rio's grasp and dropped into the water below the 1983 eyrie. It flapped its wings strongly but was not able to lift itself out of the water. Rio made several passes at it without trying to snare it. Finally, he alighted on the ledge above his victim, where he was soon joined by the female. Intermittently, each adult flew by the dove but neither tried to recover it from the water.

Marine Parkway. On June 21, Dave Gardner, Tom Renner, and I arrived at the Marine Parkway Bridge site at 8:00 A.M. and immediately heard the plaintive calls of the young peregrines. We could not see them but we spotted the adult female perched on the north tower and the adult male near the nest box. Suddenly, several peregrines were aloft near the north tower; they alighted on it. There were two fledglings there and shortly the adult female delivered prey to them. I was able to read both figures on one fledgling's alphanumeric band and the numeral on the other's band. We could not find the other two fledglings.

We surveyed nearby Floyd Bennett Field in search of another peregrine since one youngster had been observed there. Unfortunately, not only were we unable to find any peregrines but also a park ranger informed us that the body of a dead peregrine fledgling had been discovered in nearby Rockaway. This news corroborated a feeling we had held for several days, that one of the four fledglings had to be considered lost because it had not been seen with the others for too long a period of time. Adding to our dismay, we had observed only two of the four fledglings this day, indicating the distinct possibility that the other might also be lost. We hoped for the best and continued our journey, to the Verrazano-Narrows Bridge site.

Verrazano-Narrows. During the hour we were at the Verrazano, two fledglings alighted on electrical cables at the Brooklyn tower. Then the adult female carried prey into the area but we did not see either her or the young take food. Try as we might, we could not find either the adult male or the other fledgling. The Verrazano is an extremely large structure with many recesses within which birds could be hidden from our view. We hoped that this was the reason we had not seen the other members of this peregrine family.

The Throgs. In the afternoon at the Throgs, I observed a man walking along the southbound roadway. Although he wore an orange-striped vest with the letters "DOT" (Department of Transportation) emblazoned on it, he looked suspect because it was Fathers' Day Sunday. When he raised his long-lensed camera, it became evident that his mission was photographic. The female peregrine flew out to intercept him and circled above him, calling all the while. I worried that, in her zeal to drive away the stranger, the female might come into contact with a vehicle. I called the TBTA office to advise them of the trespasser. Within ten minutes, they had whisked the fellow off the Throgs.

In the late evening, Red and Rio were soaring near the anchorage. There were many other birds traveling through the area, getting ready for nightfall by returning to the safety of their night roost. Red suddenly did a wingover and, with lightning-speed acceleration, dove at a passerine. It was difficult to surmise whether this was a serious hunting attempt or merely juvenile zeal. Either way, the maneuver was adult-like in its execution.

The next day was cold for the first day of summer. The temperature measured in the low fifties, Fahrenheit, and northwesterly winds were blowing strong. These climatic conditions primed the peregrines for increased flying sorties. They relished the updrafts which effortlessly buoyed them up over the Throgs and the Cryder House. Their wings were needed only for capturing the force of the wind as they soared and glided. In fact, many of the other birds in the area such as gulls, pigeons, and cormorants were using the strong air currents too, but not with the elan and utter majesty as did the peregrines. Red had been on the wing for less than two weeks and already had substantially mastered the soaring, gliding, and climbing attributes afforded by this type of wind condition. It was extremely gratifying to witness this rapid developmental transformation from a fearful youngster to an adept flier. During one of his flying runs, Red took the opportunity to dive at a cormorant, all the while exhibiting complete control and the usual peregrine self-assuredness. This one healthy, active fledgling almost made us forget the loss of the other three young at the Throgs.

June 23 was the first day in which I did not observe the Throgs fledgling. My observation periods had been rather short and irregular, leading me to hope that the fledgling might merely be evading my detection. Illness compelled me to forego my usual observation periods for June 24 and the next day's observations were inconclusive about the status of the fledgling.

In the succeeding days, the situation became abundantly clear: all of the four young at the Throgs were lost. On June 26, I was advised that a dead peregrine chick had been found washed up on the shore of City Island. Thus, two young had been found dead and two others were unaccounted for; one had not been seen since June 15, the other since June 22. The 1992 season was a disaster at the Throgs. We were nonetheless heartened by the facts: that a total of twenty-one chicks had been produced in the region; that a new breeding site had been established at the Pan Am Building; and that Tappan Zee Bridge had reemerged as a producing site.

Marine Parkway. The Marine Parkway Bridge site had suffered from only one known loss of a fledgling to this point. To ascertain the status of the fledglings there and to possibly read their leg bands, Dave Gardner and I visited the site. We were on the bridge walkway by 8:00 A.M. Sunday, June 28. Immediately, we found two fledglings aloft, and we observed them as they came to rest on the south side of the north tower. They were about eighty feet above us and in a position that allowed us an excellent view. I read the alphanumeric band numbers of one bird; it was the same band which I had read one week earlier. The youngsters called loudly. It sounded like a food-begging call but no adult responded to their vocalizations. Eventually, the adult female appeared and was aggressively pursued by the young. She gained altitude and the fledglings followed her lead, soaring higher and higher and soon forgetting their original demands. It was splendid to witness three free spirits on the wing. However, there was still an unanswered and nagging question concerning the well-being of the unseen third fledgling. It began to appear that there remained only two of the original four fledglings at the site. Although we observed the site diligently for three hours, we could account for only two young.

Tappan Zee. On July 3, Dolores and I observed the Tappan Zee site for an hour, focusing our attention on a chick that was sitting on the nest box beam. It moved very little and we could not determine whether the bird had already been on the wing or had merely clambered across the beam. A second peregrine caught my attention as it alighted near the first one. It appeared to be a fledgling with brown plumage. Its landing was less than graceful. We did not see the adults during this observation.

A visit to the Tappan Zee two weeks later proved to be very rewarding. An adult and a fledgling were feeding when we arrived. The adult flew away and a second youngster appeared aloft. The first fledgling joined its sibling and both flew exuberantly. They flew toward each other in mock attacks, flew in tandem formation, and crabbed repeatedly. Skimming close to the water was obviously great fun. In one instance, the young female displaced the adult female from her perch on top of the bridge tower. It was wonderful to see two healthy fledglings on the wing, especially at a site that had failed to produce young in the two previous breeding seasons.

Having accomplished the primary goal of establishing the presence and condition of the two fledglings, I was eager to make my second visit of the day, a Cooper's hawk nest in Purchase, New York. Two one-year-old Cooper's hawks were nesting in a pine tree in the front yard of Polly and Jesse Rothsteins' home. It was very rare for both Cooper's hawk of a producing pair to be only one year old. Three nestlings were thriving seventy feet up in their nest above the watchful eyes of Polly, Jesse, and many others who visited the site on daily basis. The Cooper's were alert to the activities below them but seemed quite indifferent to their human neighbors. After all, they had chosen the site and they knew the environmental conditions. Unlike peregrines, which attempt to obtain synchronous hatching, Cooper's often have a wide spread in the ages of their young. These three nestlings showed marked differences in their development. The last-born had much more down and stayed within the nest cup most of the time, while its two siblings had already discovered the joys of jumping from branch to branch and making short flights to adjacent trees. The female fed the young every two to three hours. The male was observed infrequently because he did not approach the nest closely but delivered his catches to the female, usually out of the observers' view. It was an interesting change of pace to observe a nesting raptor that leads such a strikingly different lifestyle from that of peregrines.

Marine Parkway. The news from the Marine Parkway Bridge site was not encouraging. Ron Bourque visited the Floyd Bennett Field on July 4 and observed an adult peregrine and a fledgling, no doubt the Marine Parkway Bridge birds. The adult was bathing in a rain puddle on one of the runways while the youngster watched it, calling loudly. The following day, Ron observed both adults and only one fledgling, observations which were consistent with mine of the ensuing day.

The Throgs. Our observation sessions at the Throgs were being carried out less frequently now because we had given up hope of seeing any young. I did continue to monitor the Throgs regularly, however, mostly because it had become an ingrained habit but also on the slight chance that I might find a youngster. I trained my scope on Rio one evening and watched as he jumped off the pier with a purposeful attitude. He zoomed down to the water level at the anchorage to help his new partner, who was in pursuit of a pigeon. I did not see the actual strike but the victim soon was bobbing in the water vainly, flailing its wings. The peregrines circled it a few times and then alighted on the anchorage ledge to watch their hapless victim. The pigeon showed extraordinary stamina as it flapped its wings scores of times without missing a beat. It made no progress, either in rising from the water or moving toward a haven, because the wind-driven currents were too strong. Rio and his mate were on the ledge, close together, waiting for the right moment to pluck their soggy prize from the water.

Suddenly I could no longer see the pigeon and, evidently, neither could the peregrines. They searched the area, first visually from their perch and then by flying circular patterns. The pigeon was gone; and so was their interest.

They were a handsome couple as they perched on the ledge. Rio's mien could almost be described as dainty. He was so much smaller than the female and his very white bib looked as if it had been bleached and starched. The female seemed regal. She had stronger barring on her chest and light, thin stripes on her off-white bib. Seeing them together, at ease and hunting, was an elixir in these troubled times.

Marine Parkway. Several days later, I traveled to the Marine Parkway Bridge, hoping against hope to find more than one fledgling at the site. The adult male alighted at the top of the nest tower. From this vantage point, he flew at a pigeon and struck it lightly. On being hit, the pigeon dove directly down to the safety of the bridge fender. The male then alighted on the nest box perch pole. I heard the plaintive calling of a fledgling and resumed my search for it. I found the adult female but I still could not locate the youngster. To enhance my viewing position, I ascended a staircase. Increased elevation would allow me to check the tops of the beams between the towers, a favorite resting place of the young. Reaching the first level, I saw nothing, so I climbed to the second level. Again, I failed to find any birds. The adult male was eighty feet above me but did not protest my presence, as he had during my previous visit. I went to the third level but was unable to discover the fledgling's location.

As I began to make my descent, I was astounded to see a fledgling lying flat on the top of a beam within six feet of the first stairway I had climbed. Its left wing was splayed out to the side and it had a doleful look on its face. My first impression was that it was injured but I dismissed that idea because fledglings frequently flatten themselves into odd positions. The adult male, all the while, failed to come to the defense of the youngster. I thought that this related to the fledglings having been out of the nest for more than a month. Adult protectiveness declines with time and a fledgling's improved flying ability.

At first, I was reluctant to retrace my steps because I feared that I might flush the bird from its position and unnecessarily cause it distress. Rethinking the situation prompted me to return to the walkway. If the bird were healthy and were to flush, it would merely fly to another perch with no harm having been done. It seemed highly improbable that the bird's safety would in any way be compromised by my close passage. I descended to the walkway and photographed the bird as I went by it. I would wait until the bird took to flight and demonstrated that it was in normal condition. Shortly, it stood erect and my fears about its condition were allayed. The bird appeared to be getting ready to fly off so I ventured back up the stairway for a try at reading its leg band. The bird watched me climb up to within several yards of it with no visible anxiety on its part. Finally, it flew off and alighted on a beam at the north end of the bridge. I pursued it and set up my scope, again trying to read its band, but the unfavorable viewing angle only allowed me to ascertain that it had an alphanumeric band on its right leg. No other fledgling was in view during my observation session. It was possible that a second fledgling could still be alive and well and merely not within my view. However, the realistic chances for this possibility were slim.

The last two observation sessions at the bridge failed to produce any sightings of a fledgling although its cries were heard once. A reliable observer reported seeing a fledgling at nearby Floyd Bennett Field. This fledgling had very probably survived to dispersal but it was doubtful that any of its other nestmates had been as fortunate. Young peregrine fledglings need four to six weeks to develop their flying and hunting skills satisfactorily enough to survive independently.

Bike Tour. Sunday is the best day for a long bicycle ride when coupled with a peregrine run. I set out on August 2 and arrived at the Pan Am Building by 9:00 A.M. I scanned the nest building, the Chrysler Building, as well as other likely perching locations, but to no avail. My next stop was at the Riverside Church. Both adults were aloft but no young were visible, though I searched for half an hour. I pedaled on to the New York Hospital site. Again. there were no peregrines to be seen there during my short visit. This was to be expected because, as is the case at the Pan Am Building, there are many high perches on many buildings in the vicinity of the nest building which cannot be seen from ground level. At any rate, I had had a wonderful bicycle ride and had seen two peregrines.

The Throgs. Routine observations at the Throgs were enlivened on August 25 when a brown-plumaged, immature female peregrine appeared at the site. Rio immediately went on the attack. He called loudly and dove at the intruder. Rio's repeated dives finally persuaded the visitor to leave the area.

Hospital. On September 10, Chris informed me that the sole male fledgling from the New York Hospital eyrie had been found dead at the JFK Airport. Each season we receive these reports with resignation because their inevitability is certain. We sadly accept the reality that only a few of each year's young are destined to survive to even their first birthday.

Migration

September through October is the major time period of the fall raptor migration through the New York City metropolitan region. I spent from three to nine hours on each of thirty days during this period identifying and enumerating raptors as they moved past Fort Tilden on the shore of the Atlantic Ocean in Rockaway. My viewing platform, on top of an old gun emplacement, is nine-tenths of a mile from the peregrine eyrie at the Marine Parkway Bridge. On most days, I was able to observe one or both of the resident adult peregrines perched on the bridge or flying near it.

On September 21, I observed two peregrines moving southwest just offshore past my Fort Tilden position. They were traveling at a much greater altitude than were the other raptors. Their height, combined with the poor light available, did not allow me to identify their age or their plumage characteristics. Their side-by-side formation was very unusual for migrators. I watched them until they became specks and disappeared from view. I checked the sky behind me frequently, hoping to spot the two peregrines I had seen earlier should they return. Within ten minutes, a second pair of peregrines approached from the southwest, also flying in tandem. This time, however, they were flying at a much reduced altitude and were easily identifiable as adults. I followed their flight path to the Marine Parkway Bridge. It was as I had surmised; the resident pair had been taking their morning constitutional. I was invigorated by the sight of these wild animals in their natural state.

Fort Tilden had an even more spectacular peregrine-watching session in store for me. On October 2, I trained my spotting scope on an adult peregrine winging furiously past me in the usual migratory direction. Its purposeful flight did not alert me to its mission but its route prompted me to consider that it might be one of the bridge birds. I observed the speeding peregrine until it had traveled almost beyond the instrument's viewing range. Suddenly, there was a second peregrine in view. The two came together. There was a substantial size difference between them. Their talons intertwined and, clasped together, they cartwheeled downward, several times moving out of my field of view, until they disappeared below the treeline. During almost a decade of watching peregrines and other raptors, I had never had the good fortune of witnessing this exact type of behavior. Undoubtedly, one of the resident peregrines was defending its territory against the intrusion of a migrating peregrine. This type of dramatic display usually causes no harm to either player. The unwelcome traveler is merely being escorted from the resident bird's territory. An animal's inherent predisposition to protect its breeding territory does not allow for the subtle discrimination necessary to decide whether an interloper is a threat or merely traveling through.

Conference

The Raptor Research Foundation conference was convened at Bellevue, Washington, in the fall of 1992. Dr. Dean Amadon and I attended and, fortunately, I met David Hancock, my esteemed publisher for this volume. I very much appreciated the full-day seminar devoted to the burrowing owl because of my work on burrowing owl projects during my winter sojourns in Florida.

Heinrich (World Center for Birds of Prey, Boise, Idaho) delivered a paper stating that "by the late 1970's no peregrines were known to be breeding in Montana, Idaho, or Wyoming, and only small remnant populations were known to exist in Colorado, New Mexico, Northern Utah, Washington, and Oregon. . . . Since 1978, over 1,650 peregrines have been released in the Rocky Mountains and Pacific Northwest . . . . The Peregrine Fund . . . plans to continue releasing about 130 peregrines a year through 1995. After that time we believe state and federal recovery objectives will have been achieved."

Redig and Tordoff's 1992 "Midwest Status Report" advised that

773 falcons had been released during the previous decade. "Given the productivity and stability of this restored population, it is likely that hacking of falcons will occur at a greatly diminished level in 1993 and cease altogether thereafter."

21

Our First Decade

(1993)

The New York City metropolitan region enjoyed its most productive nesting season in 1993, having hosted at least thirty-four chick hatchings. The seven established eyries produced twenty-six chicks while two new eyries, one of which is located at 48 Wall Street and the other at the Goethal's Bridge, each produced four chicks. Each one of these nine nests contributed a minimum of three young. To our amazement, the New York Hospital site produced five chicks, a rare event in the "wild."

I had the pleasure of personally witnessing the banding of the chicks at the 48 Wall Street site. A later visit to the Goethal's Bridge rewarded me with several hours of viewing the adult male and several fledglings. The birds alighted close enough to my viewing position that I was able to read both the adult's and one of the fledgling's band numbers.

To the observer in the field, the world of nature offers an unending treasure of gifts. Surprise and rarity are the watchwords. As my first decade of watching peregrines was drawing to a close in April of 1993, Rio and Chelsea, Rio being the resident male at the Throgs Neck Bridge for that site's eleventh consecutive season, were defending their eyrie against the intrusion of two bridge workers. I watched in horror as Rio plummeted into the water, during the execution of a defensive maneuver, without making an attempt to arrest his fall. Logic dictated that a bird that was unable to keep from falling would not be capable of rising from the water because that would require a much more demanding effort. However, a few seconds later, he inexplicably rose from the water and flew to a platform on the tower. At first, he seemed perplexed, but he soon regained his composure and flew flawlessly up to the eyrie. This observation was one of a kind. No one at any of the New York sites had ever witnessed an adult peregrine descend into the water, let alone extricate itself from it.

Another raptorial drama of rare proportions was unfolding at the same time. A pair of adult red-tailed hawks had built their stick nest on the decorative arch above a window on the top floor of a twelve-story building on Fifth Avenue at 74th Street, adjacent to Central Park. Red-tailed hawks nesting on a city building is an unprecedented event in the annals of raptorial literature. They appeared to be incubating eggs, but sadly, the unique nesting attempt failed.

The hawks often perched on the nearby buildings. Pigeons were regularly on their menu and, in one instance, one of the hawks actually snared one from a group in flight, a la its peregrine neighbors. In fact, the peregrine eyrie at the New York Hospital site is located less than one mile distant.

After the nesting effort had been abandoned, an adult red-tailed hawk was found dead only one block from the red- tails' nest. It proved not to be one of the resident hawks. The most likely explanation is that it had been attacked by the resident hawks in defense of their territory. The promise of future red-tail nesting in the area assuaged the disappointment felt by the many Central Park observers who had hoped to observe fledgling hawks in New York City.

During a late May bicycle ride, I found the red-tailed hawks at their nesting site and later observed the adult peregrines and their three chicks at the Riverside Church site. My third visit was to the MetLife Building site, where I observed a peregrine adult and two young. The crowning event of the trip occurred at the New York Hospital site where I watched as both the adults tended to the needs of their five youngsters. Wonderfully, I had seen fifteen peregrines and a pair of red-tailed hawks during a brisk four-hour bicycle ride. Only New York City offers such a plethora of peregrines to the urban raptorphile.

The Throgs. At the Throgs, the summer of 1993 was filled with the sounds of two exuberant peregrine fledglings. The male and female survivors of the original four-chick clutch were visible daily from our home. They perched so close to us that we were able to read their large alphanumeric bands regularly. We could clearly hear their loud vocalizations from within our apartment, though the windows were shut against the summer's heat. The peregrine youngsters announced their arrivals with calls that were neither those of food begging nor of alarm; they seemed merely to be enjoying life and voicing their youthful enthusiasm.

After five weeks on the wing, the fledglings began to capture prey. They often had to make a score of hunting forays before they were successful. However, their strength and determination augured well for their survival in the days subsequent to their eventual departure from the safety of the Throgs. Chelsea and Rio still provided them with prey but the youngsters would soon be on their own.

The 1993 nesting season was a glorious one, boasting a record number of chicks and two wonderful fledglings at the Throgs. Dolores and I look forward to many more years with our peregrine neighbors.

Epilogue

Rewards

In the spring of 1983, when Dolores and I commenced observing and chronicling the activities of the peregrine falcons, we could never have predicted the extent to which our involvement with them would have grown in the subsequent years. To this day, Dolores cannot divine the reason why she felt compelled to record our observations of the peregrines from our very first encounter with them. However, her more than a score of years as a nurse educator, in which field the documenting of behavior and conditions is routine, almost assuredly was the underlying force. The log became both the foundation and the portent of our future deepening involvement with the peregrines and the writing of this book. We still record peregrine observations and data and doubtless will continue this practice for as long as we and the peregrines are present.

Our enjoyment of peregrines has never waned. Each new peregrine nest, which is created in the New York City area, rekindles our spirits. Their success radiates a feeling of renewal and is a beacon that brightens our path. Sadly we recall the barren years when there were no peregrines nesting in the eastern United States. Every new nest reaffirms the renaissance of the peregrine and demonstrates the power of the environmentally aware citizenry that has supported the peregrine reintroduction program. The growing peregrine population is a testament to the efforts of many people who have worked to redress the ecological damage wrought in the past.

These past ten years have been very rewarding to us. As Dolores aptly stated, "Seeing one, two, or more peregrines flying, soaring, or diving at prey is a spectacle for the eyes and a balm for the soul. Having them as neighbors and sharing with them the beautiful area in which we live has been a unique experience. As we observe the peregrines from our "eyrie," we are awed by their beauty, regal mien, and incomparable flying skills." Dolores and I still interrupt our meals to observe our peregrine neighbors whenever they fly by or call out.

Personally, the practice of two virtues have come to the fore during our decade of monitoring and studying peregrines. First, patience is necessary to properly observe them. Hours often pass by without a meaningful activity taking place. However, in the next instant, a nest exchange may occur or a hitherto unobserved fledgling might fly into view.

The second virtue of great value is humility when studying wild animals. One must forsake some of one's usual thought processes. Logic often serves to deter an observer from understanding the sights before his eyes because it frequently tends to be anthropomorphic. Attributing human traits to wild animals leads to erroneous analysis. The observer must accept each happening for what it is without reading too much into it. Only after considerable study should one begin to analyze the true meaning of one's observations of wild creatures.

Dolores and I have been gratified to have had the pleasure of meeting so many devoted and knowledgeable raptor enthusiasts. Whether they were professional or amateur, we have shared with them a common bond of love and protection of the peregrine. Unassisted, we began our decade of watching at a time when there were in existence only two working nests. In the following period of five years, no new nests were established but serendipitously we came to know other peregrine and hawk watchers. At present, there are nine chick-producing nests within the parameters of our study area. Our network of raptorphiles has grown in proportion to the increase in peregrine nesting successes.

Now, having reached our retirement years, Dolores and I spend our winters in Florida. The plight of Florida's burrowing owl captured our interest and, as a result, we joined the owl study project at Florida Atlantic University. In addition, we have initiated our own long-term census project of nesting burrowing owls in suburban Palm Beach County, Florida. It seems that we are attracted to raptors suffering habitat loss. Thus, we fortunately have worthy undertakings in the vicinity of both our homes.

We predict that the New York City area peregrine population will continue to prosper and that new territories will be established. There are so many more bridges and buildings that can provide them with nesting sites. Dolores and I look forward to future living in harmony with and admiration of this most magnificent creature, the city peregrine falcon.

Appendixes

APPENDIX A

Locations of Peregrine Falcon Nesting Sites and Territories
in the New York City Metropolitan Region

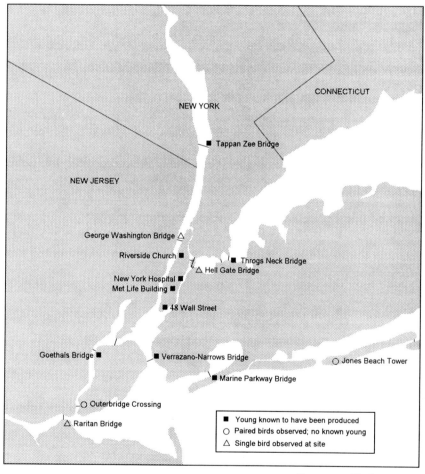

Map prepared by Steve Walter

APPENDIX B*

Breeding Season Recapitulation for
Peregrine Falcons in New York City and Environs

1983

Location	Eggs	Hatched	Fledged	Dispersed	Notes
Throgs Neck Bridge	3	2	1	1	[1]
Verrazano Bridge	3	3	3		
	6	5	4	1	

NOTES: [1] One chick possibly lost to vandalism.

1984

Location	Eggs	Hatched	Fledged	Dispersed	Notes
Throgs Neck Bridge	3	3	3	2	
Verrazano Bridge	3	3			
	6	6	3	2	

1985

Location	Eggs	Hatched	Fledged	Dispersed	Notes
Throgs Neck Bridge	4	4	3	3	
Verrazano Bridge	2	0			[1]
	6	4	3	3	

NOTES: [1] Adult female found dead on bridge in July.

* Information in part furnished by New York State Department of Environmental Conservation, Endangered Species Unit (DEC). Inaccuracies are the responsibility of the author.

1986

Location	Eggs	Hatched	Fledged	Dispersed	Notes
Throgs Neck Bridge	3	3	1	1	
Verrazano Bridge	3	1	1	0	[1]
	6	4	2	1	

NOTES: [1] Fledgling disappeared and was not accounted for.

1987

Location	Eggs	Hatched	Fledged	Dispersed	Notes
Throgs Neck Bridge	3	0			[1]
Verrazano Bridge	4	0			[2]
	7	0			

NOTES: [1] Continued disturbance at eyrie by contractors.
   [2] Adult female found dead on bridge; 1984 issue.

1988

Location	Eggs	Hatched	Fledged	Dispersed	Notes
Throgs Neck Bridge	4 + 4		1	1	[1]
Verrazano Bridge	2	0			[2]
N. Y. Hospital	3	2	2	2	
Tappan Zee Bridge	3	3	3	2	[3]
	16	5	6	5	

NOTES: [1] Two 4-egg clutches taken for laboratory rearing and hacking. One (non-related) chick fostered.
   [2] Adult female found dead on bridge; not thought to be the resident nesting female.
   [3] One fledgling rescued from the Hudson River and placed back on the bridge but only two were observed at season's end.

293

1989

Location	Eggs	Hatched	Fledged	Dispersed	Notes
Throgs Neck Bridge	4	4	3\4	2	[1]
Verrazano Bridge	4	2	0		[2]
N. Y. Hospital	3	3	3	3	
Tappan Zee Bridge	1	1	1	0	[3]
Riverside Church	2 + 4	2	2	2	[4]
40 Wall Street	4	0			[5]
Hell Gate Bridge					[6]
42nd Street area					[7]
Outerbridge Crossing					[7]
	22	12	9	7	

NOTES:
[1] One chick unaccounted for.
[2] One egg disappeared, one egg unhatched, one chick died (several days old), one chick removed.
[3] Minimum number of eggs; nest box not inspected. Fledgling killed on bridge roadway.
[4] First clutch fell from ledge. Second clutch: 1 egg disappeared, 1 cracked egg removed.
[5] 3 eggs disappeared, 1 addled egg removed.
[6] Adult pair; apparently failed nesting attempt.
[7] Adult pair; no known nesting attempt.

1990

Location	Eggs	Hatched	Fledged	Dispersed	Notes
Throgs Neck Bridge	4	4	2	1	[1] [2]
Verrazano Bridge	4	4	3	3	[1]
N. Y. Hospital	3	3	3	1	[3]
Tappan Zee Bridge					[4]
Riverside Church	4	2	2	2	
Wall Street area					[4]
Hell Gate Bridge					[5]
Pan American Building	1+	0			[6]
Outerbridge Crossing					[4]
Goethal's Bridge					[4]
Marine Parkway					
Hodges Memorial Bridge					[7]

Location	Eggs	Hatched	Fledged	Dispersed	Notes
Barrett Station					[5]
Island Park					
	16	13	10	6	

NOTES: [1] One nestling taken for hacking elsewhere.
            [2] One nestling died on bridge, one fledgling unaccounted for.
            [3] Female fledgling found dead and male fledgling found injured (not releasable) on adjacent building.
            [4] Adult pair; no known nesting attempt.
            [5] Single adult at site.
            [6] At least one egg laid; disappeared. No known renesting.
            [7] Subadult pair at site.

1991

Location	Eggs	Hatched	Fledged	Dispersed	Notes
Throgs Neck Bridge	4	3	2/3	1	[1]
Verrazano Bridge	3	3	3	2	[2]
N. Y. Hospital	4	4	4	3	[3]
Tappan Zee Bridge	3	0			
Riverside Church	5	3	3	3	
Wall Street area	0				[4]
Pan American Building	3	0			[5]
Outerbridge Crossing					[4]
Goethal's Bridge					[4]
Marine Parkway					
Hodges Memorial Bridge	2	2	2	2	[6]
	24	15	15	11	

NOTES: [1] One chick drowned at bridge.
            [2] One chick found dead on roadway.
            [3] One fledgling found dead in waters at LaGuardia Airport.
            [4] Adult pair; no known nesting attempt.
            [5] Each egg laid in different location.
            [6] Resident female killed May 16, 1991.

1992

Location	Eggs	Hatched	Fledged	Dispersed	Notes
Throgs Neck Bridge	4	4	2	0	
Verrazano Bridge	4	3	3	2	
N. Y. Hospital	4	4	4	4	
Tappan Zee Bridge	2	2	2	2	[1]
Riverside Church	4	3	3	3	
Pan American Bldg.	4	1	1	1	
Marine Parkway					
Hodges Mem. Brdg.	4	4	4	1	
Wall Street area					[2]
Outerbridge Crossing					[2]
Goethal's Bridge					[2]
Bayonne Bridge					[3]
	26	21	19	13	

NOTES:
[1] Minimum number of eggs; nest box not inspected.
[2] Courtship behavior; no known nesting attempt.
[3] Single adult at site.

1993

Location	Eggs	Hatched	Fledged	Dispersed	Notes
Throgs Neck Bridge	4	4	2	2	
Verrazano Bridge	4	4			
N. Y. Hospital	5	5	5	5	
Tappan Zee Bridge	4	4	2		
Riverside Church	3	3	3	3	
MetLife Building	4	3	3		
Marine Parkway					
Hodges Mem. Bridge	4	3	1		
48 Wall Street	4	4	4		
Goethal's Bridge	4	4	4		
	36	34	*	*	

* No totals—data incomplete.

296

APPENDIX C*

1983–1993 Breeding Summary: New York City Area

	'83	'84	'85	'86	'87	'88	'89	'90	'91	'92	'93
Nests	2	2	2	2	2	4	6	5	7	7	9
Eggs	6	6	6	6	7	16	22	16	24	26	36
Hatched	5	6	4	4	0	5	12	13	15	21	34
Fledged	4	3	3	2	0	6	9	10	15	19	
Dispersed	1	2	3	1	0	5	7	7	11	13	

1983–1993 Breeding Summary: New City York Area

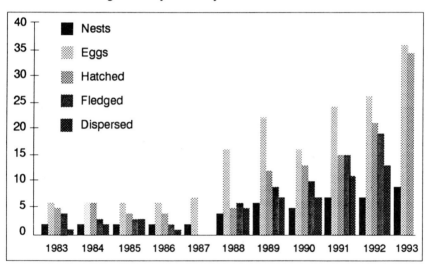

* Information in part furnished by New York State Department of Environmental Conservation, Endangered Species Unit (DEC). Inaccuracies are the responsibility of the author.

APPENDIX D*

Throgs Neck Bridge

	Eggs	Hatched	Fledged	Dispersed	Notes
		Nesting Results			
1983	3	2	1	1	[1]
1984	3	3	3	2	
1985	4	4	3	3	
1986	3	3	1	1	
1987	3	0			
1988	4 + 4		1	1	[2]
1989	4	4	3/4	2	[3]
1990	4	4	2	0	[4]
1991	4	3	2/3	1	[3] [5]
1992	4	3	2	0	[6]
1993	4	4	2	2	
	44	30	20	13	

NOTES:
[1] One chick possibly lost to vandalism.
[2] Two 4-egg clutches taken for lab rearing and hacking. One nonrelated chick fostered.
[3] One chick unaccounted for.
[4] One female nestling taken for hacking elsewhere. One female nestling found dead on bridge. One fledgling unaccounted for.
[5] One fledgling drowned at bridge.
[6] One fledgling found dead on bridge. One fledgling found dead at City Island. One chick unaccounted for.

* Information in part furnished by New York State Department of Environmental Conservation, Endangered Species Unit (DEC). Inaccuracies are the responsibility of the author.

Verrazano-Narrows Bridge

	Eggs	Hatched	Fledged	Dispersed	Notes
		Nesting Results			
1983	3	3	3		
1984	3	3	3		

	Eggs	Hatched	Fledged	Dispersed	Notes
1985	2	0			[1]
1986	3	1	1	0	[2]
1987	4	0			[3]
1988	2+2	0			[4][5]
1989	4	2			[6]
1990	4	4	3	3	[7]
1991	3	3	3	2	[8]
1992	4	3	3	2	
1993	4	4			
	38	24	16	7	

NOTES: [1] Adult female found dead on bridge in July.
        [2] Fledgling disappeared and not accounted for.
        [3] Adult female found dead on bridge; 1984 issue.
        [4] Two clutches laid at different locations.
        [5] Adult female found dead on bridge; not believed to be the resident nester.
        [6] One egg disappeared. One egg unhatched. One hatchling died at age of few days. One nestling removed.
        [7] One nestling taken to be hacked elsewhere.
        [8] One chick found dead on roadway.

New York Hospital/Cornell Medical Center

Nesting Results

	Eggs	Hatched	Fledged	Dispersed	Notes
1988	3	2	2	2	
1989	3	3	3	3	
1990	3	3	3	1	[1]
1991	4	4	4	3	[2]
1992	4	4	4	4	
1993	5	5	5	5	
	22	21	21	18	

NOTES: [1] Female fledgling found dead and male fledgling found injured (not releasable) on adjacent building.
        [2] One fledgling found dead in waters at LaGuardia Airport.

299

Tappan Zee Bridge

	Eggs	Nesting Results Hatched	Fledged	Dispersed	Notes
1988	3	3	3	2	[1]
1989	1	1	1	0	[2] [3]
1990	0				[4]
1991	3	0			[5]
1992	2	2	2	2	[2]
1993	4	4	4		
	13	10	10	4	

NOTES: [1] One fledgling rescued from Hudson River and placed back on bridge but only two were observed at season's end.
[2] Minimum number of eggs; nestbox not inspected.
[3] Fledgling was rescued from roadway area and placed back on bridge but later was found dead on roadway.
[4] Adult pair; no known nesting attempt.
[5] Minimum number of eggs; 3 unhatched eggs recovered at close of breeding season.

Riverside Church

	Eggs	Nesting Results Hatched	Fledged	Dispersed	Notes
1989	2+4	2	2	2	[1]
1990	4	2	2	2	
1991	5	3	3	3	
1992	4	3	3	3	
1993	3	3	3	3	
	22	13	13	13	

NOTES: [1] First clutch fell from ledge. Second clutch: one egg disappeared, 1 cracked egg removed.

48 Wall Street

Nesting Results

	Eggs	Hatched	Fledged	Dispersed	Notes
1989	4	0			[1]
1990					[2]
1991					[2]
1992					[2]
1993	4	4	4		
	8	4	4		

NOTES: [1] Three eggs disappeared; 1 addled.
        [2] Adult pair; no known nesting.

Marine Parkway/Gil Hodges Memorial Bridge

Nesting Results

	Eggs	Hatched	Fledged	Dispersed	Notes
1990	0				[1]
1991	2	2	2	2	[2][3]
1992	4	4	4	1	[4]
1993	4	3	3		
	10	9	9	3	

NOTES: [1] Resident pair were 1989 nestmates at New York Hospital.
        [2] Minimum number of eggs; nest not inspected.
        [3] Adult female killed 5/16/91.
        [4] One fledgling found dead at Rockaway.

	Eggs	Nesting Results Hatched	Fledged	Dispersed	Notes
1990	2/3	0			
1991	3				[1]
1992	1	1	1	1	[2]
1993	4	3	3		
	10	4	4	1	

NOTES: [1] Each egg laid in a different location.
        [2] Egg(s) laid in nest box.

APPENDIX E*

1983–1993 New York City Area Peregrine Falcon Nests at Bridge Sites

	'83	'84	'85	'86	'87	'88	'89	'90	'91	'92	'93
Pairs	2	2	2	2	2	3	3	2	4	4	5
Hatched	5	6	4	4	0	3	7	8	8	13	19
Fledged	4	3	3	2	0	4	4	5	8	11	
Dispersed	1	2	3	1	0	3	2	4	5	5	

1983–1993 New York City Area Peregrine Falcon Nests at Bridge Sites

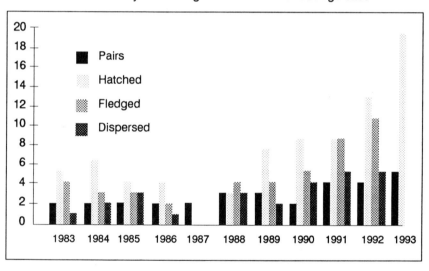

* Information in part furnished by New York State Department of Environmental Conservation, Endangered Species Unit (DEC). Inaccuracies are the responsibility of the author.

APPENDIX F

1988–1993 New York City Peregrine Falcon Nests at Building Sites

	1988	1989	1990	1991	1992	1993
Pairs	1	3	3	3	3	4
Hatched	2	5	5	7	8	15
Fledged	2	5	5	7	8	
Dispersed	2	5	3	6	8	

New York City Peregrine Falcon Nests at Building Sites

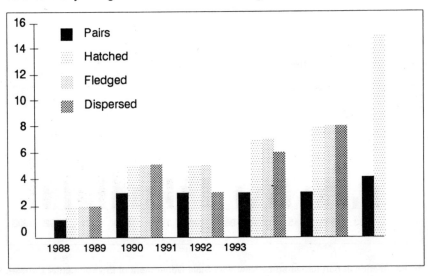

* Information in part furnished by New York State Department of Environmental Conservation, Endangered Species Unit (DEC). Inaccuracies are the responsibility of the author.

APPENDIX G

NYC Area Peregrine Falcons Average Survival Rate to Dispersal Per Egg-laying Pair

	'83	'84	'85	'86	'87	'88	'89	'90	'91	'92
Bridges	0.5	1	1.5	0.5	0	1	0.67	1.5	1.7	1.25
Buildings						2	2.5	1.5	3	2.67

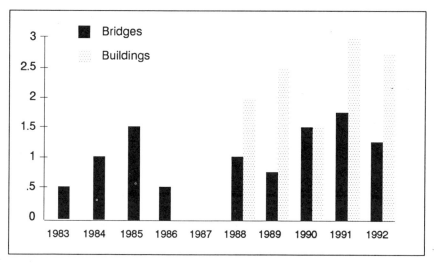

Success Rate: Bridges vs. Buildings

Ten years of peregrine nesting in the New York City metropolitan region provide data which show a pronounced difference in the success rates of bridge versus building eyrie sites. Based on 30 clutches, the overall success rate at bridges was 1.4 chicks per brood vs. 2.4 chicks for buildings. Working solely with chick-producing nesting attempts allows a comparison of the danger levels experienced by chicks at bridges and buildings related to the physical characteristics of the individual sites. Thus, it eliminates most of the biological elements of procreation which are not associated with site attributes.

Bridges attract peregrines because they provide the nest-site attributes that peregrines require: elevation relative to the adjacent topography, an abundant prey base (pigeons), and unhindered hunting space (water). But the double dangers of the bridges' vehicular traffic and the waters below frequently nullify the beneficial site characteristics. The low success rate at bridges occurs despite the fact that all of the current nests are housed in nest boxes. One may only imagine how much lower the productivity rate would be without human intervention.

APPENDIX H

Locations of Major New York City Metropolitan Region Hawk Watches

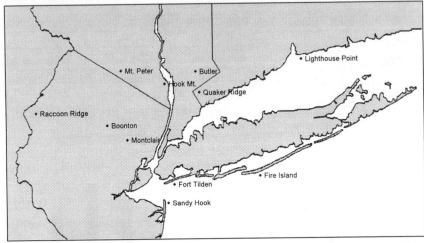

Map prepared by Steve Walter

Boonton (NJ): I-80 exit 53, Route 23 north 11 miles to Kinnelon/Butler exit, Kinnelon Road 6.5 miles to intersection, 6/10 mile to sign on right "DOWTY RFL;" continue on driveway to main parking lot, take dirt road to right and pass metal gate, and swing to left. Park and look for Bill Gallagher in the field.

Butler (Mount Kisco, NY): I-684 exit 4, Route 172 west 1/3 mile, left onto Chestnut Ridge Road, about 1.5 mile to 2nd overpass over I-684 (Butler Sanctuary). Park on west side of overpass and take trail.

Fire Island (NY): East end of Robert Moses State Park.

Fort Tilden (NY): In the west Rockaways, left at first traffic signal west of the southern terminus of Marine Parkway Bridge. Watch conducted from bunker closest to fishermens' parking lot at southwest end of Fort Tilden.

Hook Mountain (near Nyack, NY): I-87 exit 11, Route 9W north about 2 miles (passing Christian Herald Road). Park on right shoulder; room for about 6 cars. Blazed trail to summit.

Montclair (NJ): Garden State Parkway exit 151, Watchung Avenue west 2.1 miles to Upper Montclair Road, right 7/10 mile to Bradford Avenue, left 1/10 mile to Edgecliff Road, right 1/3 mile to parking on right.

Mount Peter (NY): Near the New Jersey border at the intersection of Routes 17A and 210 in Greenwood Lake. Proceed northwest on Route 17A for about 2 miles to the top of the hill. Park in restaurant lot on right. Walk 200 feet to ridge crest behind the lot.

Quaker Ridge (CONN): Merritt Parkway to Round Hill Road, north about 2 miles to John Street (look for church), left to Riversville Road and Greenwich Audubon Center.

Raccoon Ridge (NJ): I-80 exit 12, Route 521 north about 6 miles to Route 94, left about 2 miles (through Blairstown) to Yards Creek sign at Walnut Valley Road, right 4 miles to entrance.

Sandy Hook (NJ): Garden State Parkway exit 117, Keyport, Route 36, east 13 miles. Cross over Navesink River and turn left into Gateway National Recreation Area (Sandy Hook Unit). Go several miles north past maintenance yard on right. Watch site is on elevated land on the right.

Lighthouse Point (CONN): I-95 exit 50 to 2nd traffic signal. Turn right onto Townsend Avenue. Go 2 miles past Morris Cove, on the right, to signal. Right for 1 mile to Lighthouse Point Park entrance.

APPENDIX I

American Museum of Natural History
79th Street / Central Park West
New York, New York 10024

Canadian Wildlife Service
Twin Atria Building / 4999–98 Avenue
Edmonton, Alberta TGB 2X3

Golden Gate Raptor Observatory
Building 201, Fort Mason
San Francisco, California 94123

Hawk Migration Association of North America
Braddock Bay Raptor Research
432 Manitou Beach Road
Hilton, New York 14468

Hawk Migration Association of North America
Northeast Region
377 Loomis Street
Southwick, Massachusetts 01077

The Peregrine Fund, Inc.
World Center for Birds of Prey
5666 Flying Hawk Lane
Boise, Idaho 83709

Raptor Center at the University of Minnesota
College of Veterinary Medicine
1920 Fitch Avenue
St. Paul, Minnesota 55108

Raptor Research Foundation, Inc.
12805 St. Croix Trail
Hastings, Minnesota 55033

Glossary

ALLOPREENING: the preening of one bird by another, usually of the same species and normally a mate; frequently mutual.

BANDING: the placement of a band around a bird's leg. The band is usually circular, numbered, metal, permanent, and does not interfere with the bird's normal functioning. In the United States, the U.S. Department of the Interior, Fish and Wildlife Service provides prenumbered bands to licensed banders. They record the number and data of each banded bird and transmit this information to the Bird Banding Laboratory of the Fish and Wildlife Service. Minimum data pertaining to each banded bird includes species, age, and sex, to the extent possible. If a bird's band number is ever read again (because the bird was subsequently trapped, found dead, band number read in the field, etc.), the band number and information regarding the location and condition of the bird when the band was read should be forwarded to the Bird Banding Laboratory. Their computer prepares two reports: one for the bander, stating the conditions under which the bird's band was read; and one for the person who read and reported the band number, providing the information given when the bird was banded. Nearly two million bands have been recovered and reported. These reports provide information on migration routes, survival rates, harvest patterns of game species, behavior, and other aspects important to the study of bird populations.

BINDING: a raptor's grasping, with its talons, of its prey or any other item with the purpose of holding fast to it.

BIRD OF PREY: predacious, flesh-eating birds, including eagles, hawks, falcons, owls, and vultures; the term raptor also used.

BROOD: all of the young hatched from a single clutch of eggs.

BROODING: the act of parent birds sitting on nestlings to maintain satisfactory body temperature in them and also to shade them from direct sunlight to prevent overheating, to shield them from precipitation, and to conceal them from predators.

BROODY: the urge of parent birds to sit on nestlings, an innate response following the laying and hatching of eggs.

BROOD PATCH: one to three spots on a bird's abdomen which are not covered with feathers and which usually receive an enhanced blood supply during the egg incubation and chick brooding phases of its breeding season, enabling it to transfer warmth from its body to the eggs and chicks.

TO CACHE: the storage of a carcass for later consumption.

CARCASS: the dead body of any animal.

CASTING: the undigested parts of birds' food intake, such as bone, feathers, fur, etc., which are regurgitated in the form of a pellet.

CHICK: a young bird still in its nest.

CLUTCH: a group of eggs produced as a unit by a bird in a single nesting.

COPULATION: the sexual act leading to fertilization of the female ova by the male sperm.

CRABBING: two raptors aloft with intertwined talons; usually in an antagonistic interaction but also engaged in during courtship or by youngsters in play.

DARK-MORPH: a color type; gyrfalcons, for example, come in light, medium, and dark shades, which they keep through life.

DEPLUME: a raptor's removal of the larger feathers from a carcass prior to feeding on it or feeding it to its young.

DISPERSAL: a fledgling's leaving of the vicinity of its nest as a normal developmental phase. Satisfactory dispersal occurs when a fledgling has developed hunting skills enabling it to be self-sufficient. Peregrine young normally disperse from several weeks to several months after fledging.

DOUBLE-CLUTCH: the laying of a second set of eggs as a response to the artificial removal of the first clutch in order to stimulate relaying. Triple-clutching is the laying of a third clutch of eggs after the first two clutches are removed.

DUCK HAWK: one of several names formerly applied to the peregrine falcon because of its heavy predation on ducks in certain regions.

EYRIE: (aerie) the nest of a bird of prey, usually in a high place.

FALCONRY: the sport of flying falcons, hawks, and eagles to capture prey. The raptors are caught during fall migration, frequently their first one, taken from their nest, or bred in captivity. In the United States, federal and state statutes regulate and severely restrict falconry activity.

FEAKING: a raptor's wiping of its beak on a fixed object after eating.
FLEDGE: a nestling's first leaving of its nest as a normal developmental stage. This does not include accidental leaving of the nest due to its destruction, high winds, predators, or any other interference.
FLEDGLING: a young bird during the period after leaving the nest and prior to its dispersal.
FLUSH: a bird's reactive movement away from its perching, sitting, or other position caused by the intervention of another creature or event that appears threatening.
FOOTING: a raptor's grasping of any object in its talons: carcass, prey on the wing, a sibling, etc.
FOSTERING: rearing young that are unrelated to the parents.
HACK: a technique used to release captive-reared birds into the wild. Groups of three to nine chicks about four weeks old are placed in an enclosure (hack-box) at the release site. The chicks are provided with food, in the box, through a chute so that they do not associate food with humans and become imprinted. The chicks are released, at the age of 40-45 days, when they are capable of sustained flight. Food continues to be provided at the hack-box for five weeks or until the fledglings become self-sufficient and disperse from the hacking area.
HATCH: the emergence of young from an egg.
HATCHLING: a recently hatched bird in its nest.
HOOD: an object placed over the head of a raptor to block its vision in order to calm it to facilitate handling or transport.
IMPRINTING: a hatchling's identification with the parent birds or any other objects that it experiences. Human imprinting occurs when a bird is fed or handled by humans directly during its earliest developmental stages and before it reaches independence. When a bird identifies humans as its own species, this usually causes it to lose its fear of humans and also its wildness.
INCUBATION: the act of a parent bird in sitting on eggs and applying its body heat to them in order to maintain a relatively constant, high temperature in the developing embryo. Species having synchronous hatching do not incubate their eggs until the last egg of the clutch is laid. During this pre-incubation period, the eggs are sometimes covered by the parent's body but full heat is not applied so that embryonic development does not commence. The eggs are

311

protected against undue temperature but it is not true incubation. Peregrines try for synchronous hatching and usually delay incubation until their clutch, usually four, laid at two-day intervals, is nearly complete except in cold climates where more egg warming is required.

JESSES: leather thongs attached to the legs of raptors that are used in falconry to facilitate their handling.

KILL: an item of prey that has been killed.

MANTLING: a raptor's spreading of its wings over prey to hide it from the sight of others that might try to take possession of it.

MIGRATION: a bird's movement from its breeding grounds to another habitat after the breeding season activities are completed and the spring return flight. Usually, all members of the species migrate: breeders, nonbreeders, fledglings, and subadults. Raptors in the United States usually migrate, during the September through November period, from their northern breeding regions to a southerly wintering area because their prey base becomes unavailable in the fall and winter. Migration is thought to be instinctual and genetically based.

NESTLING: a young bird in its nest prior to first leaving it.

PASSERINE: a specific group of "land" type perching birds. However, some common perching, land birds are not passerines, such as raptors, pigeons, woodpeckers, hummingbirds. Passerines comprise the highest number of prey items taken at most urban peregrine nest sites but the favored prey of the peregrine is the pigeon, closely followed by the dove, which provides the largest quantity of "biomass," that is, weight of food.

PREDATOR: an animal that kills other animals for food.

PREEN: a bird's act of cleaning or arranging its feathers, using its bill and oil from its preen gland.

PREY: any live or dead creature that is a food source for a predator.

PREY TRANSFER: the act of one raptor giving a prey item to another of its kind; usually occurs between adult pairs during courtship and between adult and young during the nurturing stage. Often done while in flight.

RAPTOR: a bird of prey.

SOAR: to maintain sustained flight without wingflapping, using air currents such as thermals or updrafts.

STOOP: the attack dive onto prey from above, used by some falcons. Peregrines may attain 200 miles an hour in a stoop and use it to kill or disable their prey by raking it with their hind talon.

TALON: the curved, pointed claws of birds of prey.

TERMINAL BAND: the last or outermost band on a bird that has different colored horizontal stripes on its tail.

THERMALS: warm air currents rising from the earth's heated surface.

TRAPPING: the legal, licensed capture of wild birds for the purpose of banding. Captured birds are released immediately. Additional information is often gathered, such as size, weight, physical condition, etc., for scientific studies.

TREMOR: the slight shaking or vibration that is a natural movement inherent in humans. It is most obvious when high magnification optical equipment is handheld. Bridges, especially the suspension type, exhibit tremor induced by its traffic and climatic conditions.

WAIT-ON: maintaining a position aloft awaiting an opportunity to stoop at prey.

WHITEWASH: the name given to a raptor's excretions which are visible as white streaks below its frequently used perches. Also referred to as mutes."

Falconry Titles
From Hancock House Publishers

HAWKING GROUND QUARRY
A TREATISE ON HAWKING

Martin Hollinshead

Martin Hollinshead
5½ x 8½ 176 pp. HC   ISBN 0-88839-320-2

The Compleat Falconer
Frank L. Beebe

8 1/2 x 11 336 pp. HC
ISBN 0-88839-253-2

North America's most famous falconer, Frank Beebe, presents the sports most up-to-date and elegant tome, *The Compleat Falconer,* with 32 of Beebe's most exquisite paintings.

A Falconry Manual
Frank L. Beebe

5 1/2 x 8 1/2 198 pp. SC
ISBN 0-88839-978-2

This is Beebe's review of falconry techniques and extensive examination of the biology of the birds of prey. A classic contribution to falconry literature.

Over 178 photographs and instructive line drawings.

The Hunting Falcon
Bruce A. Haak

5 1/2 x 8 1/2 240 pp. HC
ISBN 0-88839-292-3

This is a practitioner's book on modern falconry in North America. Bruce Haak's goal is to impart a philosophy that, when combined with his practical techniques, yields success and enjoyment in this age-old sport.

Hancock House Publishers Game Bird Books

Pheasants of the World

Their Breeding and Management
Keith Howman

8½ x 11 184 pp. HC
ISBN 0-88839-280-X

Over 340 magnificent color photos. The first ever major photographic collection of all the world's pheasants.

Keith Howman, one of the world's most successful rare pheasant breeders and chairman of the World Pheasant Association, has traveled the world championing the pheasant's cause.

Keith brings together his keen behavioral observations from aviary and the wild in this concise treatise.

Produced in cooperation with the World Pheasant Association

Commercial and Ornamental
Game Bird Breeders
Handbook

Alan Woodard, Pran Vohra, Vern Denton

5 1/2 x 11 1/2 496 pp. SC
ISBN 0-88839-311-3

Three of the most imminent researchers in the keeping, rearing, and nutritional studies of pheasant, quail, and partridge have combined their sixty years of experience to produce this bible of aviculture. These men have tailored their knowledge for the backyard breeder, the serious aviculturist, and the commercial breeder—an indispensable tool.